James P. Goodrich,
Indiana's
"Governor Strangelove"

James P. Goodrich, Indiana's "Governor Strangelove"

A Republican's Infatuation with Soviet Russia

Benjamin D. Rhodes

SUP

Selinsgrove: Susquehanna University Press
London: Associated University Presses

Associated University Presses
440 Forsgate Drive
Cranbury, NJ 08512

Associated University Presses
16 Barter Street
London WC1A 2AH, England

Associated University Presses
P.O. Box 338, Port Credit
Mississauga, Ontario
Canada L5G 4L8

The paper used in this publication meets the requirements
of the American National Standard for Permanence of Paper
for Printed Library Materials Z39.48-1984.

Library of Congress Cataloging-in-Publication Data

Rhodes, Benjamin D.
   James P. Goodrich, Indiana's "Governor Strangelove" : a
Republican's infatuation with Soviet Russia / Benjamin D. Rhodes.
      p.   cm.
   Includes bibliographical references and index.
   ISBN 0-945636-82-2 (alk. paper)
   1. Goodrich, James P. (James Putnam), 1864–1940—Views on Soviet
Union.   2. Goodrich, James P. (James Putnam), 1864–1940—Journeys—
Soviet Union.   3. United States—Relations—Soviet Union.
4. Soviet Union—Relations—United States.   I. Title.
F526.G67R48   1996
977.2'042'092—dc20   95-25533
                                                          CIP

PRINTED IN THE UNITED STATES OF AMERICA

Contents

Preface   7

1. "A Country Lawyer from Over at Winchester"   13
2. A Hoosier Caesar?   30
3. A Short Retirement   44
4. Goodrich Converts Congress   74
5. Snowbound in Russia   88
6. An Indiana Banker in the "Inner Temple" of the Kremlin   107
7. Goodrich Is Forced to Start Over Again   128
8. Goodrich's Final Trip to Russia   140
9. "A Vote for Hoover is a Vote for Jim Goodrich"   156

Notes   171
Bibliography   184
Index   187

Preface

THIS study is based upon the James P. Goodrich Papers, which are housed at the Herbert Hoover Presidential Library, West Branch, Iowa. In 1982, forty-two years after the death of the former Republican governor of Indiana, the Hoover Library acquired the James P. Goodrich manuscript collection of twenty-eight boxes from the estate of Pierre Goodrich (whose first name was pronounced "Pier"). West Branch was, in most respects, a logical last resting place for the Goodrich papers, as the governor had been associated with Hoover in the Russian operations of the American Relief Administration between 1921 and 1923. Furthermore, Goodrich was an enthusiastic supporter of Hoover's presidential bids in 1928 and 1932 and had thereafter tried to draft Hoover for another contest with Franklin D. Roosevelt. As much as Hoover and Goodrich agreed on most matters of domestic policy and Republican politics, they failed to see eye to eye on the question of American policy toward Soviet Russia. Both men were convinced that Soviet Communism, which they regarded as a foolish and illogical economic system, had failed miserably. They agreed that America should extend humanitarian aid to the destitute asking nothing in return. And both favored developing trade with the Soviet state. However, Goodrich was far more enthusiastic than Hoover about encouraging trade with Russia, and Goodrich consistently insisted that the Soviets were deserving of diplomatic recognition. The exchange of ambassadors and the flowering of trade, Goodrich believed, would lead to the integration of a more capitalistic Russia into the world community. One of the few times in his entire life that Goodrich agreed with a Democrat came in November 1933 when President Franklin D. Roosevelt exchanged ambassadors with the Soviet Union, an action that substantially vindicated Goodrich.

The Goodrich Papers do not present the reader with a comprehensive record of the life of James P. Goodrich. With the exception of his uncompleted autobiography (written for Pierre Goodrich in 1938–1939), Goodrich's papers contain little information on his early life, his eight years as Indiana's Republican Party chairman, or even his four years as governor. Most of his correspondence as governor concerned routine invitations or his numerous illnesses and not matters of politics or policy. The collection is equally opaque about Goodrich's financial affairs and legal career. Goodrich, or perhaps his secretary, carefully saved scrapbooks of newspaper clippings relating to his governorship, after carefully removing the name of the newspaper and the date of publication, thus throwing future readers into a state of confusion.

From Goodrich's perspective, based on the volume of material he preserved, his four trips to Russia represented the high point of his life. It was Goodrich's great good fortune that on three of the four trips he was accompanied by Stanford University historian Frank A. Golder. Although Goodrich valued Golder's experience and command of Russian history, geography, and culture, the governor took pains to make up his mind on the basis of the "brass-tack" facts before him. Christian A. Herter, Hoover's administrative assistant, once expressed the view: "I think the Governor's views are quite largely molded by Golder. . . ."[1] But in reality, Goodrich had taken positions on recognition and trade with the Soviets that were far to the left of Golder's. Eventually Golder came reluctantly to agree with Goodrich rather than vice versa.

On each of his journeys Goodrich maintained a detailed diary account. However, he preserved only one handwritten journal, which covered the events during his first trip to Russia in the fall of 1921. The subsequent diaries are typewritten and lack the spontaneous unexpurgated quality of the single handwritten journal; Goodrich now deleted mention of such activities as poker games or song-singing. In the course of his travels Goodrich was frequently careless about dates, times, and spellings. Probably because he was intimidated by Russian names, Goodrich often recorded the title of the Soviet official with whom he had spoken but not his name.

The diary accounts served as the basis for Goodrich's numerous reports to Hoover, Hughes, Harding, and Coolidge. Yet Goodrich also intended to present his ideas and experiences to the public through magazine articles, speeches, and a book. For a time he experimented with a unique format; he recast his diary in the form of letters to his son. Apparently dissatisfied with the result he reverted to a more conventional book arrangement. Much of the information contained therein was drawn from memory, as only a portion of the material described in the book manuscript is duplicated in the diary. Oddly, he confined his account purely to travel details and omitted any mention of the political aspects of his mission. Readers of his book manuscript would not have discovered that Goodrich favored trade and diplomatic ties with Soviet Russia. As was the case with his autobiography, which abruptly ended in 1919, Goodrich's book project was never completed beyond a first draft.

With the decline of interest in Russian recognition in the mid-twenties, Goodrich's correspondence was largely confined to business and politics. His correspondents included Presidents Taft, Harding, Coolidge, and Hoover, as well as numerous Indiana Republicans such as Will Hays, Harry S. New, Raymond Springer, Will Wood, James Watson, and Wendell Willke. Strangely there is a dearth of correspondence with advocates of Russian recognition such as William E. Borah, Raymond Robins, or Alexander Gumberg. In the entire collection of Goodrich papers there is hardly a single document which reflects unfavorably upon Goodrich, with the possible exception of Goodrich's admission in his autobiography that he personally paid the state statistician four thousand dollars to relinquish his office. The question arises as to whether Goodrich, or possibly his son, culled the collection to produce a sanitized product.

Historically James P. Goodrich has virtually disappeared from sight. He is rarely mentioned in histories of the progressive era or in studies of Soviet-American relations. Usually his name is simply included in a list of businessmen and politicians who favored establishing trade and diplomatic ties with Soviet Russia. Surprisingly he is not even mentioned in the memoirs of Indiana Senator Jim Watson, Goodrich's friend, law partner, and sometimes rival in the Indiana Republican Party. Even Herbert Hoover's *Memoirs* make only passing mention of Goodrich as a special investigator of the American Relief Administration, as an early Hoover supporter in 1928, and as a member of the Commission on Conservation and Management of the Public Domain.[2] The most complete discussion of Goodrich is in James K. Libbey's study of Alexander Gumberg and Soviet-American relations.[3] In a two-page sketch, Libbey presented an excellent brief portrait, even though he did not have access to the Goodrich Papers. For the most part, however, Goodrich has been either unknown or written off as just another mid-western mediocrity. The conventional verdict, as rendered by William E. Wilson, found Goodrich to have been merely one of a "creditable but not very distinguished list" of Indiana governors.[4] Half a century after his death Goodrich appears as a pragmatic progressive and as a distinguished statesman of substantial, if not perfect, vision. Perhaps the most intriguing aspect of his career is that much of what Goodrich was saying about the USSR seventy years ago has suddenly come to pass.

I would like to express my thanks to Robert Wood, the former director of the Herbert Hoover Presidential Library, for calling my attention to the Goodrich papers. Dale C. Mayer capably arranged the collection and assisted my research. In addition I would like to acknowledge the support of the University of Wisconsin-Whitewater for two research grants and for permitting me to spend a semester at the Institute for Research in the Humanities at the University of Wisconsin-Madison where I began work on Goodrich in 1986. My research and writing was also assisted by a semester spent at the University of Jyväskylä, Finland as a Fulbright lecturer. Much of the manuscript was written in a magnificent building designed by Alvar Aalto. Finally, I would like to thank the *Indiana Magazine of History* for permission to include in this study my article "Governor James P. Goodrich of Indiana and the 'Plain Facts' about Russia, 1921–1933," which appeared in March, 1989.

James P. Goodrich,
Indiana's
"Governor Strangelove"

1

"A Country Lawyer from Over at Winchester"

WHEN James Putnam Goodrich died of heart failure on 15 August 1940, two decades after having served as Indiana's wartime governor, he seemed to merit only the briefest historical footnote. Respectfully, if blandly, his obituaries traced his career as attorney, banker, Indiana Republican state chairman and national committeeman, governor, and elder statesman. In passing, the *New York Times* recalled that after his retirement from the governorship of Indiana, Goodrich had made four trips to Russia between 1921 and 1925 in connection with American famine relief efforts. But at the time of his death at age seventy-six no one remembered or saw fit to recall that Goodrich had advocated the diplomatic recognition of the Soviet Union and the restoration of trade at a time when America's official Russian policy was one of hard-line nonrecognition. Based upon his tours of the country, his meetings with ordinary Russians and such Soviet leaders as Dzerzhinsky, Kamenev, Radek, Rykov, Krassin, Sokolnikov, Zinoviev, Litvinov, Trotsky, and Stalin, Goodrich came to the pragmatic conclusion that the Russian Revolution of 1917 was a permanent event with which the West had to come to terms sooner or later. "Every prediction made concerning Russia," he wrote in 1922, "has failed for the simple reason that men have been guided by their prejudices and their hopes and have ignored the plain facts before them."[1]

By 1940 his deviations from orthodoxy were long since forgotten and he was remembered as the very personification of Old Guard Republican respectability: as an organization man who had supported William Howard Taft over the Bull Moose insurgency of Theodore Roosevelt, as a Republican loyalist who had made generous contributions to the party's campaign coffers, and as one who had been appalled by the "folly" of the New Deal. Practically the only occasion in his entire lifetime when he agreed with a Democrat was in 1933 when President Franklin D. Roosevelt exchanged ambas-

sadors with the Soviet Union, an action which substantially vindicated Goodrich. Only two weeks before his death, Goodrich had
been a delegate to the Republican convention at Philadelphia, where
he had hoped for the nomination of New York district attorney
Thomas E. Dewey, Ohio senator Robert A. Taft, or former President Herbert Hoover instead of the more liberal and charismatic
Wendell Willkie of Indiana. His reputation as a practical Republican
businessman was reinforced by a deathbed story related by the Washington correspondent of an Indianapolis newspaper. Suffering from
recurrent heart fibrillations, Goodrich was quoted as saying, "I
know I am very sick and I know I am going to die. And I hate it
terribly because I know there will be a lot of money made in the
next few years." Or the author of one of his obituaries, alluding to
Goodrich's successes in the world of business, recalled that the
governor often described himself as a man who consciously had "to
check on himself to keep from making too much."[2]

For a man who was identified with substantial wealth, James Putnam Goodrich (Jim Goodrich to anyone knowing him for even a
few minutes) came from unpretentious origins. He was born at Winchester, Indiana, on 18 February 1864 and he was the third of the
five sons of John and Elizabeth Goodrich. His father, whom Goodrich only slightly remembered, operated a farm four miles northwest
of Winchester. The venture was sufficiently successful to enable John
Goodrich to build a new home for his family in the city of Winchester. An ambitious man, he twice (in 1860 and 1864) was elected
county clerk and while holding that office read law with a local
lawyer and was admitted to the bar. In 1872, only forty-two years
old, he died of tuberculosis, leaving a thirty-two-year-old widow
and five sons. Jim Goodrich was only eight years old at the time of
his father's death. He retained few clear memories of his father, but
did recall once having been disciplined with a switch for failing to
replenish the wood supply for the kitchen stove. He remembered
also his father's easygoing relationship with the employees on the
Goodrich farm and his initiative and ambition.[3] Of the five Goodrich
brothers, Jim was most like his father in that he intended to make
something of himself.

Goodrich's life in Winchester was marked by simplicity and frugality, but it was not poverty-stricken. Elizabeth Goodrich inherited
the family farm, which she operated with the assistance of her sons.
Jim and his brothers thus became experienced at all aspects of farm
labor: clearing trees, digging ditches, cutting wood, shearing sheep,
cleaning the chicken house, and planting and harvesting wheat, oats,
and hay. During mild weather Jim and his older brother Percy would

drive a team of horses to the farm and haul wood back to town for sale. Wood was also sold to the local railroad, that established a station at the Goodrich farm where each morning the local freight would "wood up." Jim's finest hour as a farmer came during one threshing season when he was asked to serve as the ricker, whose job it was to stack the straw in a symmetrical shape so that it would shed the rain. On this occasion Henry Vanscoy, the best ricker in the neighborhood, was too intoxicated to work and Goodrich was drafted to take his place. The resulting hay stack was said to have been the equal of any in the neighborhood. "After that," Goodrich recalled, "I was on several occasions used as a substitute for Henry when he was incapacitated."[4] Thirty-five years later, when Goodrich ran for governor of Indiana, one of his friends related the ricker tale to the press to prove that Goodrich was just as good a farmer as his principal Republican rival, Warren T. McCray, who was a genuine farmer.

Goodrich received his elementary education at the local grammar school. The basic instruction was thorough enough, but it was sometimes accompanied by such punishments as a dunce cap and the corporal punishment of those who violated school regulations. Goodrich retained a vivid recollection of an occasion when a classmate was spanked before his class by the superintendent, who intoned "The way of the transgressor is hard" before each blow on the boy's posterior. If Goodrich can be believed, he managed to avoid either the dunce cap or a humiliating spanking.

Even as a boy Goodrich possessed an active political mind. When he was just twelve his mother permitted him to go to Philadelphia with his older brother to attend the celebration of the nation's centennial. Later that year he attended a rally at Winchester held on behalf of the Republican presidential candidacy of Rutherford Hayes of Ohio. A hollow sycamore tree in the town square was set afire and hundreds of torch-bearing men paraded in support of the Grand Old Party.[5]

As Goodrich entered high school his interest in Republican politics was further stimulated by the selection of his maternal uncle, John W. "Chess" Macy, as Republican chairman for Randolph County. During the campaign of 1880 young Goodrich was greatly disappointed when James Garfield of Ohio won the Republican nomination instead of the party's "Plumed Knight," James G. Blaine of Maine. But the sixteen-year-old was highly flattered when he was permitted to attend local caucuses and he "had great fun hauling in voters and running errands for the County organizations." One of his assignments introduced him to the seamier side of political life.

He was enlisted to escort vote repeaters or "floaters" to several poll-
ing places where they would cast a straight Republican ticket. Goodrich would then return with his charges to party headquarters where
they were liberally paid in "spirits." Between political campaigns
Goodrich attended to his high school courses in Latin, algebra, ge-
ometry, and trigonometry. When he completed his senior year in
1881 his class numbered only nine survivors. Besides Goodrich, who
was a future governor of Indiana, the graduates included James E.
Watson, later a Republican representative and senator, John R. Commons, who became a prominent economist at the University of Wisconsin, and Cora Frist, whom Goodrich married in 1888.[6]

Goodrich did not immediately attend college nor for several years
did he have a clearly defined long-range plan of action. One rather
romantic possibility, one which was especially appealing to a young
man without much financial backing, was to secure an appointment
to the United States Naval Academy. In the meantime, having passed
the examination for a state teacher's license, Goodrich became a
teacher at a country school five miles from Winchester. It was his
intention to teach his twelve students throughout the school term
while he contemplated his future. Only four weeks into the term
Goodrich broke his hip while gathering hickory nuts with a group
of friends. The nuts were being shaken from the tree by crashing a
large log into it. One of the forks holding the log unexpectedly
shifted, causing the "bumper" to strike Goodrich instead of the hickory tree. His first thought on regaining consciousness was that he
wouldn't have to return to the school. According to Goodrich the
accident ended his chance of becoming a naval officer. But, in any
case, his hope of attending Annapolis was more of a teenage pipe
dream than a fully matured idea.

Over the winter Goodrich made a rapid recovery from his injury.
By the fall of 1882 he was well enough to take a second teaching
position, this time at a country school three miles to the northeast
of Winchester. Living at the family farm, he hiked to school during
good weather and rode a horse when the roads were muddy. Although he "enjoyed the work most thoroughly," teaching sixty students ranging from first graders to high school freshmen was not an
occupation he wished to continue indefinitely. In the fall of 1883,
therefore, he decided to attend DePauw University at Greencastle,
Indiana. Because of his good high school grades in advanced courses
he was admitted as a sophomore. Already his friend Jim Watson was
a student there and he also became a good friend of Albert Beveridge,
a future Indiana senator. Goodrich fondly remembered the "many
splendid professors" at DePauw from whom he took courses in

chemistry, mathematics, history, biology, and physics. Looking back on his college experience Goodrich characterized his years at De-Pauw as "both happy and profitable."[7] Yet, he dropped out at the end of his second year and rarely did he mention DePauw again. His failure to complete his studies and the fact that he later selected Wabash College and not DePauw as the object of his financial beneficence casts some doubt on whether Goodrich was actually as happy during his two years of college as he recalled when writing his autobiography some fifty years later.

When Goodrich left DePauw he still had no clear career plans and was in fact "completely unsettled as to my future." For one year he tried farming in the Red River Valley of North Dakota on a ranch owned by Uncle Chess. By the fall of 1885 he was back in Winchester and, on the advice of his uncle, began the study of law. Together Goodrich and Jim Watson—the two Republican "Jims" of Indiana politics—began to work as law clerks for two local attorneys, Enos Watson (who was Jim Watson's father), and his partner Jim Engle. Each morning Goodrich and Watson would recite to their mentors from their readings in the law and they obtained practical experience in preparing such documents as deeds, abstracts, mortgages, and contracts. In 1887 Goodrich passed the bar examination and began to practice law in a firm headed by Uncle Chess Macy, with Good-rich and Jim Watson as junior partners. What accounted for Good-rich's newfound drive and direction? Certainly a large part of the explanation lay in Goodrich's engagement in 1885 to Cora Frist of nearby Lynn, Indiana. As Goodrich noted in his autobiography, "I am sure that the wish to consummate that engagement had much to do with my desire to get into something whereby I could earn an income sufficient to justify our marriage." In June, 1888 Goodrich became a married man and six years later a father, with the birth of his son, Pierre.[8]

In the practice of law Goodrich found satisfaction both from a substantial income (he earned the impressive sum of $720 in his first year of practice), and from the opportunity to keep active in Republi-can politics. Yet Goodrich was a thoughtful and not a dogmatic Re-publican. Probably his determination to make up his own mind—a characteristic Goodrich retained throughout his life—was derived from his strong-willed mother, who remained a Democrat even when her husband ran for county clerk on the Republican ticket. As a young man Goodrich demonstrated a streak of political independence by joining the Grange and the Knights of Labor. The Grange or Patrons of Husbandry had been in existence for fifteen years before Goodrich joined in 1881. The organization, which sought to

advance the interests of farmers, was partly social, partly educa-
tional, and partly political. Goodrich was primarily interested in the
agricultural information distributed by the Grange and less attracted
to its political program of bringing railroad corporations under state
regulation. At least nominally he remained a member of the Grange
until he retired from the Indiana governorship in 1921.

He was far more active in the Knights of Labor, which he joined
a year after becoming a member of the Grange. Under the leadership
of Terrence V. Powderly the Knights sought to organize a comprehensive national union. All who toiled were eligible for membership
and Goodrich qualified by virtue of his farm work and his having
worked one summer cutting grass and digging graves for the local
cemetery. What Goodrich particularly enjoyed was participating in
monthly debates upon such issues as the secret ballot, voting rights
for women, prohibition, child labor, and workmen's compensation.
Thirty days in advance the master workman would assign a topic
for debate and appoint members to present arguments on either side
of the question. The experience taught Goodrich to prepare himself
thoroughly before participating in such an exercise and not to under-
estimate the reasoning power of the ordinary man. In particular he
recalled a debate in which he presented what he thought was a convincing case against woman suffrage. Goodrich found his arguments
promptly demolished by a workman who arose and stated, "I can't
answer your argument, but my mother pays tax on a lot of property
[and] I wish you would just tell me why some worthless cuss who
pays no tax at all should be permitted to vote and elect people who
tax her and she be denied the ballot." Needless to say, when the
group voted on the issue, Goodrich found himself on the losing side.
Looking back, Goodrich regarded his participation in the Grange
and Knights of Labor "with a great deal of satisfaction."[9] No doubt
one reason for his sense of pride was that his memberships turned
into a considerable political asset when he decided to seek the governorship in 1916.

Until 1894 Goodrich and Watson practiced law together at Winchester. From the beginning theirs was a love-hate relationship. In
Goodrich's opinion, Watson was intellectually brilliant and a gifted
orator. On the negative side, claimed Goodrich, Watson was too
conservative, too lazy, too self-centered, and too opportunistic.
Throughout his autobiography Goodrich frequently praised Watson's abilities, but he could not resist the temptation to take periodic
potshots at his friend. "The truth of the matter," Goodrich complained, "is that Jim, throughout his entire life, never once made a
sacrifice for the party." According to Goodrich, the height of Wat-

son's folly came in 1910 when, contrary to the clear advice of Good-rich, Watson unwisely agreed to endorse the stock of a newly formed automobile insurance company. Soon the company failed and Watson found himself in "a hell of a fix." To save Watson from public embar-rassment and possible prosecution it was necessary for Goodrich and his friends to quickly raise $25,000, which Goodrich then presented to his friend along with a tongue-lashing. "I don't think I ever talked straighter or harder to any man than I did to Jim. He promised to quit [shady business dealings], but forgot his promise as soon as he left office." From Goodrich's rather self-righteous perspective, he himself set at all times an impeccable example of selfless public serv-ice. When asked to sign a letter recommending that investors pur-chase stock in the same auto insurance company endorsed by Watson, Goodrich ostensibly agreed, provided he could add a sentence read-ing: "This letter is written in consideration of the $12,000 per year salary for no service except presiding at the meeting of the board, and I also received as a bonus $20,000 worth of stock." When told that no stock could be sold with such a statement attached, Goodrich rejoined, so he recalled, "This deal is crooked . . . and I don't want to have anything to do with it."[10]

Throughout their association as law partners the two young Re-publicans found ample opportunity to discuss politics and their re-spective ambitions. Of the two, Watson was by far the more anxious to lead a public life. According to Goodrich, Watson's oft stated ambition was to become governor of Indiana and eventually to seek the presidency. For his part, Goodrich regarded himself as better suited for the role of behind-the-scenes organizer and wire-puller. Goodrich was keenly aware that he lacked the powerful voice and oratorical flamboyance which were then essential qualifications for potential candidates. In 1896 Goodrich, in his role as precinct com-mitteeman, made the first political speech of his life before 2,000 county Republicans at Winchester. For several months Goodrich had been "bewildered" by the debate between those who defended the existing gold standard and those who advocated a new monetary standard based upon silver. Having attended the Republican conven-tion at St. Louis, that nominated William McKinley and endorsed gold, Goodrich returned home convinced that a silver monetary standard would be "folly." The theme of his speech, therefore, was that all party members should support the Republican platform and its nominee. "I carefully prepared myself," he recalled, "but I must confess that it was a sorry effort." At least Goodrich was vigorously applauded. Still, it was the last public political address attempted by Goodrich for nearly twenty years.[11]

McKinley's defeat of William Jennings Bryan in the 1896 election indirectly assisted Goodrich's rapid rise in Indiana politics. The new McKinley administration promptly named thousands of deserving Republicans to federal positions. Soon the chairmanship of the Republican Party in Randolph County became vacant when the incumbent accepted a minor position in Washington. Largely due to the influence of Uncle Chess, Goodrich was elected in 1897 by the county Republican executive committee as county chairman. The chief criticism of Goodrich was that at age thirty-two he was too young and inexperienced for the position. However, the doubts of his detractors were speedily wiped away by Goodrich's energetic stewardship of the local organization. He resolved that his county would deliver as high or higher a percentage of the vote to the Republicans as any county in the state. To that end he tried to meet every Republican in every precinct of the county. He drew up a list of one thousand Republican farmers who were suspected of having voted for Bryan in 1896 and arranged for them to receive free subscriptions to the St. Louis *Globe Democrat,* a newspaper which, in Goodrich's view, was "one of the soundest papers in the middle west which had been consistently right on the money question." And he learned how to dispense patronage positions to the party faithful, which consisted chiefly of $40-a-month positions as rural mail carriers. In the 1898 election Goodrich was gratified when the Republican candidates for secretary of state and Congress carried the county by 700 votes more than McKinley had polled two years before.[12]

In 1900 Goodrich was urged by Congressman George Cromer to be a candidate for Republican eighth district chairman. Under the impression that he faced no real opposition, Goodrich somewhat naively agreed to run. Soon he learned, from a tip supplied by a telephone operator, that conservative Republicans were clandestinely supporting a rival candidate and intended to keep Goodrich in ignorance of the fact until the day of the district convention. In response, the thirty-six-year-old Goodrich demonstrated that he could play political hardball if necessary. From Cromer, Goodrich obtained lists of supporters and held a series of "secret meetings" to line up the election of friendly delegates. Goodrich's counterattack paid off handsomely as he controlled ninety percent of the delegates and easily carried the day.[13]

As district chairman Goodrich was now automatically a member of the Republican state committee. On the state level the new committeeman found the party leadership to be badly split between the older, conservative supporters of Senator Charles Fairbanks and the younger, more progressive supporters of Senator Albert Beveridge.

Goodrich took the politically artful position that he belonged to neither faction and that the party should unify behind President William McKinley and the Republican candidate for governor Winfield Taylor Durbin, who happened to be from the eighth district. Although Goodrich felt his colleagues on the state committee were not pleased by his position, they elected him to a three-man executive committee which was to direct the 1900 campaign. Most of his own effort in the election was concentrated in the eighth district, where he strove to promote the reelection of Representative Cromer by holding conferences with every precinct committeeman. Goodrich was surprised and pleased when the party elected all its candidates in Indiana and also by the fact that his district showed a larger increase in the Republican share of the vote than any other district in the state. As a result Goodrich received many congratulations for his organizing ability. The truth was, Goodrich candidly confessed, that "I was given credit for much work that Cromer had done."[14]

When it came time to select a new state chairman in 1901 Goodrich had managed to ingratiate himself with both Republican factions. It did not, therefore, come as a great surprise to Goodrich when Senator Fairbanks let it be known that he favored as the new chairman either Goodrich or another member of the state executive committee, Warren Beigler of Wabash. According to Goodrich's recollection, Beigler flatly refused to consider the position and graciously said to Goodrich, "Jim, you've got to take it, there's no one else who can do the job as good as you." Goodrich then discussed the situation with Fairbanks, the first time Goodrich and the "Indiana Icicle" had personally discussed politics. The meeting went well, as Fairbanks was conciliatory and agreed with Goodrich that the party must not accept contributions from utilities or large corporations having direct business dealings with the state. Fairbanks also agreed that the state chairman should be free to take positions on public matters based upon considerations of merit rather than the dictates of partisan politics. And Fairbanks agreed to Goodrich's suggestion that the position of secretary of the Republican state committee be offered to a Beveridge supporter, Fred A. Sims of Frankfort, in order to unify the party. Finally, Goodrich told Fairbanks he would accept the chairmanship and a special meeting of the state committee went through the formality of electing Goodrich to head the party. Within a few days Goodrich's resolve to distance himself from special business interests was severely tested when he was offered the huge annual retainer of $5,000 to represent a telephone company owned by J. P. Morgan. With characteristic good sense Goodrich declined, pointing out that such a connection would be construed as a blatant conflict of interest. The real goal of the company, Goodrich maintained, was "to employ the Chairman of the State Committee and not a country lawyer from over at Winchester."[15]

For the next eight years (1901–1909) Goodrich was in his element as state chairman. "I might say without egotism here," he rather egotistically wrote in his autobiography, "that from that time on down until 1921, the general policy of the Republican party so far as the organization was concerned was directed by me." Nevertheless, in leading the state organization, Goodrich was often compelled to perform a delicate balancing act between the competing ambitions of Fairbanks, Beveridge, and Watson. Goodrich found that each of the rivals coveted the presidency and that they were intensely suspicious of each other. His challenge was to steer a middle course that would offend the jealous rivals as little as possible. For the most part he succeeded, especially in the 1904 election, when the entire Republican ticket swept the state. President Theodore Roosevelt, who had named Fairbanks as his running mate, overwhelmed Judge Alton Parker; J. Frank Hanly was easily elected as governor; the Republicans carried eleven of the thirteen congressional districts; and the party swept both houses of the legislature to gain a three to one advantage over the Democrats. Afterward, Goodrich thought seriously of retiring at a time when the party was unified and triumphant. He changed his mind when the Beveridge faction endorsed a rival for state chairman. And Fairbanks's supporters urged Goodrich to stay, in part because they were not sure of being able to elect anyone else. "With a good deal of reluctance I consented to do so," Goodrich recollected, "and had ten of the thirteen votes of the [state] committee." When the legislature convened in January, 1905, Goodrich used his influence to insure that both party factions shared in the spoils of victory. The progressive wing was pleased by the selection of Beveridge for a second term in the senate. And to fill the remaining four years of Fairbanks's term the legislature selected Congressman James A. Hemenway, who was favored by Fairbanks and regarded by Goodrich as "one of the most levelheaded men in Indiana politics."[16]

During the stormy four-year term of Governor Hanly, Goodrich several times questioned his decision to remain as state chairman. In the opinion of Goodrich, the new governor was "a fanatic on the temperance question" and unwisely roiled the legislative waters by seeking the passage of a bill giving each county the option to permit or prohibit the sale of alcoholic beverages. As a matter of personal choice Goodrich did not patronize saloons, but he was not enthusiastic about legislation which was disruptive to party unity. Another controversial issue was Hanly's pledge to enact a public depository law prohibiting public officials from investing tax collections for personal gain or for speculative purposes. Traditionally such "cross-eyed banking" had been tolerated by both parties. As the bill bogged down in the legislature, due to the opposition of local officials, Hanly asked Goodrich to draft amended legislation. When the bill was introduced for debate Goodrich, who was not a member of the legislature, sat in the seat of Representative John Edwards of Mitchell handing him the text of the revised bill along with an abstract justifying each of the 124 changes. Goodrich regarded his role in the passage of the reform bill with a good deal of satisfaction, although the Democratic minority "howled" afterward about the impropriety of Goodrich having been present on the floor of the assembly directing Republican strategy. Next Goodrich was called upon to help contain a scandal involving the charging of excessive fees by the Indiana secretary of state. Acting on Goodrich's advice, Hanly cleaned house and those responsible were quietly forced to resign. Despite the troubles, Goodrich regarded Hanly as an essentially able governor who had cleared the atmosphere in the state house.[17]

When Hanly retired in 1908 Goodrich saw that the political situation facing Indiana Republicans "looked none too good." According to Goodrich, Hanly urged him to run for governor, but Goodrich declined on the ground he had no desire for public office. Jim Watson, now a veteran of six terms in the House of Representatives, won the Republican nomination for governor. But in the opinion of Goodrich, Watson proceeded to make "a beautiful mess" of the campaign. Against the wishes of Goodrich, the chief issue in the election became the emotional and explosive question of state control of alcohol. Watson, in the view of Goodrich, "lost his head" by endorsing the dry cause. To make matters worse, Governor Hanly called a special session of the legislature which, after a divisive debate, enacted a local option law. To Goodrich it was now "perfectly clear that we were headed straight for defeat." As Goodrich had foreseen, Watson was overwhelmed in the governor's race by attorney Thomas R. Marshall, who had never before run for public office. William Howard Taft, the Republican presidential candidate, carried Indiana against William Jennings Bryan. But the Republicans managed to lose eleven of the thirteen house seats and lost control of the state legislature to the Democrats.[18]

For Goodrich the election reverse meant that it was high time to leave the chairmanship. Senator Beveridge was about to run for reelection and was entitled to name his own chairman. Besides, after eight fairly successful years in office, Goodrich was anxious for a

respite from political headaches. On the whole Goodrich's sense of
timing had been excellent. He had become chairman when Republican fortunes were on the rise and by leaving without major enemies
in 1909 he had managed to cut his losses. Fortunately for Goodrich's
reputation he was out of office when Beveridge, who received only
lukewarm support from the Fairbanks wing of the party, was defeated for a third term in the Senate. By retiring he also escaped
blame for the debacle of 1912 in which the Democrats captured
twelve of the thirteen Indiana house seats and won control of both
houses of the legislature. In recognition of Goodrich's eight years of
service to the party, the state organization in January, 1910 held a
"very delightful farewell dinner" for the retiring chairman, presented
him with a gold watch, and in after-dinner speeches said many "com-
plimentary, fulsome, and foolish things." It was Goodrich's intention, so he told Watson, "to retire from politics myself and devote
the rest of my life to business."[19]

For the next six years Goodrich, while never abandoning politics,
basically kept his promise to stick to business. Several projects demanded his time and energy. First of all, Goodrich organized and
became president of the People's Loan and Trust Company at Winchester in 1907. Another of his ventures was a coal mining company,
the Patoka Coal Company, and he became president of the local gas
and water companies. One of his severest business challenges came
when he served as the receiver of the bankrupt Chicago, Cincinnati,
and Louisville Railroad, a post to which he was appointed by Federal
Judge Albert B. Anderson in 1908. Actually, his acceptance of the
assignment casts some doubt on Goodrich's claim that he consistently avoided any conflict of interest between his private financial
interests and his public role as state Republican chairman. Goodrich
had no experience whatsoever in the railroad business, and the conclusion is inescapable that he received the appointment because of
his political standing. Concerned about Goodrich's lack of railroad
training, an attorney for the railroad's bondholders asked for the
appointment of a co-receiver. Goodrich was present in court when
the judge summarily rejected the suggestion and expressed great confidence in the business acumen of Goodrich. Afterward Goodrich
heard the disappointed attorney ask, "What kind of a damn judge
have you down here?" Goodrich, needless to say, felt that Judge
Anderson had demonstrated sound judgment.[20]

Getting the business back on its feet proved a more formidable
task than Goodrich had expected. "I never worked harder in my life
than I did in the four years when I was actively running the railroad,"
he recalled. One of his troubles was the discovery that the railroad

industry was riddled with corrupt practices. Managers often sought kickbacks from suppliers and the railroads then received substandard materials in return. Goodrich admitted that he was almost deceived by such a scheme when he decided to "retie" his railroad's entire roadbed and signed a contract to purchase one hundred thousand ties. The tie company delivered to Goodrich's office a sample of the product they agreed to provide. Yet when Goodrich inspected the construction work it appeared to him that the ties were smaller than he had expected. "I had the conductor drop me off and soon ascertained that the ties were at least two grades under the sample and not according to the contract." Back in Chicago Goodrich demanded and received a $30,000 credit from the dishonest tie company. At the same time he dismissed the supervisors who had acquiesced in the fraud and replaced them with young "hustlers." After four years of labor Goodrich returned the railroad to profitability and sold it to the Chesapeake and Ohio Railroad at a price that enabled most of the bondholders to break even. Having worked himself out of the railroad business, Goodrich then entered a law practice at Indianapolis with Judge Leander J. Monks, who had just retired from the state supreme court, and two prominent Republican legislators, John Robbins and Harry Starr.[21]

Despite his immersion in business ventures, Goodrich continued to find time for Republican politics. As a delegate-at-large he attended the acrimonious Republican convention of 1912 at Chicago that rejected the candidacy of former president Theodore Roosevelt and renominated William Howard Taft. With reservations Goodrich decided to support Taft, who was the organization candidate. His objection to Roosevelt was that he believed no person ought to serve more than two terms as president. On the other hand, Goodrich regarded Taft as an inept executive who had kept the party in turmoil through repeated blunders. In his heart, said Goodrich, "I really was not for either one." His political instinct told him that the party split would likely leave deep and lasting scars and he therefore took the initiative in advancing a compromise. His idea was to convince both Taft and Roosevelt to withdraw in favor of a compromise candidate, possibly Governor Herbert S. Hadley of Missouri. According to Goodrich, Roosevelt expressed interest in the idea, but concluded that his supporters wanted him to fight to the bitter end. On the national level the divided party went down to a decisive defeat at the hand of Woodrow Wilson. In Indiana the Democrats achieved a clean sweep as they carried the presidential vote, elected Samuel M. Ralston as governor, won both houses of the legislature, and carried all thirteen seats in the House of Representatives. An incidental result of the election was that James P. Goodrich had managed to remain on good terms with both major factions of his party. One indication of his continued influence in Republican circles was his unanimous selection as national committeeman by the Indiana delegation at the Chicago convention; even the Roosevelt delegates supported him. In his new post Goodrich promptly went to work "to put the pieces together again."[22]

His first step in the rebuilding process was to promote the candidacy of Will Hays for the post of state chairman. In a sense Hays was a Goodrich protégé. The two had first met when Goodrich was state chairman in 1902 and Hays was county chairman of Sullivan County, a hopelessly Democratic area. Goodrich was greatly impressed when Hays, with financial support from the state committee, "delivered the goods" by electing a member of the legislature and part of the county ticket. Thereafter, recorded Goodrich, "I was greatly interested in the boy." With the backing of Goodrich, Hays was selected as state chairman in February, 1914. Despite Hays's "splendid job" the Democrats managed to retain control of the legislature and they reelected Senator Benjamin F. Shively. In the judgment of Goodrich the Republicans lost because Indiana Progressives, remnants of Theodore Roosevelt's Bull Moose movement, insisted on entering a slate of candidates. But the Progressives made a dismal showing with even Beveridge, their candidate for the senate, finishing a distant third. The Progressive debacle of 1914, thought Goodrich, did a great deal to convince the defectors to rejoin the Republican Party.[23]

By 1916, therefore, as the Indiana Republicans prepared to select candidates for the governorship and the Senate, the party was more unified than it had been in a decade. Goodrich, who was fifty-two years old, financially secure and without major enemies, found himself under pressure from "the boys" to run for governor. Consistently he had disclaimed any intention of seeking public office, but he was highly flattered by the widespread encouragement he received from the party leadership. The prospect of running with united Republican support was a further reason for giving the race serious consideration. Another favorable factor was that no major candidate appeared to oppose him. Former state chairman Fred Sims declined to make the race, and Watson decided to run for the Republican nomination for the Senate, which was also being sought by Harry S. New, a former national committeeman. Provided he could win the March, 1916 primary election, the first ever to be held in Indiana, the nomination for governor belonged to Goodrich. "The die was cast," wrote Goodrich in his autobiography. "There was nothing for me to do but to make the race." To finance his primary campaign Goodrich wrote a personal check for $40,000 and he refused to accept any contributions.[24]

His main opponent was Warren T. McCray of Kentland who, through full-page newspaper ads, sought to win the farm vote by stressing his agrarian roots. Yet Goodrich had a distinct organizational advantage based upon the personal contacts he had made while directing five statewide campaigns. Goodrich felt the key to his success was a letter-writing campaign in which he asked all 25,000 precinct committeemen for their support. The results fully justified the effort since, recalled Goodrich, "By the time these letters reached their destinations and the boys in the precincts had time to think it over there wasn't much difficulty about it as I carried 87 of the 92 counties in Indiana." (Almost as gratifying was the discovery that his election effort cost less than expected, and his campaign chairman was able to return to Goodrich an unexpended $2,000.) To oppose Goodrich the Democrats selected as their gubernatorial candidate John A. M. Adair of Portland, a ten-year veteran of the House of Representatives. In the Republican Senate primary, New defeated Watson in a bitter contest in which Watson claimed to have been fraudulently "counted out." Fortunately for Republican unity, Senator Benjamin F. Shively died and the Republicans, who now had to select two candidates for the Senate, were able to offer nominations both to New and Watson.[25]

To his discomfort Goodrich found that being a candidate was far more stressful and complicated than he had remembered from his days as state chairman. He had no difficulty in developing a platform for his campaign. He stressed the need to revamp the state property tax, and called for the abolition of unnecessary bureaucrats and the consolidation of the state executive machinery. The problem for Goodrich was how to find the time for statewide campaigning and at the same time write speeches and issue press releases. In a word, said Goodrich, "I needed publicity." Fortunately the state committee came to his aid in the form of Chairman Will Hays, "the best publicity man that ever lived," and two talented journalists, George Lockwood of the Muncie *Press,* and Carl Mote of Indianapolis. On the advice of Hays he delivered his first speech at Greencastle, Indiana, the home of DePauw University. In drafting the document Goodrich found that he had no trouble in summarizing his basic ideas. But he realized the address was terribly dull and that it lacked "that polish, that oratorical finish necessary in a campaign document." Frankly admitting his limitations, he "turned it over" to Lockwood, who recast it in a form which made "a very favorable impression." The

general facts and framework were his, recalled Goodrich, "but the
language in which it was clothed was George Lockwood's."[26]

Mote's contribution was just as valuable. Goodrich detailed the
former reporter to research the shortcomings of the Democratic ad-
ministrations of Thomas R. Marshall and Samuel Ralston. He would
then prepare, under Goodrich's name, a press release criticizing the
Democrats for such vices as excessive state spending. Another of
Mote's favorite themes was to question Adair's knowledge of state
government because, as a congressman, he had not lived in the state
for nearly a decade. Goodrich found that he could say whatever he
pleased during his campaign travels as the press did much of his
work for him by printing Mote's articles verbatim. According to
Will Hays, a great Goodrich admirer, the strategy placed Adair in
"an amazing situation" in which he was forced to admit "that it was
useless for him to answer the Goodrich accusations."[27]

In response to Goodrich's newspaper campaign, his Democratic
opponent attacked several vulnerable aspects of Goodrich's record.
Probably the most embarrassing revelation was Adair's discovery
that Goodrich had paid only thirteen dollars in property tax the
previous year. How could a man paying so little have the effrontery,
he asked, to offer advice on changing the tax laws? In rebuttal Goodrich pointed out that most of his property and investments were
registered in the name of a corporation which had paid substantial
taxes. Besides, he argued, even the smallest taxpayer had the right
to demand that tax money be managed conservatively and honestly.
Goodrich was also forced to defend himself against the insinuation
that his public utility companies had profited excessively at the expense of the general public. And much of his time was spent denying
reports that he had been seen drinking in saloons; apparently he was
confused with his brother Ed. Goodrich freely admitted to having
entered saloons while campaigning, but he denied having consumed
any beer. Edward S. Shumaker, the head of the Anti-Saloon League,
pointedly asked Goodrich if he minded explaining why he had been
seen in a saloon. "No, not at all," replied the candidate. "I was
looking for votes."[28]

Voter interest in the election was naturally high because two Senate
seats and the governorship were at stake. Moreover, both vice presidential candidates, Thomas R. Marshall, who ran for reelection with
Woodrow Wilson, and Charles Fairbanks, the running mate of Republican Charles Evans Hughes, were from Indiana. The indefati-
gable leadership of Hays was a great asset to Goodrich's candidacy.
With missionary zeal Hays established direct mail and telephone
contacts with county and precinct committeemen, and he saturated

the state with Republican literature and motion picture films, the latter being a novel step for 1916 which perhaps foreshadowed Hays's later role as the "czar" or "Judge Landis" of the movie industry. Hays recalled that when national Republican officials visited that state they were openly surprised by the degree of Republican unity and by the thoroughness of the organizational preparations. The only disappointment on 8 November was that Hughes lost the presidency to Wilson even though he carried Indiana by more than 7,000 votes. Both Republican senatorial candidates were victorious and the Republicans won nine of the thirteen congressional seats and a majority of both houses of the legislature. Leading the ticket was Goodrich, who defeated Adair by 12,771 votes, a higher margin of victory than polled by New (who won over Senator John Kern by 11,501 votes), or Watson (who was elected by 9,616 votes over Boss Tom Taggart). Despite feeling pride and relief in his victory, Goodrich was not anxious to repeat the experience of running a statewide campaign. "I became pretty thoroughly disgusted with being a candidate," he recorded in his autobiography. "I did not like it, and think I was somewhat indifferent as to whether or not I should be elected."[29]

2

A Hoosier Caesar?

As an experienced politician heading a united party and having control of both houses of the legislature, Goodrich should have been a successful governor. Assuming that he would be the beneficiary of a political honeymoon at the beginning of his administration, Goodrich confidently presented to the legislature a moderate program of progressive reform. His most controversial proposal was to enact an excise tax on corporate property so as to equalize the state tax burden between agriculture and industry. His objective, said the governor, was to remedy a "deplorable" tax situation in which the poorer counties in the south were overassessed and overtaxed, while the northern counties and industrial centers paid less than their fair share. Goodrich further advocated establishing a nonpolitical department of conservation to protect the natural resources of the state. Likewise he would reorganize the state highway commission on a nonpartisan basis. Another of his pet projects was to repeal the oil inspection law whereby about seventy politically appointed inspectors pocketed fees merely for certifying as accurate a chemical analysis provided by private oil companies. Goodrich contended that the existing system should be abolished, as it "rendered no service either to the state or the consumers of oil." Also for the purpose of improving governmental efficiency he proposed to make the office of state geologist appointive rather than elective and he called for abolishing the unnecessary post of state statistician. Statistician Henry A. Roberts, Goodrich complained, "had not a single qualification in the world for the job, and could not even spell the name of his office." Goodrich was realistic enough to anticipate opposition to his program from the Democrats. But he expected to receive solid Republican support for his progressive program. During the campaign, after all, his fellow Republicans had often said to him, "This is good stuff—go to it." But as governor he discovered "that the 'boys' all thought opportunities for service to the state should be reserved for Republicans only."[1] The result was a legislative fiasco that left Goodrich discouraged and humiliated.

Almost immediately Goodrich experienced personal criticism when he removed Edwin Lee, a progressive Republican, from the Public Service Commission. Goodrich contended that Lee, an appointee of Governor Ralston, had been incompetent in supervising public utilities. Primarily the governor's action was motivated by politics, however, as Goodrich viewed Lee's appointment to the commission as a Democratic plot to keep the Progressive Party alive and thereby divide and conquer the Republicans. Still it came as a shock when Democratic legislators and newspapers condemned the dismissal of Lee as an act of political "terrorism" on the part of the governor. Democrats, joined by dissident Republican senators, then managed to defeat the oil inspectors bill. One Democratic senator, who urged Goodrich to postpone action, frankly said to the governor, "I cannot afford to vote to put sixty-seven Democrats out of office." (In March Goodrich got his revenge by naming Carl Mote chief oil inspector. All sixty-seven Democratic inspectors were dismissed and replaced by Republicans. "I got a great deal of satisfaction out of that," Goodrich recollected.)[2]

The greatest embarrassment suffered by Goodrich during the legislative session was the defeat of his excise tax bill by Republican senators of "small mind and narrow vision." After his years of faithful service to the party, Goodrich was appalled by the unexpected back stabbing by his fellow Republicans. "It was a strange situation in which I found myself," he recalled. "The men who had been associated with party politics ever since 1900 complimented me during the campaign on the promises made and almost invariably said that it was 'good stuff.' But after my inauguration, they began to express grave doubts as to the wisdom and political expediency of so many new and unusual things." The most dismaying defection of all was that of Lieutenant Governor Edgar Bush who, according to Goodrich, "tried to sabotage every policy of my administration," and who "swelled up like a poisoned pigeon" as he was courted by corporate interests. Goodrich could not, however, deny that he was himself responsible for having selected Bush, a dry, to run for lieutenant governor instead of John Lewis of Seymour, a wet. "As it turned out," recalled Goodrich, "I would have been better off with John Lewis drunk than Ed Bush sober." About all Goodrich could take credit for as a result of the legislative session was a prohibition law and a woman suffrage law. Actually, on the latter measure, Goodrich had not changed his mind since his youth when he had opposed woman suffrage as a member of the Knights of Labor. "I never subscribed to the idea that it would in any way purify politics as so many advocates had suggested," he noted, "nor did I believe it would improve the political situation in any way, holding that the doubling of voters would very greatly increase the expense of carrying on a campaign."[3] At least Goodrich was a good enough politician not to express his views in public.

The governor's legislative frustrations were soon overshadowed by America's declaration of war against Germany. Preoccupied by his battles with the legislature, Goodrich had paid little attention to such ominous European developments as Germany's decision to conduct unrestricted submarine warfare, the interception of the sensational Zimmermann telegram which proposed a German-Mexican alliance, or the sinking of American merchant ships near the British Isles—which Wilson in his war message termed "overt acts of war." Nor did the governor pay much attention to the collapse of the monarchy in Russia, the formation of a pro-western Provisional Government, or the arrival in Russia of Lenin aboard a sealed German train—events which later had a profound influence on Goodrich's life and fortunes.

Back at home Goodrich had his hands full organizing state support of the war effort. Will Hays was appointed head of the State Council of Defense to coordinate all aspects of the state's war effort, including publicity, the encouragement of voluntary enlistments, and the sale of liberty bonds. Goodrich appealed to farmers to increase food production and he established a clearinghouse to seek war contracts for state businesses and their workers. But he met stiff resistance when he urged coal producers to accept a fair price for coal. One coal operator, who demanded a price of three and a half dollars a ton, bluntly told Goodrich in the governor's office, "We propose to get ours while the getting is good." The imbroglio was especially embarrassing to Goodrich because he was a stockholder in two unpatriotic coal companies that demanded excessive profits. To prevent price gouging Goodrich prepared to call a special session of the legislature. Immediately, however, a way out appeared when the President imposed, on 22 August 1917, a national coal price of two dollars a ton, which Goodrich regarded as a fair solution. Thus the special legislative session became unnecessary, which was fortunate for Goodrich because on the same day that Wilson fixed the price of coal, the governor experienced the first distressing symptoms of typhoid fever.[4]

For two months he was hospitalized with a high temperature, headache, and general exhaustion. Afterwards Goodrich was told by his doctors that he had been close to death. Frank Litschert, the governor's private secretary, shielded Goodrich's privacy by releasing little specific information about the governor's medical condition. As a result, Litschert later recalled, "I do not think that the general public ever realized how ill he was." As late as 11 October Goodrich was still too weak to answer his mail. By 21 October, two months after becoming ill, he was finally strong enough to sit up and receive a few visitors. To complete his convalescence he decided to return on 22 October to his home at Winchester. Six days later Fred Sims, a Goodrich ally and the head of the state board of tax commissioners, came to Winchester with the news that acting governor Bush was about to announce appointments to the state supreme court and the state public service commission. Goodrich was enraged and decided to return immediately to Indianapolis to reclaim his office. In making the trip by ambulance Goodrich rejected the advice of his physician, who told him that such an ordeal could endanger his life. Weak though he was, Goodrich got great satisfaction from observing Bush's surprise when the lieutenant governor arrived at the state house and found Goodrich sitting in the governor's chair. "The expression on his face was worth seeing," Goodrich remembered. Following a brief reception in his honor, Goodrich "got away from the office as quickly as I possibly could," and embarked on a month-long trip to New Orleans and New Mexico. "Every muscle in me was completely burned out," he wrote a friend, "and while I am feeling better than I have in years, yet it is necessary to take a very brief rest in order to recover my physical strength." Not until the end of November was Goodrich back in his office, having been out of action for three entire months.[5]

His second year as governor was no more satisfying than the first. "The new year [1918] started out with the [Goodrich] administration faced with all sorts of difficulties," he noted in his autobiography. His troubles included a serious coal shortage, a January blizzard which disrupted freight and passenger traffic, and the destruction of the state reformatory at Jeffersonville in a fire. He also lost the services of Will Hays as head of the state council of defense because Hays, with the strong support of Goodrich and Theodore Roosevelt, was elected on 14 February to the prestigious and powerful position of chairman of the Republican National Committee. Already the preliminary skirmishing was under way in preparation for the 1920 presidential campaign. The selection of Hays was designed by Roosevelt's supporters as the first step toward again nominating him for the presidency. According to Goodrich, Roosevelt himself suggested that Goodrich would make an excellent running mate, an idea that was not politically farfetched in that two recent vice presidents, Fairbanks and Marshall, had come from Indiana. Goodrich answered that the question was premature and maintained "that I had no ambition whatever in that direction."[6]

Amid the political maneuvering Goodrich continued to be plagued by a parade of relatively minor difficulties that demanded his personal attention. "It seemed that there was scarcely a week passed that some problem or question did not arise," he recalled. As governor he was called upon to protest the draft quotas assigned to Indiana on the ground that the federal authorities failed to give the state sufficient credit for its many previous voluntary enlistments. Then he was faced with the "disagreeable task" of trying to enforce Indiana's prohibition law. Next, Goodrich had a "disagreeable experience" with Dr. Horace Ellis, the state superintendent of public instruction. Goodrich was first upset when he received reports that Ellis had accepted a substantial sum of money from a book company. Another of the governor's concerns involved allegations of personal misconduct by Ellis. "He had a young lady in his office with little or no duties to perform," recalled Goodrich. "Her presence and her relations with Dr. Ellis were a source of common gossip around the state house that was not at all helpful." Finally, Goodrich was disillusioned because the superintendent had placed his son, Howell, on the payroll of his office. In a painful interview, Goodrich delivered an ultimatum giving Ellis twenty-four hours to withdraw as a candidate for reelection. Although Goodrich prevailed, he incurred the lasting ill will of Ellis and his son. (According to Goodrich, Howell Ellis later got his revenge when, as a member of the Indiana Public Service Commission, he ruled "without any justification whatever" against a case brought by Goodrich's son, Pierre.) At least the Republican state convention went well, as the delegates applauded Goodrich's keynote address and endorsed the state ticket without opposition.[7]

Soon the governor's discontent returned. "We had all kinds of trouble toward the middle of 1918," he noted. The railroads, now nationalized by the Wilson administration, were unable to furnish sufficient cars to carry the state's war production. Furthermore, Goodrich was displeased when the president, unnecessarily in his opinion, raised the price of grain in order to increase farmers' profits and stimulate production. Goodrich maintained that no increase was justified and that existing rates were high enough.

Then on 28 August came the most painful personal experience of his life. Goodrich had been invited to the home of an Indianapolis physician, Dr. Amelia Keller, who was giving a farewell dinner for a number of medical officers about to depart for the western front. Personally Goodrich did not want to go, but changed his mind when his wife called with word that Dr. Keller had telephoned his home and urged the governor to attend. On his way home, Goodrich was involved in a serious accident when his automobile was struck broadside by a streetcar. He was thrown from the car and suffered fractures of the hip, skull, ribs, collarbone, and left hand, in addition to bruises "too numerous to mention." For the next two months he was confined to the hospital in a plaster body cast and he described himself as being "pretty badly knocked out." He was also understandably discouraged. "Fate seems to be against me," he wrote to one friend. To another he confided, "I think I have had about my share of trouble. . . . My only regret is that I am not able to accomplish the things that I had hoped to work out—so many complicated ambitions, so many selfish interests that one makes progress too slowly."[8]

From his hospital room Goodrich was able to read and answer his mail and generally carry on the affairs of state, but his physical recovery was discouragingly slow. By the first of the year he was able to get around "on four legs" through the use of crutches. However, his hip—the same hip he had fractured as a young man—was slow to heal properly. In a state of distress former senator Albert Beveridge urged Goodrich to consult "the very best and most expert and *trustworthy* specialist to be had. Take no chances, dear friend. Fellows like us are scarce—'there are so few of us left.'" As late as June 1919 Goodrich was forced to cancel a planned trip to Toledo, because his doctor advised "very strongly" against excessive use of his leg. Even after he was able to give up crutches in the fall of 1919, Goodrich complained that it was very difficult for him to get around because of "red neuralgia" in his feet and ankles.[9] For the rest of his life the governor walked with the aid of a cane.

On balance the final two years of his governorship, marred neither by illness nor accident, were far more bearable for Goodrich than the first two. From Goodrich's perspective the most welcome development was an improvement in his relations with the legislature. The key factor behind the governor's newfound legislative influence was the decisive Republican victory in the November 1918 election. To Goodrich's amazement, President Wilson unwisely upset the nation's wartime mood of bipartisanship by appealing for the election of a Democratic congress. It was the governor's opinion that Wilson's blunder enabled the Republicans to carry all thirteen congressional seats and to gain "full control" of the legislature. Moreover, Goodrich followed up the election gains by calling a unity meeting of all Republican members of the legislature and congress which met at the state capital on 15 November. At least superficial unity was achieved as all present, including Watson and Bush, pledged to support the state party platform. But privately, complained Goodrich, party conservatives gave him only "lukewarm support" and caused "all kinds of trouble" in their attempts to "sabotage" his administration.[10]

For the most part, however, Goodrich prevailed during the winter session of the legislature, as several of his proposals which had been blocked two years previously were passed on their second introduction. One of the governor's greatest legislative victories was the approval of a department of conservation. Much of the credit belonged to State Forester Richard Lieber, who prepared the bill and effectively lobbied members of the legislature. The governor was also pleased by the passage of workmen's compensation and by the passage of his proposal to place state highway construction and maintenance under the control of a four-member nonpartisan commission. On the tax question Goodrich accepted a compromise bill which maintained existing rates, but purported to distribute the burden more equitably. He liked to call it the "Goodrich Tax Bill," although it was written by a legislative conference committee and fell far short of his sweeping excise tax proposal of 1917. Several progressive measures failed to pass, including a ban on child labor, a measure giving cities the right to establish the commission form of government, and a proposal to regulate the hours of women workers in industrial occupations. Nevertheless, Goodrich was pleased enough to issue a statement calling the legislature's record the most constructive in fifty years.[11]

This extravagant judgment was in part based on the approval of several of the governor's most cherished personal projects: the work of the oil inspectors was transferred to the Pure Food and Health Department, and the offices of state geologist and state statistician were abolished. In congratulating the legislature for its actions on behalf of increased efficiency, Goodrich did not disclose that he had personally paid the campaign expenses of the state geologist amounting to "something over a thousand dollars" with the understanding that the official would resign when requested to do so by the governor. And Goodrich offered the public a highly selective accounting of the facts behind the resignation of Henry A. Roberts, the chief of the State Labor Bureau and the Bureau of Statistics. All that appeared in the press was a letter from Roberts to Goodrich stating that the former statistician had decided to pursue unspecified commercial opportunities and would not accept Goodrich's offer to appoint him to the post of state fish and game commissioner. In submitting his letter of resignation to Goodrich, Roberts included the cryptic statement: "I want to assure you personally that I felt you have more than discharged the public obligation which you voluntarily assumed toward me when the movement to abolish the office to which I had been elected assumed definite form." The letter did not reveal that Goodrich had personally presented to Roberts liberty bonds with a face value of $4,000 (after having carefully removed interest coupons which were due within a few days.)[12]

Several days later, recalled Goodrich, Roberts appeared to say that his attorney advised that he was entitled to the unpaid coupon interest in addition to the face value of the bonds. Anxious to end the matter, Goodrich agreed and directed his secretary to write a check to cover the modest additional amount. According to Goodrich, when the clerk of the Supreme Court learned of the secret arrangement he remarked, "I am going to sell out to the Governor. For four thousand dollars he can have my office too." Fortunately for Goodrich's reputation as a man of integrity, word of his under-the-table payments did not reach the press or the opposition. No doubt the information would have made choice campaign ammunition for Democratic critics who, like Claude Bowers of the Fort Wayne *Journal-Gazette*, delighted in characterizing Goodrich as a "Hoosier Caesar."[13] Had he been forced to explain himself, Goodrich could have plausibly defended his actions as motivated by a desire to improve governmental efficiency and save money for the taxpayers.

The completion of the legislative session meant that Goodrich was at last free to concentrate on the more agreeable subject of presidential politics. Originally it had been the intention of Goodrich to join with national chairman Will Hays in rallying the party machinery behind the candidacy of Theodore Roosevelt. But the unexpected death of Roosevelt from a stroke on 6 January 1919 left the governor and the party chairman "pretty much up in the air." One possibility for Goodrich was to support Roosevelt's former military associate and heir apparent, General Leonard Wood. When Goodrich, on crutches, traveled to New York in April 1919 to greet returning Indiana doughboys, he found that Wood's supporters had started a newspaper campaign proposing a Wood-Goodrich ticket in 1920. According to Goodrich, Wood was well aware that Goodrich and Hays had been promoters of Roosevelt's candidacy. Therefore, it appeared to Goodrich that the "Goodrich for vice president" rumors were a transparent attempt to attract the support of the two Indiana Republicans to Wood's candidacy. In reality the rumors were mere speculation and there is no record of there having been any discussion or correspondence between Wood and Goodrich about the topic. No doubt Goodrich was flattered to have been mentioned, but the

governor was thoroughly disillusioned with public life and had no
interest in seeking further public office. His position was "that under
no circumstance would I accept the nomination for vice president in
order to accommodate the friends of General Wood."[14]

Goodrich's determination to return to private life was reinforced
during the final months of his administration by accumulated labor
troubles, personal attacks by Democrats, and the usual insatiable
demands on his time. In the fall of 1919 Indiana was brushed by the
national Red Scare, as the state experienced strikes in steel and coal.
Goodrich had to send the National Guard to Gary and Hammond
where quantities of revolutionary literature were discovered. But the
governor refused to believe press reports that the strike was a plot
to overthrow the government or that the strikers had been subverted
by Red propaganda. The coal strike, which began simultaneously,
posed a more serious problem since John L. Lewis, the leader of the
United Mine Workers, refused to guarantee that his union would
provide sufficient fuel to operate state institutions and public utilities.
"I was very much disappointed in John L. Lewis," Goodrich noted.
To the great relief of the governor, both strikes petered out by the
end of the year. But to his acute annoyance, Goodrich had to contend
with repeated Democratic sniping at his record. One legislator publicly called Goodrich a socialist for having appointed Carl Mote and
Richard Lieber to his administration. (Possibly Goodrich provoked
the outburst by referring to President Wilson as an international
socialist for advocating American membership in the proposed league
of nations.) Goodrich was also "unjustly criticized," at least in his
opinion, for having pardoned 662 criminals during his first two and
a half years as governor, whereas governors Ralston and Marshall
had only extended clemency to 210 and 225 respectively. Goodrich
was infuriated because his critics told only a portion of the story.
They left out the fact that he only extended clemency to first-time
offenders in cases where a pardon was recommended by the prosecut-
ing attorney, the judge, and the local draft board. Ninety percent of
those pardoned performed well once drafted into the army, argued
Goodrich, and his actions, therefore, deserved understanding rather
than condemnation.[15]

To defend the record of his administration, Goodrich accepted
more public engagements than usual during the summer and fall of
1919. In June he attended commencement ceremonies at the Muncie
Normal School and the meeting of the Imperial Council of the Murat
Temple of Indianapolis. On the Fourth of July he denounced the
evils of Bolshevism at the Indiana Soldiers' Home at Marion. In
subsequent speeches to Republican groups at Magnesia Springs and

Wabash he defended his administration's tax policy. And in an address to the National Grain Dealers Association at Kansas City, he criticized the Wilson administration for failing to deal decisively with strikes caused by radical agitators. Despite his heavy work schedule Goodrich found some time for play. On Memorial Day he accepted the invitation of the Indianapolis Motor Speedway (which included a private box and six free tickets) to attend its annual 500-mile race. And a month later he accepted an invitation from the Commerce Club of Toledo to be a guest of honor during a cruise on Lake Erie. "We have chartered the steamship South America and the indications are that we will have a splendid time. It will be a stag affair," read the invitation. Occasionally even the disillusioned Goodrich found that being governor of Indiana carried with it some enjoyable privileges. And he was genuinely disappointed when his doctor advised that his broken hip had not healed sufficiently for him to make the trip.[16]

For the most part Goodrich's final year as governor was devoted to preparing for the national and state elections of 1920. This time Goodrich found it difficult to muster his usual election year enthusiasm. Three turbulent years as governor, his bout with typhoid fever, and his automobile accident had all taken their toll on his political energy and ambition. Furthermore, he had trouble deciding which of the many Republican candidates to support for the nomination. Since the death of Roosevelt a host of contenders had materialized, including General Wood; Senator Hiram Johnson of California; Governor Frank Lowden of Illinois; Herbert Hoover, the mining engineer and humanitarian; and Senator Warren G. Harding of Ohio. Personally Goodrich found none of them particularly appealing. A related question was whether Goodrich should permit his name to appear on the 4 May presidential ballot as Indiana's favorite son. Will Hays urged Goodrich to enter the race so as to discourage the other candidates from entering and dividing Indiana's vote between them. Goodrich was naturally flattered by the suggestion, but on mature reflection concluded that he had "no real ambition" to get involved in the contest. "If I was moved by a consuming ambition to hold office," he wrote Will Hays, "it would be different, but after three years of it, the glamor has all disappeared and I really want to be out of official life and get back again to the work in which I have always been reasonably contented." On 28 January Goodrich settled the question once and for all by announcing that he would not permit his name to be placed on the ballot.[17]

Briefly he considered supporting Herbert Hoover, for whom he had "very great admiration." However, he was wary of Hoover because he was not a party regular. Finally, without much conviction, he decided to support the California progressive and isolationist, Hiram Johnson. His decision was based less upon ideological grounds than upon his feeling that Johnson would make the strongest national candidate of all the Republican contenders. In the Republican race for governor he used all his influence to block the ambitions of Ed Bush. And when Bush was forced to withdraw from the race in March for lack of financial backing, the governor gloated, "He never had a chance." Quietly Goodrich tried to pick his successor by discreetly supporting the candidacy of Edward C. Toner over Warren McCray. On the day of the primary election, Goodrich was mildly disappointed when Toner finished sixty thousand votes behind the front-runner McCray. Goodrich was better pleased by the results of the presidential primary, in which Senator Johnson finished a close second to General Wood, with Lowden placing third and Harding a distant fourth. Yet the result demonstrated that Goodrich was less than a master politician in that he had failed to back a winner in either race. Moreover, by spurning the chance to run as Indiana's favorite son, Goodrich let slip a splendid opportunity for enhancing his national status in the party. More than likely Goodrich, running with the support of the state organization, would have easily carried the primary and won all or most of the delegates. With a united delegation Indiana Republicans would have possessed at least some leverage in the presidential selection process at Chicago. As it was, the delegation was hopelessly fragmented and even Goodrich admitted "the result was [that] our state carried little or no influence in the convention when it met in the spring of 1920."[18] After ten ballots, Senator Warren G. Harding, the handsome and available choice of the party leadership, received the presidential nomination. Then the unexpected occurred and the convention chose for vice president the obscure favorite son of Massachusetts, Governor Calvin Coolidge. If political lightning could strike Massachusetts, it must have occurred to Goodrich that the same fate could have happened to a favorite son of Indiana—a state which had provided two recent vice presidents.

Nearing the conclusion of his term, Goodrich had no second thoughts about leaving public life. As he wrote to Senator Harry S. New, "I have no desire or ambition to do anything but finish my administration as best I can then go back to my business. I am done with politics for ever and a day." But as long as he was still governor he could not completely avoid political duties. In July he was compelled to call a special legislative session which debated for eighteen days before passing a modest tax increase and a deficiency appropriation to finance state institutions and increase teachers' salaries. He also succeeded in getting a $2 million appropriation for a soldiers' memorial at Indianapolis, and a bill establishing a state coal commission to regulate the price of coal in the public interest. But his proposal to give the State Purchasing Commission authority to buy a coal mine so as to guarantee the state an ample supply of coal at a fair price was deemed too socialistic and died in committee. Fulfilling his political duty he busily campaigned on behalf of Republican candidates. Speaking at Muncie, he defended his administration as having set a model of economy and efficiency. Had James Cox, the Democratic governor of Ohio and his party's presidential candidate, been governor of Indiana an $8 million tax increase would have been required, he contended. But on the campaign trail he once again demonstrated a tendency to be accident prone. Visiting the state fish hatchery at South Bend with Richard Lieber he managed to fall into a pond while attempting to feed a frog to a large bass. For the rest of the tour Goodrich was compelled to wear a game warden's uniform.[19]

Goodrich spent the final month of the campaign traveling throughout southern Indiana. Ostensibly he was inspecting the condition of the state highway system and examining proposed highway routes. In the process he seized the opportunity to defend the integrity and frugality of his administration and to advocate the election of the national ticket of Harding and Coolidge. His travels and contacts left no doubt in his mind that the Republicans were headed for a decisive victory. Writing to Harding, Goodrich urged the candidate to say nothing further one way or the other about American membership in the proposed league of nations. "This fight is won," he contended. "Why take any chances of throwing it away?" He predicted that Harding would carry every state west of the Mississippi except for Arkansas, Louisiana, and Texas, and would carry every state north of the Ohio River including Indiana. "If you never come in the state," he advised, "we will carry it by at least seventy-five to a hundred thousand. I know I am not deceived in this, because I have taken the trouble to go out in the counties and to send for men and get at this thing from the 'grass roots'. You will have no trouble to be elected. That matter is already settled. Your troubles will come after the fourth day of March."[20]

On election day all of Goodrich's predictions came true, except that he was wrong about Harding's margin of victory in Indiana which was 182,000 votes, almost twice what Goodrich had anticipated. The Republicans carried all thirteen Indiana congressional seats, won both houses of the legislature, and elected McCray to succeed Goodrich as governor. The outgoing chief executive could hardly wait to lay down the burdens of office. With just two months of his term remaining, he wrote a friend, "I will be the happiest man in Indiana when the tenth day of January comes and I can once more be free. Never again will I even think of rendering any service to the people in an official capacity." His final official duty was to attend the swearing in of his successor. According to newspaper reports, Goodrich appeared elated and in his prepared remarks he made no secret of the great personal relief he felt in completing his term. "The hour of my deliverance is now at hand," he stated. "I feel like saying: 'Lord now lettest thou thy servant depart in peace.' Gladly did I take up the burdens four years ago and gladly do I lay them down."[21]

For Goodrich his term as governor had been the most difficult period of his life. In his naivete he had assumed the governorship would be a bed of roses. Presumably his fellow Republicans, in gratitude for his years of service to the party, would rally about his program. Instead, Goodrich learned the hard way that many elected Republican legislators were resentful about accepting the leadership of a wealthy man who had never held elective office. As chief executive he had learned to "beware of Greeks bearing gifts."[22] He had discovered that his "friends" approached him as champions of the public interest when in fact they were representatives of special interests. Disillusioned by the disloyalty, backbiting, and logrolling of his fellow Republicans, discouraged by his bout with typhoid fever and his crippling automobile accident, Goodrich came to regard the governorship as a personal prison. It was an experience that had failed dismally to live up to his expectations.

His unhappy memories of the governorship aside, Goodrich could look back on his record in law, banking, and politics with a good deal of satisfaction. Starting as a mere "country lawyer from over at Winchester" he had excelled in the world of business despite, he said, having given half of every dollar he made to his wife. The governor's net worth is unknown, but he undoubtedly qualified as a self-made millionaire, a luxury which later enabled him to donate almost $400,000 to Wabash College at Crawfordsville, Indiana. Goodrich to the contrary, there is no evidence he made much of an effort "to check on himself to keep from making too much." But professional politics, not money-making, was his first love and real calling. In his uncompleted autobiography, written for Pierre Goodrich in 1938–1939, the governor devoted just 28 pages to his childhood and education and 160 pages to his political career. Quietly and inconspicuously, while demonstrating a great capacity for work and thorough organization, he had come to dominate the Republican political machinery of one of the midwest's most pivotal states. At heart he was a conservative organization man, but as state chairman he had had the good sense not to take public sides in the disagreements between the opposing Fairbanks-Beveridge party factions. His rather self-righteous streak of independence, earlier expressed in his memberships in the Grange and the Knights of Labor, had again served him well by enabling him to remain above the fray and to stay on fairly good terms with both conservative and progressive Indiana Republicans.

With good reason Goodrich looked upon his governorship as a personal time of troubles. That he was forced to spend much of his term in the hospital must have been deeply discouraging. Yet Goodrich tended to magnify his disappointments. After his initial legislative reverses, Goodrich regrouped his forces and, with the exception of a corporate excise tax, he eventually secured passage of the bulk of his program—including the establishment of a department of conservation, a nonpartisan highway commission, a state coal commission, and the elimination of the useless oil inspectors and the nonessential posts of state geologist and state statistician. Despite his reservations on woman suffrage, Goodrich had slowly emerged as a moderate champion of progressive reform; he had been a professional politician who actually reduced the number of patronage positions available for distribution via the spoils system. Leaving office, Goodrich could truthfully say that he had fulfilled his personal goal (as expressed to Jim Watson in January 1917) "to give Indiana a good business administration and make it easier for the boys who are to come after me to be elected." Entering his retirement, Goodrich longed for peace and quiet and the opportunity to travel abroad for the first time. He vaguely told a correspondent that one of his ideas after leaving office was to visit Russia to observe Bolshevism in action. No timetable was mentioned for such an undertaking which, like his youthful idea of joining the navy, was probably a bit of romanticizing on Goodrich's part.[23] Unlike his vision of life on the high seas, Goodrich's dream of visiting Russia came true sooner than anticipated, but under circumstances that were completely unexpected.

3

A Short Retirement

In 1922, a year after Goodrich left office, Sinclair Lewis published *Babbitt*, a novel which was both a satirical and a serious examination of the Midwestern businessman. The star of the work, the hustling real estate salesman George F. Babbitt, was the personification of thoughtless American conformity and his last name became a new word in the English language. Certainly the novel was not written with Goodrich in mind, but there were at least some superficial similarities between James P. Goodrich and George F. Babbitt. Both were provincial Midwestern businessmen, joiners, boosters, Presbyterians, and Republican loyalists. Neither had ever traveled outside the country and neither was given to deep theorizing. Yet the apparent simile between the two men was far from perfect. Goodrich was not a moral hypocrite or social climber, and—unlike Babbitt—he could not have made a superpatriotic and anti–intellectual speech to a convention of realtors. Moreover, Goodrich was not a conformist; he was perfectly able to make up his own mind based upon the facts as he saw them. Surprisingly Goodrich soon came to demonstrate a high degree of political independence in the domain of foreign policy, an area where he lacked experience and expertise. It is inconceivable that Sinclair Lewis's Babbitt could have committed so awful a heresy as to urge, contrary to the considered advice of both political parties, the establishment of normal diplomatic and commercial relations with Soviet Russia.

As governor of Indiana Goodrich had had only the most limited contact with foreign policy. In 1917 he had supported America's entry into World War I as an act of patriotism. Preoccupied with state matters, he had had little time or inclination to think or offer advice about the war's consequences. Insofar as he had thought about foreign relations, he was influenced largely by partisan political considerations. Both of Indiana's Republican senators, Harry New and Jim Watson, were opposed to American membership in the proposed league of nations and so was Goodrich. Based on his soundings of public opinion, he maintained that Wilson's league concept was politically doomed. As he wrote Harding: "The people of this country are against the League of Nations 'lock, stock and barrel.' I do not care what the intellectuals and some newspapers say about it. I know I am not mistaken. Taft, Root, Wickersham, and their like don't represent the sentiment of this country and they don't understand how the people feel about the question." Even when his views on foreign policy were free of partisanship, his opinions were often superficial. Speaking at the National Military Home during the Red Scare, the governor said that Bolshevism was doomed to failure and that any Red tendencies in America would be overcome not with force but with justice. "Americanism will prevail," he concluded. "Our country will continue its onward march and the work of our fathers, started nearly a century and a half ago will go on to completion." And in a speech at Indianapolis on 1 March 1920, Goodrich announced, "You don't make Bolshevists or Socialists out of men that have money saved in the form of life insurance or in a home."[1]

To Goodrich Bolshevism was synonymous with anarchism. He had never seen a Bolshevik and knew little about the course of the revolution which had brought Lenin to power in November 1917. He distantly knew that the Bolsheviks had signed a separate peace with Germany in the spring of 1918, that civil war had broken out between Reds and Whites, and that the Allies had intervened weakly in Siberia and North Russia. During his final year and a half as governor most of his time was spent on politics, but from press reports he became vaguely aware that the civil war and foreign intervention had ended, that Lenin and the Bolsheviks were holding on to power, and that the country was generally exhausted and disorganized. As a good practicing capitalist Goodrich had been startled by the repeated Bolshevik appeals for proletarian revolution to overthrow the governments of the West. But during the Red Scare he had refused to panic, because he was convinced that Communism was too alien and too artificial to appeal to the mass of American workers. His general impression of the Bolshevik leaders was that they were honest but ignorant idealists who would be forced by circumstances to modify their Communist ideology. Soon concrete support for Goodrich's view emerged when Lenin, in March 1921, introduced the New Economic Policy. Under the NEP the peasants were permitted to retain a portion of their grain, small-scale private manufacturing was permitted, and a system of state banks was established to finance new ventures and attract foreign accounts. Seemingly Russia was returning to more traditional economic values.[2]

His neglected business affairs, rather than Russia, primarily oc-

cupied Goodrich's mind in the first six months after his retirement
from public office. In particular he was involved in negotiations to
become one of the major stockholders in the National City Bank of
Indianapolis. Having completed that project Goodrich and his wife
left Indiana in mid-August for an extensive vacation trip to the state
of New York. Their itinerary took them to New York City, Albany,
and Saratoga Springs, where they planned to remain for a few weeks.
The governor's leisurely vacation journey came only a few weeks
after the West became aware of the latest disaster to strike Russia:
the catastrophic famine of 1921 which swept the Ukraine and the
Volga region. Drought was the immediate cause, although the civil
war—which led to the confiscation of food reserves by both sides—
and Poland's invasion of the Ukraine were contributing factors. The
distress created a mass movement of refugees frantically searching
for sustenance. As traditional food supplies were exhausted the use
of food substitutes such as roots and flour made from grasses and
weeds became common. Seed grain, draft animals, cats, dogs, and
rodents were consumed, parents abandoned their children and numerous cases of necrophilism and cannibalism were recorded. A fa-
mous appeal for aid by the writer Maxim Gorky, published on 13
July 1921, made the world aware of the calamity. "I ask all honest
European and American people for prompt aid to the Russian people. Give bread and medicine."[3]

Speaking for the United States, Secretary of Commerce Herbert
Hoover signified his willingness to organize a program of famine
relief. Hoover had been in such a situation several times before.
During World War I he had earned an international reputation as a
humanitarian for his work in organizing Belgian relief. During the
Paris Peace Conference he had headed the American Relief Administration, an official agency that distributed food supplies on credit to
war-torn Europe. Once the war was over, the ARA remained in
existence in New York as a private organization with close ties to
the American government, and Hoover continued to serve as chairman. As a veteran of bureaucratic and political infighting between
rival humanitarian organizations, Hoover saw that the only way to
avoid waste and duplication of effort was to concentrate all relief
activity under the direction of one organization. Aggressively the
sometimes introverted Hoover moved to assure that his organization
was solely in charge of America's response to the famine. At Riga,
after two weeks of negotiation, the ARA's European director, Walter
L. Brown, signed an agreement with Soviet Deputy Commissar for
Foreign Affairs Maxim Litvinov. By the terms of the Riga pact (20
August 1921) the ARA was permitted to distribute relief supplies in

the famine regions and promised to refrain from all political activity whatsoever. As a result of arm-twisting by Hoover and President Harding, other American relief organizations (such as the American Friends Service Committee, the American Red Cross, the Federal Council of Churches, the Jewish Joint Distribution Committee, the Knights of Columbus, the National Catholic Welfare Council, the Young Men's Christian Association, the Young Women's Christian Association, the American Mennonite Relief Committee, the Volga Relief Society, and the National Lutheran Council) were persuaded under some duress to coordinate their efforts in Russia under the direction of the ARA.[4]

Selecting personnel for the Russian program was Hoover's next step. To head the operation he named Colonel William N. Haskell. A West Point graduate (class of 1901), Haskell was a logical choice because he had directed ARA operations in Roumania and Armenia during the Peace Conference. Because of his previous relief experience and his service in Eastern Europe, Haskell was justifiably regarded by Hoover as "an expert along this line." The possibility that Goodrich might be available was first mentioned to Hoover by Postmaster General Will Hays following a Cabinet meeting. Hoover responded enthusiastically and asked Hays to tell Goodrich "to come in to see me at once." Hoover's thought was that Goodrich could be appointed as "one of the important divisional heads" under Haskell. "I believe," wrote Hoover, "that it would be of substantial benefit to this country to have a man of such experience as Governor Goodrich obtain a real knowledge of what the real difficulties of this foolish economic system are."[5]

Throughout these discussions Goodrich and his wife were preparing to leave New York where they were vacationing at the Hotel McAlpin, fashionably located at Broadway and 34th Street. Their next destination was the resort community of Saratoga Springs. After a week's stay they planned to return to Winchester at the end of August. While still in Manhattan Goodrich unexpectedly received a note from Hays describing Hoover's ARA Russian operation and asking whether he would consider serving with the organization. Reading the letter (which Goodrich did not retain in his papers), the governor was surprised, excited, and perplexed. His first thought was that going to Russia would complicate his business plans. He was not at all certain, he wrote Hays, that he could get his affairs in order. As he thought more deeply about the idea he was excited by the prospect of undertaking a new and exotic adventure. And he was plainly flattered at being asked to go. "The fact that Hoover might look with favor on the proposition is a compliment in itself," he wrote his friend. By now there was no question that Goodrich wanted to go in the worst way, even though he claimed a bit transparently, "It will not disappoint me in the least if I am not asked."[6]

Upon his arrival at Albany on 24 August, Goodrich found a telegram from Hoover waiting for him at the Western Union office. It read simply, "Would be glad if you could conveniently come to Washington to discuss Russian situation." His interest now thoroughly whetted, Goodrich abandoned his vacation, took the next train for Washington, and made a reservation at the Willard Hotel. (His letters and later writings do not reveal how his wife felt about the turn of events, but presumably she encouraged his interest in serving the ARA. On his first trip to Russia a month later, Goodrich was accompanied by his wife to western Europe, although it was felt that sanitary and travel conditions were too risky for her to proceed further.)[7]

The next morning (25 August) Goodrich was able to meet Hoover and Haskell for the first time. In a brief interview with "the Chief," Goodrich candidly admitted, "I don't know anything about Russia." "That's why I want you to go," Hoover shot back. At the urging of Hoover and Haskell, Goodrich then agreed to go to Russia "with an open mind to investigate the entire famine situation, learn the truth about Russia and return as soon as the preliminary investigation was completed." Impulsively Goodrich said he could sail from New York on 2 September. However, on his return to Winchester, he found he had been far too optimistic and that it would take at least two weeks to get his affairs in sufficient order to leave. Haskell and Hoover readily agreed to a revised departure date of 17 September. "I am delighted to know you will be going to Russia," Hoover wrote. "I believe you can do a great service not only on the ground but in enlightening the American mind when you return."[8]

On the surface Goodrich was not very well qualified for such a mission. His entire experience had been in the world of business and domestic politics. Certainly his knowledge of foreign affairs was slight. But it would be an exaggeration to label him an irreconcilable isolationist on the basis of partisan remarks he had made against Wilson's league of nations while he was governor of Indiana. He was even less well informed about the history, geography, and culture of Russia than he was about foreign policy. Goodrich himself readily admitted: "I had never been in Russia and knew nothing about the country of the Great Bear excepting what I had learned at school and what I had read since in the American newspapers and magazines."[9] Yet, in a sense, his lack of preparation was an advantage in that he undertook his mission without holding intense anti-Soviet convictions (with the exception that Goodrich, like most westerners, regarded the Communist economic system to be contrary to human nature). Demonstrating a rather youthful curiosity, he saw his position with the ARA as an opportunity to combine a worthwhile humanitarian service with a last great adventure. At the age of fifty-seven, having achieved financial security and having attained all he desired in politics, Goodrich was at peace with himself and politically obligated to no one, Hoover included. He took literally Hoover's request that he approach the subject with an open mind. And as a result of his observations he was soon to begin a campaign to enlighten the American mind, but not quite in the direction anticipated by Hoover.

For the first two weeks of September Goodrich rushed to organize his affairs and gather a traveling kit. Sensing that he was about to undertake a journey of unique personal and historical significance, Goodrich purchased a compact diary so as to be able to make a daily record of his experiences. It was his intention to use the diary as the basis for a book about Russia, a project he began in 1922 but abandoned after completing a first draft of 300 pages. By mid-September steamship tickets for Goodrich and his wife arrived from ARA headquarters in New York. Illustrative of the hurried nature of the Russian operation, ARA officials at New York found that they were in the dark as to what title should be assigned to Goodrich. The New York office wondered also what financial arrangements Hoover had made with the governor. Perrin Galpin, the secretary of the ARA's New York office, assumed he was to pay the travel expenses of the Goodriches but not carry Goodrich on the payroll.[10]

The inquiries from New York quickly revealed that Hoover (perhaps casting some doubt on his reputation as a master administrator) had neglected to discuss with Goodrich such details as his title and compensation. Hoover's assistant, Christian A. Herter, confidentially replied to Galpin that the ARA "could well afford to pay any and all bills" which might be submitted by the Goodriches. And why could the ARA afford the luxury of paying the Goodriches' expenses? "Again confidentially," explained Herter, "Goodrich himself has loads of money and expects, I believe, to put some forty or fifty thousand dollars into Russian relief when he gets over on the other side so that we would probably be losing much more than we gained if we haggled over any expense accounts." In fact the new "special investigator," as Goodrich was now entitled, had no intention of asking the ARA for more than his own travel expenses. Apparently neither Hoover nor any other ARA officials specifically solicited the governor to contribute "loads of money." For his part

Goodrich was concentrating on last minute travel arrangements and thus did not discover the designs of the ARA upon his bank account.[11]

The Russian education of James P. Goodrich began with a ten-day crossing of the Atlantic aboard the liner *Kroonland*. The voyage to England gave the governor an enforced opportunity to recuperate from the rigorous preparations of the preceding three weeks. He also used the time to read newspaper and magazine reports about the famine and he perused a report prepared by the League of Nations. By chance he found another good source of information in the person of George Repp of Portland, Oregon, who was en route to Russia in his capacity as general secretary of the Volga Relief Society. Repp had been born in the Volga region and had immigrated to America at the age of two. His organization was composed of descendants of Germans who had settled in the Volga region during the reign of Catherine the Great. Subsequently Repp reported to his members, "Before we arrived in London, Gov. Goodrich was fairly well acquainted with our German colonies, how they got there and in fact, I told him all I knew regarding them."[12] As a result of Repp's efforts, Goodrich developed a lifelong fascination with the history and fortunes of the Volga Germans. Perhaps it was just as well that Goodrich did not live through World War II, as he would have been deeply distressed by Stalin's forced deportation of many of those who had been saved from starvation by the efforts of the ARA.

Following "a smooth and uneventful" voyage, Goodrich and his wife landed at Plymouth, where they visited memorials to Sir Francis Drake and the pilgrim fathers of the *Mayflower*. The only problem, Goodrich noted in his diary, was that he had difficulty in sleeping because he missed the motion of the boat. By the next day he had regained his land legs and proceeded by train to London. Reflecting his background as a frugal businessman, Goodrich approvingly noted that English charges for hotels, meals, and cab and train fares were only about half of those he was accustomed to paying in America. The five-hour train trip to London in a comfortable and economical second class compartment confirmed his view that "no one traveled 1st class in England but Americans and D-d fools."[13]

Goodrich, the tourist, found the sights and sounds of London an exhilarating contrast with the pastoral mid-west. During their two days in the British capital the Goodriches toured the inevitable public buildings and museums, and they attended a two-hour service at Westminster Abbey, which was distinguished by outstanding singing on the part of the choirboys. At the same time Goodrich was acutely aware that he had serious business ahead of him. At the first opportu-

3: A SHORT RETIREMENT

nity, therefore, he called on the ARA's European director, Walter L. Brown who, with the assistance of his staff of "bright active young men," completed the governor's travel arrangements to Russia. On Brown's advice Goodrich hired a taxi to drive him about London while he purchased winter clothing, including a down-filled sleeping bag. "I think I have enough to go to the North Pole," he noted in his diary, "if the Bolsheviki don't get it all."[14]

The departure of Cora Goodrich for Paris on the morning of 30 September meant that the civilized stage of Goodrich's mission was about to end. That afternoon Goodrich and Repp took the train to Dover, crossed the channel to Ostend, and boarded the night train which took them across Belgium and France toward Berlin and Riga. As he awoke in Germany Goodrich observed a "beehive" of activity—belching smokestacks, men and women working in the fields and gardens, and "wonderful industry and efficiency on every hand." By dinner time they had reached Berlin, which from the train impressed him as a city of "beautiful streets, parks, and buildings."[15] How completely his experiences in England, Belgium, and Germany failed to prepare him for what lay ahead.

Entering Lithuania, which two years before had received its independence from Russia, Goodrich was shocked to observe run-down, unpainted houses and muddy, unpaved roads. No longer was the roadbed smooth and well ballasted. Instead the ride was rough, the service poor, and the train ran well behind schedule. On the German side of the border he found "thrift, industry, efficiency, on the other waste, laziness, and inefficiency. . . . It is hard to understand it all." Upon reaching the Latvian border he was frustrated by the slowness of the customs officials and at Riga he found that his passport photo had to be retaken. Moreover, he was angered by the "sloth and inefficiency" of the bureaucracy, which did not begin work until 9:30 A.M. and then "quit early." Goodrich was so exasperated by the repeated delays and examinations of his luggage that he recorded: "Everyone who travels thru this country ought to curse the league of nations for their fool treaty of Versailles and the little countries that it set up. I have had my baggage looked into so many times I am weary of the whole thing and the next time I go to Europe I shall not carry a trunk."[16]

While waiting at the Riga train station Goodrich came in contact with the first miserable refugees from the famine region. A party of eleven Volga Germans related to Repp vivid tales of deprivation and starvation both at home and on their travels toward Germany. To sustain life, they said, the people of the Volga region had been compelled to eat roots and clay. Goodrich was so shocked by their tale of woe that he gave the refugees an American five dollar bill and all the miscellaneous coins he could find in his pocket. As a treat for the five children in the group he contributed a bar of German sweet chocolate. Goodrich was surprised to discover that the refugees regarded the chocolate as the rarest of novelties. According to their mother, the two youngest children had never tasted candy before.[17]

Fifteen hours after their arrival at Riga their documents were finally in order and the two exasperated and apprehensive Americans set out for Moscow on what was reputed to be "one of the best sleepers in Russia." Expecting a Pullman sleeping car, Goodrich was in for a major disappointment as he found: "No heat, no hot water, no towels, no soap, no light and finally no bedding of any kind." Fortunately Goodrich's sleeping bag was accessible and thus he was able to spend a warm and reasonably comfortable night. Again the train, burning wood and traveling only twenty miles per hour, was behind schedule, which seemed to bother no one except Goodrich. One consolation was that the slow pace enabled him to observe the timbered countryside (which reminded him of eastern Canada) with its primitive villages of thatch-roofed houses and women doing field and railroad work side by side with men. In the absence of a dining car, Goodrich was forced to improvise his breakfast from an apple, some zwieback and Swiss cheese, and a chocolate drink made from hot water and a piece of sweet chocolate. To his surprise the resulting meal was "not at all bad."[18]

Upon reaching the Russian border Goodrich was subjected to another customs delay, this one lasting nine hours. His first impression of Russia was decidedly unfavorable, as the train station at the border was "dirty, cold, ill-smelling, and absolutely unlighted." Yet, in his first encounter with the Russian people, Goodrich found himself strangely attracted to the "noisy laughing crowd of dirty ragged Russians jabbering like mad in a strange tongue not a word of which I could understand." At a private home near the depot he was served a "very good dinner" consisting of a sour soup, potatoes, fish, meat, black bread, and beer, for which he was charged the equivalent of sixteen cents.[19] Surely this was not the first time in his life that Goodrich, a supporter of prohibition in America, had consumed a glass of beer. But it was not reckless frivolity which led Goodrich to deviate from his dry past. Ever the practical man, he found that the water in Russia was often unfit to drink and that the prudent traveler, therefore, drank tea or, if that were unavailable, beer or wine.

Six hours late, Goodrich's train finally reached the capital of the new Russia at dusk on 5 October 1921. To have achieved his dream of visiting Moscow would, under ordinary circumstances, have pro-

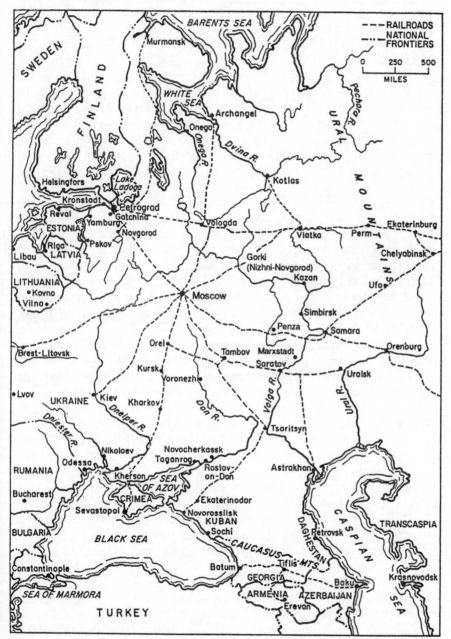

The Travels of Governor Goodrich in Russia, 1921–1925. Map courtesy of Benjamin Rhodes.

American Relief Administration identification card of Governor James P. Goodrich. Photo courtesy of James P. Goodrich Collection, Herbert Hoover Presidential Library, West Branch, Iowa.

Governor James P. Goodrich, second from right, in Samara, Russia, in March, 1992. At right is Will Shafroth, head of the American Relief Administration in Samara. Photo courtesy of the American Relief Administration, Russian Unit Collection, Hoover Institution Archives, Stanford University.

Governor James P. Goodrich, second from right in front, and Will Shafroth, head of the American Relief Administration in Samara, to his left, in a snowstorm in Russia. Photo courtesy of the American Relief Administration, Russian Unit Collection, Hoover Institution Archives, Stanford University.

Governor James P. Goodrich, at right in foreground, and unknown official in Samara, Russia. Photo courtesy of the American Relief Administration, Russian Unit Collection, Hoover Institution Archives, Stanford University.

duced a sensation of exhilaration. But on this occasion fatigue, com-
pounded by confusion, was the dominant factor. In vain Goodrich
and Repp searched the crowd for familiar faces. But Colonel Haskell
was in the field on an inspection trip and their wire announcing the
time of their arrival had not been delivered. Without much choice
in the matter the two weary travelers struggled through the crowd,
located porters, and were conveyed to the ARA headquarters in a
large residence known to the Americans as the Pink House. There
they were welcomed by Archibald Coolidge, a Harvard history professor who was on leave to serve with the ARA. Fortunately dinner
was being served late that evening and Goodrich and Repp were thus
in time to dine with the ARA workers. "It was the first good meal
we'd had since leaving London," Goodrich recorded, "and reminded
us of home."[20]

The next two days were devoted to resting, exploring his surroundings, and reorganizing in preparation for traveling to the famine region. Goodrich had a "corking good night's rest" and spent
most of the first day "clearing up" his accounts, getting a cholera
vaccination, and exchanging "90 good American Dollars for
8,920,000 worthless Russian Rubles." In the afternoon he received
a tour of the art collection displayed in the Pink House. To Goodrich
the place, with its oak flooring, hand-carved woodwork, and paintings by Rubens, Van Dyke, and Raphael, qualified as "a regular
palace." His guide was the former owner of the residence who was
now reduced to the role of building custodian. In the evening he
seized the welcome opportunity to take a bath, his first since leaving London.[21]

The following day he visited a Soviet kindergarten which he
viewed as evidence that the Soviets were adopting the American practice of universal education. In the afternoon he paid a taxi driver
5,000 rubles to give him a tour of Moscow. "To me it was only six
cents," he recalled, "but to him it seemed to mean almost a fortune."
Several hours were spent in touring a large open air market, the
existence of which seemed to prove that Lenin was "making one
concession after another to capitalism." That night Goodrich, "for
about 60 cents in our money," attended a highly professional performance of Tchaikovsky's ballet "Swan Lake." To a musical novice
from Indiana the costumes, the choreography, the sets, and the playing of the orchestra were aesthetically overwhelming. And once again
he found himself drawn to the simply dressed but attentive and ap-
preciative members of the audience.[22] Among the Moscovites who
attended the ballet, Goodrich could see no evidence whatsoever of
Red fanaticism. Yet the Russians whom Goodrich had met so far

had been mostly good-natured peasants, urban workers, or dignified
concertgoers. His travels, which were due to resume the next day,
soon taught him that the society of revolutionary Russia was more
complex than he had realized. Revolutionary zeal, he was to discover, was not just a figment of capitalist imaginations.

His inspection trip to the Volga began with a typically disorganized performance on the part of the state-owned railroad system.
Goodrich and Repp planned to travel first to Samara and then south-
ward to Saratov. They were to be accompanied by two Soviets: an
interpreter and a courier. Frank A. Golder, a history professor from
Stanford University, planned to go along as far as Samara. According
to the arrangements, the party would leave Moscow at 6:30 P.M.
on 8 October and Goodrich, therefore, intended to spend the day
completing his packing. Suddenly at noon the Pink House was noti-
fied that the train would leave five hours earlier than previously
scheduled. The message caught Goodrich with his packing only "half
done," but he and Golder hurried to the station. No sooner had
they boarded the train than it departed, leaving behind the translator,
the courier, and Repp, who had with him "all the grub." Goodrich
was understandably distraught by the wholly unexpected turn of
events. "Here I was," he recalled, "going into a famine and disease
stricken country, without an interpreter, dependent upon what food
I could forage along the way."[23]

To Goodrich's relief, he promptly discovered a new friend in the
person of Golder. A native of Odessa, Russia, Golder was the pos-
sessor of a Harvard Ph. D., a veteran world traveler, and already a
distinguished scholar. In an article published in the *American Historical Review* in 1915, he had demolished the myth that Russia had
sent its fleet to America in 1863 as a gesture of friendship for the
cause of the union. In reality, he demonstrated, Czar Alexander II
feared the outbreak of war with Britain and France and therefore
dispatched his navy to America so that it would not be immobilized
in the event of an Anglo-French blockade. Golder had also published
authoritative accounts of the settlement and sale of Alaska. In 1921
he was on leave from Stanford in order to serve with the ARA as
a "special investigator"; he was also busily purchasing books and
newspapers for the Hoover War History Collection at Stanford; and
he was keeping his eyes open for historical material to be used in his
next book: a study of the career of the American naval hero John
Paul Jones when he served as an admiral in the navy of Catherine
the Great.[24]

As he traveled across a strange land in a freezing, unlighted railroad
car, Goodrich was more interested in Golder's practical abilities as a

traveler than in his academic distinction. On this and other occasions Golder rose magnificently to the challenge. Soon he had foraged cheese and bologna sandwiches made of black bread which were augmented by hot tea prepared on an oil burning stove by the car's porter. The meal, noted Goodrich, "tasted better than it looked." Later at "a little way station," Golder performed another coup when he jumped off the train and returned a few minutes later with a roasted chicken and a dozen hard-boiled eggs for which he had paid the equivalent of forty cents. Among his ARA colleagues Golder enjoyed a deserved reputation as a resourceful traveler, a renowned cook, a lively raconteur, and a deadly poker player. At the latter diversion Golder surprisingly met his match in Goodrich. In one of the first contests between the two Goodrich trounced Golder by 120,000 rubles (the equivalent of $1.20). Perhaps it was because of the prowess demonstrated by Goodrich at poker that Golder thereafter routinely consulted the governor on matters of personal finance and investment.[25]

Having solved the immediate problem of locating enough to fill their stomachs, Goodrich and Golder turned their attention to the other occupants of the car. Their fellow travelers consisted of a mining engineer and his wife who were en route to the Ural Mountains, and two Reds, one of whom, Goodrich noted with disfavor, was traveling with "a lady not his wife." Soon Golder, who was no admirer of the Bolsheviks, got involved in "quite an argument" with the Reds over the topic of the New Economic Policy. To Goodrich the fanaticism and antagonism of the two Communists, who had probably never laid eyes upon a real capitalist before in their lives, came as a body blow. That Lenin had made concessions to capitalism the two readily conceded, but they insisted that the introduction of wages and rents was only a temporary tactic, which did not alter in the slightest the ultimate goal of destroying the exploitive economic system of the West. Furthermore, they contended, the Soviet worker was far better off than the oppressed factory laborers of America who received only "the crumbs that fall from the rich man's table." When Golder baited his adversaries by raising the subject of religion "one big, fierce looking fellow" launched a diatribe, contending that churches were "opiates" employed by the capitalistic class to dominate the masses. "Mrs. Red," the traveling companion of the ferocious Bolshevik, joined the discussion by vigorously attacking the institution of the family as another capitalist tool for enslaving the people. To Goodrich her views seemed dangerously close to free love.

After darkness and cold had ended the unproductive debate with

neither side being converted to the views of the other, the two
Americans bundled up in blankets and sang all the patriotic songs
they could think of including "America," "The Star Spangled Banner," and "Glory, Glory, Hallelujah." Personally Goodrich was appalled as he thought of the contrast between "our own blessed
country" and the Russia of Lenin. And, before falling asleep, he
"prayed God to give us men and women with a vision big enough
to measure up to the task of saving our country from the awful blight
that has fallen on Russia."[26]

Awakening the next morning in a freezing car, Goodrich and
Golder sang "There is sunshine in my soul," as the sun briefly broke
through the grey overcast. For breakfast the two shared millet bread,
raw turnips, and pumpkin rind tea. In the meantime the slow pace
of the train, which Goodrich estimated at only eight to ten miles per
hour, gave him ample opportunity to observe the black loam of the
steppes, which appeared well cultivated in preparation for the planting of wheat in the spring. Near every village were observed herds
of sheep and cattle. Often the train stopped at length to unload
freight cars, several of which were attached to the train, or to take
on wood or water. To Goodrich's exasperation the work went on
without any sense of urgency whatsoever. "It takes 5 men to do one
man's work in this operation," he noted, "and they proceed with
oriental deliberation." At one stop he observed a crew of five men
take twenty minutes to load the tender with wood one stick at a
time. Another fifteen minutes was required to fill the tender's water
tank. "All of this," Goodrich maintained, "would have been done
in America in less than five minutes." Why, Goodrich asked the
engineer, did he not let the water run while loading the wood? The
man's answer, "It does not matter," seemed to Goodrich conclusive
proof that socialism and railroading were incompatible. (Later in the
trip when Golder asked some railroad workers to move his car onto
a ferry without results he got a similar answer: "We have lost all
interest in our work.")[27]

Goodrich did not forget that he had been sent to Russia to assess
the seriousness of the situation and on the second day of his trip he
began to see for the first time signs of distress. At almost every stop
he noted crowds of refugees from the famine region who were seeking food, or who were on their way home with bags of flour or
potatoes. At one station Goodrich curiously poked a bundle of dirty
rags with his cane and found it to be alive. Beneath the pile were
three children who were crudely but effectively protected from the
cold weather while their parents searched for food. "I would have
given anything for a camera," he recalled, "as the scenes when repro-

duced would have touched the hardest heart." Despite the general
squalor, the refugees appeared strong, rugged, and surprisingly
healthy. Goodrich was so sympathetic that he was tempted to empty
his pockets. On further reflection he thought better of the idea,
because he realized it would be foolish to be left without any local
currency. That afternoon, on the final approach to Samara, Goodrich
and Golder spent two hours at "the national game" which reduced
the governor's ruble supply by 20,000, or the equivalent of twenty
cents. Typically, the train did not arrive until 6:00 P.M., six hours
behind time. Had Goodrich, who had once run an American railroad, been in charge of the operation heads surely would have
rolled.[28]

At Samara Goodrich found conflicting evidence regarding the se-
verity of the famine. For those with money he found there was no
shortage of food at all. Soon after being welcomed at the station by
"a real American boy," he and Golder were conveyed to the local
ARA headquarters, assigned the luxury of cots, and taken to a local
restaurant which was outstanding both for its cuisine and because it
was "a marvel of cheapness." For dinner the two hungry travelers
enjoyed "excellent bread and country butter, good soup made of
meat and vegetables, good steak and potatoes, tea, and dessert all for
25,000 rubles—25¢ American." The next day, as Goodrich strolled
through the streets, he observed ruddy-cheeked men and women
and food of good quality for sale in abundance and at prices far
below those in America. Some typical prices per pound, he recorded
were butter (22¢), sausage (8¢), beans (3¢), rice (12 to 15¢), "good
mutton and beef" (3 to 4¢), cheese (20 to 25¢), flour (8¢), and bread
(9¢). All but the latter two foodstuffs were plentiful, even in the
famine areas, for those with money. Nevertheless, Goodrich ac-
knowledged that the shortages of bread and flour were serious defi-
ciencies inasmuch as bread was the staff of life to the Russians who
consumed less meat than Americans.[29]

The bustle of economic activity was not confined to the sale of
food products, he observed. In one bazaar he admired a beautiful
coat of bear and skunk fur and the next morning the owner appeared
at ARA headquarters offering to sell the coat for 7,000,000 rubles.
Goodrich responded with a counteroffer of 4,500,000 rubles. After a
lengthy negotiation, punctuated by much waving of arms and chatter
which Goodrich could not understand, the price was reduced to
4,700,000 rubles; the man told Goodrich he would die before yield-
ing further. "I told him to prepare his coffin," Goodrich noted in
his diary, "for I wouldn't give another kopec." Only when Goodrich
ostensibly terminated the transaction did the owner fling the coat at

Goodrich's feet, extend his hand, and agree to accept the 4,500,000 rubles (about $46.00). Goodrich the capitalist had enjoyed himself immensely, but he could not escape the suspicion that the Russian coat merchant had actually gotten the better of the bargain.[30]

Behind the superficial evidence of prosperity Goodrich saw much disorganization and privation. Inspecting Samara's six flour mills and adjacent grain elevators, Goodrich was surprised to find them idle and empty. Nearby he saw crowds of refugees occupying vacant lots and buildings trying to flee the famine district for some destination where they had heard there was food. Among the crowded refugees communicable diseases were easily spread. Cholera was just subsiding at the time of Goodrich's arrival, but a typhus epidemic spread by lice was in full swing. Two new cemeteries were required for the victims of disease and Goodrich saw thousands of fresh mounds and crosses in each. Frequently, he was told, as many as half a dozen corpses were thrown together in mass graves. "It is beyond anyone's words adequately to describe the distressful things which I saw," he recalled. The danger of contracting typhus from the lousy refugees was strongly impressed upon Goodrich when he visited Dr. Anna Louise Strong, a Quaker relief worker from Chicago, who was seriously ill with a rash and high fever. Next he inspected the ARA child-feeding program which had just begun in Samara. Visiting one American kitchen Goodrich counted seventy-six of "the most pitiable objects I have ever seen—dirty, ragged, almost naked, lousy, emaciated little souls left to live or die according to whatever fate chance might bring them." However, Goodrich questioned the judgment of the ARA in serving meals of beans, rice, fats, and cocoa instead of the black bread, potatoes, and cabbage with which the children were familiar. Until midnight (12 October 1921) Goodrich and Golder, accompanied by Colonel Haskell, who had arrived with University of California economist Lincoln Hutchinson, met with the local Soviet authorities urging them to cooperate in the still embryonic American relief program. Soon afterward Haskell, Golder, and Hutchinson bade Goodrich goodbye as they left to catch the train eastward to Penza. Goodrich's plan was to travel by boat down the Volga River to Saratov with Repp, who had arrived in the company of a new Soviet translator, the first one having been dismissed for missing the train at Moscow.[31]

When Goodrich finally retired to the luxury of his cot he nervously tossed and turned thinking of all he had seen that day. In particular, he noted, "Had thot of Dr. Strong and typhus lice so much I could feel them crawling over me all night." The next morning Golder unexpectedly appeared with the news that the train to

Penza had not left after all and that its departure would be delayed until sometime in the afternoon. Goodrich, he said, was welcome to travel with himself and Hutchinson following a triangular rail route eastward to Penza and then south to Saratov. "This is a fair sample of Soviet railroading," Goodrich noted, "one day six hours ahead of time, another 24 hours behind time—they take it as a matter of course in this country and their patience is exasperating." Goodrich, who had an appointment to have his dental work repaired, decided to accompany the two professors. Repp, however, decided to proceed to Saratov by boat. And so, at 5:00 P.M. on 13 October, only three hours late, the three Americans set off on what they were assured was the quickest and most convenient route to Saratov. True to form the interpreter assigned to Goodrich missed the train and the Americans were left with a first class compartment in which to pursue their poker game. By daybreak their train had reached the junction at which the Moscow line branched to Penza, but they were told they would have to wait a day or two for the next train. On this occasion Goodrich had no opportunity to become frustrated by the vagaries of Russian railroading as half an hour later a freight train unexpectedly appeared. Soon they were coupled to the rear, crawling toward Penza at six miles an hour. At 9:30 P.M. their car arrived at Penza's main rail yard; they learned they would be moved to the Saratov station early the next morning, although this was not actually accomplished until 9:30 A.M.[32]

Golder and Hutchinson then departed for government offices to seek statistics about the food situation. "I remained to guard the car," Goodrich recorded. Thus he lost an opportunity to tour the ancient city of 80,000 inhabitants. In the opinion of Golder the governor did not miss too much, as the city was "picturesque from the outside and ugly from the inside." Yet, from his vantage point in the station, Goodrich had an excellent opportunity to observe the famine refugees jammed into short boxcars about twenty-four feet long. In one such conveyance Goodrich counted thirty-two people crowded together, each with his belongings and a bag containing black bread and potatoes. Despite the "dirt and filth" the travelers appeared reasonably happy and content, as did the numerous men and women doing strenuous track maintenance work. At meal time the workers cooked a stew in a black kettle and, sitting in a circle, devoured the dish using wooden spoons, a practice that struck Goodrich as decidedly unsanitary. [33]

By 10:00 P.M. (16 October) the trio was off for Saratov and by morning had reached the midpoint of Rtischevo, having completed the scheduled six-hour journey in only ten hours. Again Goodrich observed crowds of people, often riding on couplings, locomotive bumpers, and steps, moving aimlessly in every direction. At least five hundred of the refugees, strangely enough, were moving south-ward into the famine area. A few of these, however, were returning to their homes with food they had purchased during their wander-ings. Golder interviewed a peasant woman who had left her home in Saratov a week earlier with a saw which she had exchanged for a one hundred-pound sack of flour. Everywhere there was the usual filth and lack of sanitation. During the two-hour wait for their car to be attached to a freight destined for Saratov, Goodrich "saw two young women at RR station in plain sight of two hundred people squat on the platform and relieve the pressure." To Goodrich one of the most baffling aspects of the situation was that the majority of the travelers (except for a few whose clothes and appearance sug-gested they had seen better days) were reasonably comfortable and cheerful.[34]

Three hours after leaving Rtischevo the Americans' poker playing was interrupted as the train abruptly stopped amid reports that the engine had exploded and seriously burned the engineer and fireman. Goodrich, Golder, and Hutchinson suspended their high stakes con-test and hastened forward with their ARA first aid kit only to dis-cover that "neither the engineer nor the engine was as badly injured as was supposed." After temporary repairs the train was able to resume its journey, although, noted Golder with irritation, "by ten o'clock the train began bumping and jerking so hard that we could hardly go on with our poker game." About midnight they reached Saratov and decided to spend the remainder of the night in their railroad car. Until they parted company three days later their secure and comfortable coach served as a temporary dwelling.[35]

Touring the city early on Sunday morning, Goodrich found Sara-tov a welcome and wholly unexpected contrast with the dilapidated Russia he had encountered previously. Saratov seemed to have es-caped serious damage from the Civil War and it was easily the clean-est city Goodrich had yet seen in Russia. Clear skies, mild temperatures, and the remnants of fall colors enhanced Goodrich's high opinion of the city. Now he understood, he noted, why the town was called "yellow mountain." The well swept streets, he ob-served, had recently been patched with asphalt. As it was Sunday, numerous men and women were walking about or shopping in a large hall divided into booths where individual merchants were hawking their wares. Saratov's market, Goodrich remembered, was larger, better constructed, and cleaner than the Tomlinson Hall Mar-ket in Indianapolis. And the well dressed shoppers looked more like

Americans "and less like nomads" than was the case in the other cities he had visited. After an hour's search Goodrich, Golder, and Hutchinson found the ARA headquarters, which was located in a building formerly the property of two of the town's leading merchants. A general conference was held with the "very decent lot" of ARA workers around the Russian stove ornamented with the "most exquisitely decorated tile" Goodrich had ever seen. As Goodrich had suspected, the conference confirmed that food conditions in the area were not yet desperate. After dinner Repp appeared and the Americans returned to their railroad car to resume their poker game. On the whole it had been the most rewarding day of his trip so far. His sole disappointment was summed up in his final diary entry for the day: "Went to bed in car at 11 P.M. after 2 hours at the game and after losing 18000R.—18¢ American."[36]

Early the next morning (Monday, 17 October 1921) Goodrich and Repp presented themselves at the office of the governor of Saratov province with the objective of making arrangements to go by boat to the German colonies at Marxstadt and Schilling. Presently they were assured that a boat would depart early the next morning for Marxstadt and that a government representative would convey them to the dock. To pass the remainder of the day, Goodrich and Repp strolled through several bazaars and then inspected six orphanages which, with one exception, were "models of cleanliness." The children appeared plainly but adequately dressed and in Goodrich's opinion were reasonably healthy and well nourished. Returning to the ARA offices he met an impoverished history professor from the local university who was happily working as an ARA translator, since he and his colleagues had received no pay for the past four months. Upon inquiry Goodrich learned that professors received the equivalent of one dollar a month and that the 400,000 rubles due these men was but the price of a single meal in a first class hotel.[37]

Overnight Goodrich's favorable impression of Saratov was somewhat diminished by a discouraging series of travel mishaps. First of all, when he and Repp went to the depot to board their car for the night, they found that it had been moved and almost two hours passed before it could be found. No sooner, it seemed, had they gotten to sleep than they were awakened at 4:00 A.M. and driven to the dock. Incredibly, or so it seemed to Goodrich, the boat had not arrived and no one was able to provide any information as to when it might be expected. "It would have been enough to make a saint swear," was Goodrich's reaction. Despite his anger Goodrich did his best to conceal his feelings and tried to tell himself "it doesn't matter." While awaiting further developments he and Repp retired to a restaurant where they enjoyed "an excellent meal consisting of soup, bread and butter, mutton chops, tea, pastry. Cost 19 cents American money." Afterwards Repp had the inspired idea of seeking the assistance of an organization of Volga Germans at Saratov, and shortly they were told that reservations had been made to take them to Marxstadt on the next boat. There they would be housed in a private residence and furnished with an automobile and driver to tour the area. "For the first time," wrote Goodrich, "I felt that here was something I could depend on."[38] Also for the first time Goodrich was about to witness widespread starvation.

As promised, the Volga boat arrived on time and Repp and Goodrich were shown to a "very comfortable room" in the bow of the vessel. Returning to the deck they watched as an enormous crowd sought to board the ship. "I never saw such a struggling mass of humanity in my life . . . and many could not get on," Goodrich recorded. "I helped to 'hook' two ladies on with my cane and brought down the guard on me, but I at least had the goodwill of the women." Travel on the Volga required more time than usual because the dredging of the channel had been neglected. It was not until 3:00 A.M., after nine hours of struggling against the current, that they docked at Marxstadt, where they found an automobile and driver waiting to receive them. Within an hour Goodrich was sound asleep again "in a comfortable bed" in the home of a German family. By 9:00 A.M. he and Repp were up and after a simple breakfast of tea, sausage, milk, and bread without butter, they called on local officials to gather food statistics.

They were told that in 1919 the German communes had enjoyed their most prosperous year ever, but that the crop of 1920 was short due to drought. Sufficient rye and winter wheat were then planted to assure a comfortable surplus. However, government requisitions in the spring of 1921, followed by a devastating drought and heat wave, left the region in desperate condition. Cholera and typhus had taken a disastrous toll of the undernourished, and Goodrich was told that 5,000 people had died since the first of the year. In the three previous days the death toll had been thirty-five, twenty, and twenty-two respectively and the dead were buried in their rags without coffins. The information was so detailed that Goodrich felt it must be true. "Here," he noted, "we found at least an approach to xactness of knowledge and efficiency."[39]

Any doubts Goodrich may have harbored about the accuracy of the statistics were dispelled by an automobile tour of Marxstadt. First he and Repp visited two children's homes for destitute orphans. "I never saw anything like it," he wrote in his diary. "A visit to one of these places leaves one depressed to think such suffering can xist in this 20th century civilization." For the most part the inhabitants appeared to be "normal, intelligent children." But Goodrich—not yet inured to scenes of desolation—was shocked to see that the children were "little more than skin and bones." The orphans of Marx-stadt, he recalled, were "mere skeletons, hollow eyed, naked, cold and hungry, picking lice off each other, and with that timid haunted expression of countenance which told eloquently that these tiny folks knew that death was impending." The inspection was cut short by the honking of their automobile, which was said to be the only one in the commune. As they toured a nearby village they met a cart full of potatoes pulled by a camel and a small horse. The strange sight and sound of the car caused the camel to bolt and spill the potatoes, many of which were quickly carried away by children from adjacent houses. Goodrich gave the owner of the cart 200,000 rubles which seemed to be greatly appreciated.

The car tour then resumed with stops at three additional villages, all of which had abandoned houses from which the roofs had been torn for fuel. As Goodrich and Repp passed a small shed near one of the abandoned homes two young girls, ten and twelve years old, came out shivering and crying. On inquiry Goodrich learned that their parents had died five days before and that the girls had had nothing to eat since then but cabbage leaves and carrots. Goodrich's recollection was: "They were barefooted and had on no clothing except thin cotton dresses extending to their knees. They said they were very hungry. They looked as if they were in great distress, were exceedingly thin and emaciated." When Goodrich asked the communal authorities why they did not energetically seek to discover such cases, "they did not give a very good excuse." Having given each of the girls 100,000 rubles with instructions to go to the communal hall for food, Goodrich collected statistics on rye and wheat production. According to the village leaders the Volga Germans would be able to feed themselves by the next summer provided the weather returned to normal. In the meantime, they said, about half the population would require help to survive. To Goodrich the essential accuracy of the statistics was confirmed by his observation: "No dogs in village—they say they have butchered and eaten all of them."[40]

When Goodrich and Repp returned to Marxstadt at 3:30 P.M. (20 October) they found two visitors waiting for them. Golder and Hutchinson had arrived by boat that morning and, after a whirlwind investigation, were anxious to return to their railroad car, which had been left behind at Saratov. Jointly, the four Americans agreed to return by boat to Saratov jammed into two small cabins together with a number of Russian passengers. The crowded conditions were unimportant, in Golder's opinion, because they expected to reach their destination within just three hours. Once again, however, their travels were delayed, but this time by the weather rather than by mechanical or personnel problems. Just twelve miles from Saratov their ship encountered a heavy fog and the captain decided to cast his anchor rather than risk becoming marooned on a Volga sandbar. Goodrich, Golder, and Hutchinson again played poker, in part to pass the time, but also to determine who would get the best place to sleep. On this occasion the governor's luck deserted him, and he had to settle for an empty corner; Hutchinson won the top of the table, and Golder, wearing a 10,000 ruble grin, that portion of a sofa not occupied by a sleeping Russian. (By his own account Golder now embarked on a run of gambling luck which continued the next day as he won three consecutive 10,000 ruble bets from Hutchinson.) Suddenly at 3:00 A.M. the fog lifted and Americans were able to land at last.[41]

Just four hours later Goodrich was awake and dressed, seeking to make arrangements for visiting Schilling. To his disgust he found: "No one gets up until 10:00 a.m. & at 11 the boys said we could not have the boat." Once again Repp used his influence to get the Russian authorities "on the job" and shortly after noon they were off downstream to Schilling. As the voyage started Goodrich was in high spirits because of the unusually favorable weather. "It was a wonderfully beautiful day," he noted upon leaving Saratov, "and as we sailed out of the city it was a beautiful sight. Just cold enough and with enough tang in the atmosphere to brace me up and we sat on the top of the boat for an hour." At 3:00 P.M. they arrived at Schilling and walked a mile up a two hundred-foot hill to the town offices. Along the way Goodrich, limping with his cane, was amazed to see women and mere girls, with wooden yokes across their shoulders, each carrying two three-or four-gallon pails of water from the Volga to their homes. At the commune hall he collected food statistics documenting the extent of the crop failure. Since the first of July, he was told, the community of 3,789 had suffered twenty-five deaths from cholera, thirty from typhus, and forty-five from starvation. About 800 children would require food assistance if they were to survive the winter. He and Repp then examined the nine communal warehouses and found that eight were completely empty. From talking to the farmers his general impression was "Good clean honest lot of folks. The anxious despairing look in their eyes told more eloquently than any words how desperate their plight appeared to them."[42]

As Goodrich and Repp continued their travels to the south they found that conditions steadily deteriorated. From Schilling they "dropped down the river" about ten miles to Balser, a community of about 12,000 inhabitants. Due to a misunderstanding no one was there to meet them. But after a two-hour wait in the dark a voice called out and two horse-drawn wagons appeared. A rough and slow ride brought them to a home occupied by ten people—parents, grandparents, and children. They were quartered in a room (Goodrich estimated its size as sixteen by twenty-four feet) divided by curtains and occupied by six sleeping members of the family. Before retiring Goodrich noted, "We had a dinner @ 11:30 P.M. Black bread, tea and milk. Our host apologized for lack of anything more but said on account of the famine they had little to eat." In the morning Goodrich and Repp made use of an unusual wash basin in which the cold water, laboriously carried from the river, was supplied from a bucket suspended over the basin and a small quantity of water was dispensed by operating a plunger valve in the center. Walking outside he observed and smelled numerous goats, chickens, and pigs and "the yard [was] filthy and dirty as we found all yards in every commune in Russia." For breakfast they were served almost the same meager menu as before: coffee, black bread, and apple butter "and we were in one of the best homes in Balser." For the next hour the two Americans walked through the town's bazaar and noted large quantities of inexpensive food for sale including various cuts of meat, sunflower seeds, cabbage, and apples. Yet flour was unavailable and the small amounts of bread for sale were very expensive. As Goodrich departed one painful scene remained in his mind: the memory of "a sad eyed thin faced peasant boy" about sixteen years old who had walked, Goodrich was told, eight miles to the bazaar "hoping to trade what we would send to the rag bag for a bit of bread to eat." Both of the boy's parents had died of cholera and he and his sister were left alone. "Beside the lot of this simple boy and girl our plain fare of the morning seemed palatial," he remembered, "and I resolved that I would not complain again no matter what happened."[43]

En route to the commune of Norda, Goodrich felt depressed by the dull grey sky and the endless expanses of prairie. Along the way he saw scenes which added to his sense of dejection. Several times the travelers observed teams of horses with mowers cutting what appeared to be cockle burrs, wild rose pods, and a short black weed known as "famine grass." At one stop Goodrich threshed the black seeds in his hand and found they had "a slightly bitter taste." He carefully recorded what he had seen in his diary:

> In one field we found a whole family, 9 in number: Father, Mother, 4 daughters and 3 sons all at work carefully picking up these weeds, piling them in little piles to be hauled to the barn. It may save their cattle and themselves from starvation and in a world of such abundant harvests it is a pity to see human beings driven to such straits. We stopped to inquire about the weeds for it seemed no animal would eat it. The farmer said "They won't eat it now but when all else is gone and they get hungry they will eat before they will starve." Then he said as he rolled a bit of the weeds in his hands and hulled out a few small black seeds, "We can thresh some of this and mix [it] with our bit of rye and grind [it] to make bread when all else fails."

As they passed through the commune of Kutter he was told that about 400 out of a population of 3,010 had died from starvation and the effects of cholera and typhus. Goodrich was startled when a village official blandly told him that they would not need as much American aid as before because so many had died. At Denhous, a commune of 6,232, he learned they had escaped both cholera and typhus, but still had lost 425 to starvation. Goodrich had no reason to doubt the figure, as he visited the village graveyard and counted "198 new made graves over which the grass had not started to grow." Nearby he saw a small boy wearing a sheepskin coat. "He seemed so sturdy," Goodrich noted in his diary. "I slapped him on the shoulder and was shocked to find him nothing but skin and bones. I learned on inquiry both his parents had died a few weeks ago and they were going to send him out to Marxstadt to the [children's] home. I gave them 50,000 rubles [about 50¢] and told them to get him some bread to eat on the way."[44]

At their next stop of Houk, they were received by the secretary of the commune who stated that the town's population had declined from 6,000 on 1 January 1921 to fewer than 5,000. Goodrich and Repp were served a repast of "good rye bread, splendid butter and tea [that] was more than we ought to have had with so much hunger about us." Thirty minutes later a fresh team of horses conveyed them to Norda where Repp had relatives. Soon after their arrival at the communal hall the place was packed with farmers relating tales of woe. According to several speakers the situation was so desperate that whole families had starved to death and on a single day the community of 8,500 had conducted eight funerals. Goodrich was told that the farmers were gathering weeds and carefully saving anything with food value such as cabbage leaves and melon rinds. Yet

Goodrich found that the famine stories "had begun to get on my nerves." He questioned the credibility of those telling of mass starvation because they were strong and healthy in appearance. To one "well fed bunch of farmers," Goodrich said, "Why is it when so many of you have bread to eat so many others die of hunger?" After a long silence one man slowly offered an explanation which Goodrich at first found difficult to understand: "It cannot be helped; some must die for if help does not come we all must die."[45] For an American such a statement was almost incomprehensible. But when Goodrich tried to view the situation from the perspective of the fatalistic peasant farmer, who would be left desperately short of food if he divided what little he had left, the remark made a bit more sense.

As the meeting concluded Goodrich, perhaps as a result of the famine stories he had just heard, found that he possessed a ravenous appetite. A simple but very welcome meal was then served in the honor of the two visitors. The menu consisted of boiled cabbage, mashed potatoes, rye bread, and tea. Goodrich's table was waited upon by "a very good looking barefoot girl 16 years of age." When he playfully asked if she would accompany him to America the tears came to her eyes and she replied, "Oh, that would be heaven to me, but it is not possible." Goodrich was so pleased by the meal and the courtesies shown him that he insisted on leaving a contribution of 1 million rubles for the "soup kitchen fund." His favorable impression of Norda was slightly diminished, however, during his final hour in the town. While Repp visited his relatives, Goodrich wandered alone about the community. What he saw was a primitive collection of low houses and stables with thatched roofs and yards without grass crowded with pigs, goats, chickens, manure, and dirt. Previously he had heard the saying "as dirty as a Russian." Now he concluded it should be revised to "as dirty as a Volgan."[46]

By the time Repp had finished visiting his relatives, the sun was setting and the two decided to return to Balser to pick up statistics promised them by the village authorities. On the return trip they stopped briefly at two final villages for statistics. In the dark of the night Goodrich, wrapped in his new fur coat, fell asleep and dreamed he was in his Winchester home with his family and friends until the droshky struck a pothole. Then, he recalled, "I awoke suddenly in the middle of the night to find myself not in the peaceful prosperous Hoosier state, but back in Balser in the midst of the stricken, the starved and the dying." With the statistics in hand Goodrich and Repp reached the boat landing at 1:30 A.M. (22 October), and Goodrich was soon "rolled up in my blanket" having survived one of the most strenuous days in his life. Arriving in Saratov the next morning

Goodrich picked up his belongings at the ARA office and immediately set out for Moscow by train. Still on his agenda was a final Volga inspection trip to Kazan. However, Goodrich—tired, dirty, and anxious to catch up on his correspondence—felt that he badly needed a few days of rest before returning to the field.[47]

On his return to Moscow an interpreter was assigned to accompany him, but "at the last minute with usual Russian efficiency, he missed the train and I had to go alone." At first Goodrich, who had reserved an entire compartment for his own use, traveled in peace and quiet. "Pretty soon," however, three Russians carrying large suitcases and bedrolls crowded into his quarters. Presently Goodrich found the conductor while "waving my arms in true oriental style and pointing to my compartment where the three slavs were contentedly smoking their cigarettes and mildly wondering what was the matter with the strange Americanski who was making such a fool of himself." Eventually Goodrich was moved to a separate compartment adjacent to "an intelligent Russian" and his wife. Several years later in the margin of his book manuscript about his Russian travels Goodrich wrote himself a note: "Add??? Story of visit with Russian & wife." Since he never revised his manuscript, one can only guess as to the nature of the story and must be content with Goodrich's comment, "We had a very interesting visit on the way up to Moscow."[48]

Ten days later (26 October 1921) a refreshed Goodrich began the two-day rail journey to Kazan in the company of "a crowd" of ARA workers. Also accompanying the Americans was the British journalist Sir Philip Gibbs, whom Goodrich had met the day before during a dinner at the Pink House. Promptly Goodrich and his British fellow traveler became fast friends. All day long, as the train passed through a "dreary and monotonous landscape" of seemingly endless pine forests, the two men compared notes. Goodrich found Gibbs to be "an unassuming and delightful gentleman" and he discovered that they shared a common sympathy for the long suffering Russian people. At nightfall Goodrich was inclined to continue the conversation, but the other Americans insisted on "dragging us into a session of the great American indoor sport." Protesting that he was but an innocent, Goodrich got his revenge by winning 180,000 rubles from "that gang of old players." Gibbs' showing of 120,000 rubles was almost as impressive. Afterwards Goodrich enjoyed "real luxury in Russia!" as he was provided with a clean, deloused compartment which was so secure that, for the first time aboard a Russian train, he slept in pajamas. When he arrived at his destination about noon the next day he was rested and eager to investigate food conditions in the Tartar Republic.[49]

His two days in Kazan convinced Goodrich that the food situation in the upper regions of the Volga was almost as bad as in the south. A severe shortage of grain, he was told by the commissar of agriculture, had caused at least 300,000 inhabitants to become refugees and the 3,000,000 who remained were in a weakened condition due to an inadequate diet and the ravages of cholera and typhus. Already, he found, the ARA had established a child-feeding program which was serving daily meals to 123,000. His opinion, based upon visiting orphanages, hospitals, and ARA kitchens was that the children were not in as desperate condition as those he had seen at Marxstadt. Nevertheless, he concluded, "Unless Uncle Sam himself came to the relief of these distressed people I felt that hundreds of thousands of them, many helpless children, were doomed." Originally Goodrich had intended to proceed southward from Kazan by boat, but a sharp change in the weather convinced him to return to Moscow instead. On his way to the station through a driving snowstorm, Goodrich noticed a crowd gathered about a body on the ground and he was informed that "a peasant with a little child in his arms had just been found dead." Goodrich could not determine whether the fatality was caused by starvation or disease, but the incident was a further illustration that the Tartar Republic was in "a deplorable condition."[50]

4

Goodrich Converts Congress

UNTIL his return to Moscow from Kazan (late in the day on 30 October), Goodrich had been so preoccupied with gathering information and coping with the disorganized transportation system that he had hardly had time to think. Over the next two days he seized the opportunity to write letters to his wife and to make an appointment with the commissar of agriculture to collect more statistics. His most important endeavor of all, however, was the composition of preliminary reports to Hoover and Secretary of State Charles Evans Hughes summarizing his impressions of the country, its government and people, and outlining what steps needed to be taken by America in response to the famine. His efforts, he found, were assisted by the bracing climate. "Snow everywhere," he noted, "and very cold today but I like it."[1]

Goodrich did not present himself as an instant expert on Russia. He readily admitted that he had gone to Russia without previous knowledge and that he had been able to visit only the Volga region. On the other hand, Goodrich stressed that he had not confined his investigation to easily accessible cities. Instead, he had traveled to obscure villages where he had personally examined the records of food warehouses, hospitals, and feeding kitchens while mingling with the people, sleeping in their homes, and eating their meager food. In preparing his reports Goodrich demonstrated a high degree of political shrewdness. Reflecting the fact that he had spent much of his life seeking to influence his fellow man, Goodrich shaped his message according to his listeners' predilections.

To Hughes, whom Goodrich classified as a doctrinaire opponent of everything Red, the governor stressed themes of Soviet moderation and pragmatism. "On every hand," he stated, "I see the most conclusive evidence of the return of the Government to a capitalistic basis . . . and there is a feeling everywhere I have gone that the Government has turned the corner and that every step from this time on will be a return to the capitalistic . . . form of government."

The new rulers were firmly in control, stressed Goodrich, and he saw no prospect of a successful revolution in Russia. Therefore, he reasoned, change in Russia would occur through a process of evolution not revolution. He would not go so far as to suggest that Hughes should end America's policy of non-recognition. He implied, however, that Hughes's attitude was out of date in that Russia was reverting to capitalism and was in such a state of economic collapse as to pose no threat to the West.[2]

No such political overtones were present in Goodrich's report to Hoover. Instead, the governor, assuming his role as an ARA special investigator, summarized the food situation as dispassionately as possible. He pointed out that mass starvation had not yet arrived, as evidenced by the availability of good quality food even in the main cities of the Volga region. His best estimate, allowing for the likelihood that some food supplies were concealed, was that even the Volga district had at least four to five months of food remaining. What worried him, said Goodrich, was the situation that would occur between the depletion of supplies in the spring and the next harvest in the fall. To illustrate the human toll produced by the catastrophe, he recounted for Hoover's benefit several of the worst examples of starvation he had witnessed (the dead peasant found with a child in his arms, and the two "poor hungry looking frightfully emaciated half naked waifs, shivering in the cold raw wind" he had stumbled upon near Marxstadt.) "I could tell you these things until you would be sick at heart as I have been as I saw them, but that would not help the situation, nor aid in the solution of the problem," he noted. What was needed, he recommended, was for the ARA to increase its child-feeding operations to one and a half million children a day which, he admitted, would reach only a portion of those in need of help in the Volga region. Finally he suggested that the ARA should expand its operations to include the feeding of starving adults and he recommended that the United States Grain Corporation should loan the Russians sufficient seed grain to assure that spring planting could be completed. "I am certain," Goodrich concluded, "that the situation is such that if immediate relief is not given . . . many thousands of people, men, women, and children will perish in the famine district who otherwise might live."

His four weeks in Russia left Goodrich with two dominant impressions: that Communism had failed miserably, and that the people of Russia were coping courageously with the catastrophe. Goodrich, who had not yet met any top Communist leaders, was erroneously convinced that the New Economic Policy heralded a quick return to capitalism which, in his view, was the only sensible economic system.

Neither Goodrich nor many members of the Communist Party appreciated that the NEP was meant to be only a temporary retreat from Communism. At the same time that he held Communism in utter disdain, he had nothing but admiration for the good-natured, industrious Russian population. As he wrote Hoover, "I am very impressed by the ability of the people to adapt themselves to the very trying situation that confronts them."[3]

From the moment he set foot on Russian soil, Goodrich found himself attracted to the men and women he met in train stations, concert halls, city markets, and rural communes. In their good humor and capacity for physical labor they were reminiscent of the people he had left at home in the midwest. From his car window he observed numerous small villages carved from the deep forest and was reminded of a poem by his friend George Lockwood: "God bless old Indiana, the child of the pioneer / In the solitude of swamp and wood they builded for future years / Braving the dangers of trackless wilds, patient to work and wait / Until the clearings around their cabins merged into a mighty state." At Kazan, Goodrich and Sir Philip Gibbs attended a performance of Mussorgsky's opera *Boris Godunov*, set in the "Time of Troubles" during the late sixteenth century. During the lengthy intermissions they closely watched the dress and demeanor of the audience. "All were plainly but cleanly dressed," observed Goodrich. "Tartar, Semite, Mongolian and Caucasian were mingling together, and they impressed me as a strong, clean, sort of people, so much like the average American crowd in one of our cities that the comparison was almost startling. 'What does this crowd remind you of,' I asked Sir Philip Gibbs. 'Of an English or American audience,' he replied. That same thought was in both our minds." The opera itself, one of the first that Goodrich had ever attended, lasted until well past midnight. Dramatically and musically the performance struck Goodrich as "remarkable." He was especially impressed by the basso who sang the role of the tormented czar and was convinced he should have been singing with the Metropolitan Opera in New York (could the singer have been Fyodor Chaliapin?) Sharing in the accolades were the members of the chorus, who represented the long suffering people of Russia. To Goodrich the common men and women of Russia were the real heros both of the opera and of Russia's modern time of troubles.[4]

Having placed his reports in the hands of a stenographer, Goodrich suffered through a day of disappointments. Three hours were wasted before he was able to find the office of a government translator who was to accompany him to his interview with the commissar of agriculture. To make matters worse the translator was an hour and a half late for his appointment with Goodrich and then offered no apology for his tardiness; he claimed "it did not matter" because he had rescheduled the appointment for the following morning. Goodrich's irritation was probably accentuated by the onset of a sore throat and head cold. By the following morning his health was improving and a physician pronounced his throat to be in good condition for his interview.[5]

To Goodrich's surprise the official was a slightly built youth, not a day over thirty, who was active and bright but had "much to learn about his deportment." In answer to Goodrich's request for statistics he summoned a statistician and a mechanical engineer, but Goodrich was not satisfied with their figures. "I could get little real information from them," he noted, "and came to the conclusion that I knew more about the situation in the Russian communes than he [the commissar of agriculture] did." However, one statement of the engineer made a great impression on Goodrich. He related that he was soon going to England for the purpose of inspecting tractors and intended to recommend the purchase of "a large number." How shortsighted, thought Goodrich, for America to lose such a sale merely due to the nation's failure to maintain normal commercial relations with Russia. (Alertly, Goodrich reported the comment to Hoover noting, "It occurs to me that there should be a chance for America here for we make the best tractors in the world.") Goodrich was promised that more complete figures would be available in two weeks after he returned from an inspection trip which he and Colonel Haskell planned to make to Petrograd.[6]

The trip to Petrograd came as a relief after "the grind" at the office in Moscow. On the overnight train trip, during zero temperatures and "a rather heavy snow storm," Colonel Haskell proposed that Goodrich make "a quick trip [to America] to see Hoover." The suggestion was welcome to Goodrich as he now had a fairly comprehensive idea of the nature of the catastrophe. And besides, he missed his wife, his business, and western civilization. His first day in the former capital was all business, as he and Haskell visited the docks to inspect the facilities for housing American wheat and corn. They found the warehouse to be in "good condition" and of sufficient capacity to store five thousand tons of food. In the process Goodrich observed American wheat being unloaded from a Swedish ship. On the wharf he counted 70 German locomotives, 116 switching engines from England, and he saw "a yard full of plows, harrows, and farm machinery from Switzerland." Why, the Indiana banker must have wondered, were American manufacturers not permitted to participate in such a flourishing market?

The city itself resembled a ghost town, as the population had declined from 2,400,000 before the war to about 800,000. The sense of desolation was further accentuated by the sight of numerous wooden houses being demolished for fuel. One exception to the spectacle of run-down and deserted buildings was the "palace of 24 rooms" occupied by the ARA "boys." Inside Goodrich found: "House filled with elegant furniture, floors covered with oriental rugs, walls adorned with beautiful paintings by the great masters. Two grand pianos . . . In fact a home such as few Americans can afford. 5 fires going with coal and wood, both scarce. 3 servants in the house, a cook, a maid and a man to fire stoves, furnace and do valet work. Thus in a land of famine do they care for our ARA boys."[7] Apparently the ARA "boys" at Petrograd were on their good behavior and Goodrich saw nothing amiss in the Petrograd relief operation. However, on his next visit a few months later he was instructed by Hoover to investigate reports of immoral activity in the palace where he had been a guest.

Of necessity his four days in Petrograd were devoted more to sightseeing than to inspecting. On Monday, 7 November Goodrich awoke, after a night at the ballet, to discover that the day was a holiday, the occasion being the fourth anniversary of the Bolshevik Revolution. The city was decorated with Red flags and banners and Goodrich counted seven thousand soldiers marching on a nearby parade ground. Yet he detected a general lack of enthusiasm on the part of the population and noted, "We do not find the noise and bombast of our 4th of July." Goodrich and Haskell spent the day touring various orphanages and ARA kitchens and hospitals. They came away with the impression that, because conditions in Petrograd were "nothing like as bad . . . as we found in the Volga district," the correct policy for the ARA was to confine its feeding operations to children's homes rather than to establish public kitchens. The most enjoyable aspect of the day was touring such sights as Saint Isaac's Cathedral, the Winter Palace, and the Smolny Institute—a former girls' school which had served as Lenin's headquarters for a time during the Bolshevik Revolution. Because no trains were running on the holiday, Goodrich and Haskell "made the best of it and went to the opera." Emerging from an excellent performance of Rossini's *Barber of Seville*, Goodrich and Haskell found that a heavy blanket of snow had fallen. The storm continued all the next day (8 November) and as a result "we could do little" due to the blockage of traffic and the lack of streetcars. Before the day was over hundreds of women wielding shovels had cleared most of the streets and traffic was restored through the use of sleighs and sleds. As darkness set in

Goodrich and Haskell finally departed for Moscow with the snow still falling. According to Goodrich's calculation they arrived at Moscow the next afternoon only twenty-nine hours late, which was "not so bad for Russian railroading in the winter time."[8]

Awaiting Goodrich at Moscow was a telegram from Hoover summoning him home as soon as possible. Despite his best efforts he was unable to arrange his departure until Monday, 14 November, a delay of four days. In the interim he answered his mail, telegraphed his wife to meet him in London, shopped for Christmas presents, and attended the trial of thirty-five men who were accused of stealing valuables they were supposed to be protecting. As a member of the Indiana bar, he was fascinated by the Soviet system of justice in which the judge acted both as prosecutor and jury. Aided by a translator, Goodrich recorded the following exchange between the judge and one of the prisoners: "'Why did you take the safe containing the jewels down to your house,' asked the judge. 'I just wanted to show how easy it would be for an outsider to steal it,' the prisoner replied. 'Of course I intended to return it.' 'Then why did you open the safe,' queried the judge. 'Just to prove how easy it would be for an outsider to open it,' the prisoner replied."[9] When he learned later that nineteen of the men had been executed, including the prisoner in question, Goodrich was not surprised in the slightest.

To complete his gathering of information for Hoover, Goodrich made several last minute appointments—with the commissars for foreign affairs and railroads, and with the managers of the newly organized state bank. Georgii Chicherin, the commissar for foreign affairs, received Goodrich at the unorthodox hour of 7:00 P.M. and for an hour impressed his listener with his "honesty and sincerity of purpose." Chicherin stressed that America and Russia were natural friends with common interests and that America's policy of nonrecognition was misguided. When Goodrich brought up the question of the New Economic Policy, Chicherin plainly stated that the concessions made to capitalism were only a temporary retreat designed to pave the way for "the final victory for Communism."[10] Goodrich, who was usually skeptical about the statements of Soviet authorities, should have been more attentive in this case to Chicherin's determination to establish a Communist society. With his capitalist bias, Goodrich was more inclined to listen to those who viewed the NEP as a permanent policy rather than a strategic retreat.

More to his liking, therefore, were the answers he received from the representatives of the state railroad system and the state bank. In a two-hour conference Goodrich was assured that the railroad system was sufficiently restored to ship American grain to the Volga region without delay. The introduction of a capitalistic piecework system, whereby workers were compensated according to the amount of work accomplished, accounted for part of the improvement. To make ends meet the railroads had begun to charge fares for freight and passenger traffic. A further increase in efficiency came from the purchase of 1,900 steam engines from Germany and Sweden and 500 Canadian tank cars. Why, it occurred to the Indiana banker, were Americans not permitted to participate in the economic development of the new Russia? Just as satisfactory to Goodrich were the assurances he received from two representatives of the state bank who said they welcomed foreign capital and that they had been promised full freedom of action by the government. Goodrich was especially pleased by their comment:

> The changes now going on in our government are fundamental. Mr. Lenin has had a real change of heart. It is not a mere strategic move on the part of the communists. It is not temporary. The retreat toward capitalism has actually set in. It will continue until capitalism is established and full assurance given to everyone that the right of contract and private property in Russia will be respected.[11]

Goodrich, who accepted their statements at face value, was not the only person confused about the goals and purposes of the NEP.

His return to America required an entire two weeks and was punctuated by tedious delays in changing trains and passing customs at the borders of Latvia, Lithuania, Poland, Germany, Belgium, and Britain. For once his train left Moscow on time and Goodrich, who had procrastinated in assembling his trunks, suitcases, food, candles, and "the insect powder for lice and bugs," had to hurry to the station. His new fur coat proved a wise acquisition as the unheated train crossed a snow covered landscape en route to Riga. The ARA office at Riga assisted Goodrich in transporting his luggage and in confirming his reservations to sail for America on the liner *George Washington*. In his discussions with John C. Miller, the head of the Riga ARA office, Goodrich found that, in his naivete, he had made "a rather serious mistake." Due to his lack of familiarity with the Latvian currency he had given the baggage porters the equivalent of six American dollars. According to Miller, "I had given them the biggest tips since the Tsar went thru there in the old days."[12]

Two days later he was met at London's Victoria Station by Walter Brown, the ARA's European director. Brown was about to leave for Riga and was concerned about reports of increased friction between Haskell and the Soviet authorities. But Goodrich, optimistic as ever, was confident all difficulties over transportation and bureaucratic red tape could be resolved without difficulty. For five days Goodrich, now joined by his wife, waited restlessly at the Savoy Hotel for the departure of the *George Washington*. The delay presented him with an opportunity to read through stacks of mail and to have a luncheon with George Harvey, the controversial American ambassador to Britain. According to Goodrich, Harvey was "exceedingly kind" and readily agreed that American trade with Russia should be promptly resumed. Harvey, who had frequently demonstrated questionable political judgment as ambassador, urged Goodrich to press his views on United States-Soviet trade upon Secretary of State Charles Evans Hughes, a recommendation which proved typically unrealistic. In practice Goodrich was to find Hughes rigidly unreceptive to his suggestions. Trade was also the subject of a two-hour conference between Goodrich and Leonid Krassin, the head of the Russian mission in London. Goodrich stressed that he personally favored reopening trade channels, but that his highest priority of all was overcoming the famine.[13]

His overriding sensation during the enforced five-day layover was one of discontent. The "warm, muggy, foggy" weather intensified his longing for Indiana or even Moscow. "I find myself at times wishing I was back in Moscow where the cold itself made one get up and whistle to keep warm," he noted. Having seen the tourist sights of London and completed his reports, Goodrich impatiently marked time. "This week has been a dreary one," he recorded. "Now that the work is over for the moment I find myself anxious to get started for home and have been counting the hours when the boat is to sail." Even the voyage, after the novelty of his first passage, was anticlimactic. On the third day a North Atlantic storm slowed the liner's progress and even Goodrich, who "foolishly thought I was immune," suffered briefly from nausea. No sooner had he recovered than his presence was discovered by several newspaper correspondents who "pestered" him for interviews about Russia. Convinced the American press was unreasonably anti-Soviet, Goodrich flatly rejected the requests. His views, he feared, would be distorted to fit the bias of each publisher who preferred "always propaganda, never the truth."[14]

The arrival of the *George Washington* at New York on 3 December put an end to Goodrich's enforced inactivity. While his wife returned to their home at Winchester, Goodrich made a quick trip to Washington to confer with Hoover. Because Goodrich mailed his diary home to a stenographer (with the feeling "as if I never again wanted to look at it") he left us no record of his Washington discussions.[15] Most

likely he reviewed with Hoover his impressions of the famine along
the lines of his narrative reports of 1 and 2 November. Probably the
main topic of their conversations was a document drafted by Haskell
entitled: "Memorandum for Governor Goodrich on matters to be
taken up with Mr. Hoover."

Using Goodrich as a conduit, Haskell sought to outline for Hoover the main problems faced by the ARA. Haskell stressed that he
wished to avoid the arrival all at once of large quantities of corn and
wheat so as not to overwhelm the decrepit Russian railroad system.
Gradually he would increase the American shipping of grain to two
thousand tons per day, as the railroads and government departments
demonstrated an ability to handle the load. "Governor Goodrich,"
he added, "can explain the difficulty of obtaining any correct statistics on railways or anything else in Russia." Goodrich then discussed
Russia's need for seed corn and wheat to ensure the success of spring
planting. Haskell and Goodrich recommended sending sufficient
seed to plant five million acres in corn and two million in wheat.
From the Soviet point of view, they conceded, wheat was preferable
to corn. But Haskell and Goodrich advised corn because it was less
likely to be stolen than wheat, as "everyone in Russia will steal food
at the present time." Goodrich was also asked to explain that the
unprecedented scope of the operation required far more American
supervisors than had been the case in previous ARA operations in
eastern Europe during the Peace Conference. "Our operations,"
Haskell noted, "now extend from north of Kazan to the Caspian
Sea and from Riga to Ufa and Orenburg. Each district is a great
country by itself and we are really up against it at the present moment
for the proper American supervision of our supplies."

Goodrich was asked to explain to the Chief Haskell's difficulties in
getting any degree of cooperation from the inefficient and indifferent
Soviet bureaucracy. Even the simplest request, he complained, required continual letter writing and personal pleas and "even then we
are days and sometimes weeks obtaining things that should take a
few hours." One of the most exasperating examples he had yet encountered concerned the need to go to three different departments
before a member of the ARA could travel—one to authorize the
trip, another to issue the tickets, which had finally to be presented
to the department of railroads at the start of the journey. In Haskell's
opinion the sole purpose of the multiple offices was to provide jobs
for bureaucrats and their friends and secure a guaranteed supply of
government food rations. In conclusion, Haskell mentioned that he
had had a few personnel problems of his own and had been compelled
to discharge three employees for dishonesty. Indirectly Haskell told

Hoover that a mistake had been made in sending Harvard history professor Archibald Coolidge to Moscow as an ARA staff member. According to Haskell he found it difficult to find "anything for him to do which the Professor considers of sufficient importance." Coolidge preferred holding conferences with high Soviet officials to the handling of mundane administrative details. The solution, suggested Haskell with the concurrence of Goodrich, was to discreetly dispense with Coolidge's services. As indelicately expressed by Haskell, "Most of the things he would like to do are things which can be better done by myself directly." As it turned out Haskell and Goodrich were not alone in questioning Coolidge's value to the ARA. Edgar Rickard, the Director-General of the ARA, regarded Coolidge as "absolutely impossible," and added, "The Chief and one of us spent hours in trying to get information from him and all to no avail."[16]

Armed with the reports of Haskell and Goodrich, Hoover adopted a shrewd if politically risky strategy. Speed was of the essence, he reasoned, and Hoover concluded that only a congressional appropriation could deliver sufficient corn, wheat, and seed to Russia to meet the crisis. Hoover then and later insisted that he was motivated only by humanitarian considerations. More worldly factors were also present. Since the Paris Peace Conference of 1919 Hoover had maintained a reputation as one of America's leading opponents of Bolshevism. At Paris he had advised President Woodrow Wilson that America's policy toward Russia should emphasize nonintervention, nonrecognition, and food for the destitute. While Hoover's response to the Russian famine of 1921–1922 was a logical continuation of his earlier recommendations, feeding starving Russians was more than a manifestation of compassion on Hoover's part. In general political terms he hoped that relief assistance would increase America's influence in Russia and, by demonstrating the contrast between western abundance and communist poverty, push the Soviet leadership in a capitalist direction. But he denied any grand design for overthrowing the Soviet government or the use of food as a political weapon. In 1925, when asked to comment upon the manuscript of Harold H. Fisher's official history of the Russian relief operation, Hoover stressed the humanitarian motives behind the program. He had not designed the project as "a setting up exercise to instruct the world on Bolshevism," he maintained. On the contrary, he told the public relations director of the ARA, "all these actions were for one concerted purpose—to save the lives of starving people."[17] In his approach to the disaster Goodrich, like Hoover, stressed America's humanitarian obligation. But already Goodrich was moving far

ahead of his fellow Republicans as he considered ways and means of
integrating the new capitalist Russia into the world community.

Hoover devised the ARA's strategy of seeking congressional approval for aid to Russia; Goodrich played a crucial role in securing
the appropriation. Hoover's first step was enlisting the support of
President Harding. On 6 December, in a special message to Congress, Harding endorsed purchasing ten million bushels of corn and
one million bushels of seed to halt the wave of starvation. Noting
that his administration did not recognize Russia and disapproved
of Communist propaganda, Harding stressed the nation's duty to
humanity. "The big thing," he stated, "is the call of the suffering
and the dying."[18] A week later Hoover's bill to appropriate ten million dollars "for the relief of the suffering people of Russia through
the American Relief Administration" was introduced in the House
of Representatives. The proposal to provide expensive relief to an
ideologically repugnant regime was greeted with less than whole-
hearted enthusiasm by Republican congressional leaders. Goodrich
helped to tip the balance in favor of the measure. On 13 December,
Goodrich was invited to testify on the bill before the House Foreign
Affairs Committee. His candid description of what he had seen
brought home clearly and poignantly to his listeners the extent of the
calamity. Before he was through, Goodrich had practically single-
handedly persuaded the committee to double the amount of assistance proposed in the bill.

In calm tones Goodrich carefully traced the devastating effects
of civil war and drought upon the Volga region. He sprinkled his
presentation with statistics he had painstakingly gathered from communal leaders and Soviet commissars. At his fingertips Goodrich had
available concrete figures on food production, food reserves, railroad
capacity, population density, and mortality from starvation. As he
described the distressing conditions he had witnessed in the lower
reaches of the Volga, Goodrich effectively appealed to the emotions
of his listeners:

> In going into the German and Russian communes and the Russian
> communes in the lower Volga I found an appalling situation. On going
> into the cities and observing these great, strong, round-faced, red-
> cheeked men and women in the bazaars and on the streets, one would
> think there was no famine in that country, but when you go into the
> community houses where deserted children and orphans are assembled,
> go out into the communes and into the communal homes where they
> have gotten them together, you realize how terrific the situation is, espe-
> cially when you get down to the brass-tack facts and see the small amount

of food that they have there upon which they must depend to sustain life for the next six months.

His sympathetic portrayal of the "pretty clean looking lot of farmers" at Schilling received a sympathetic hearing. Unless help arrived from abroad he estimated that at least eight hundred out of a population of four thousand were doomed to death by starvation. The serious expressions on the faces of the farmers convinced Goodrich that they were telling the truth as did his inspection of food reserves. "I went into their warehouses," noted Goodrich, "and out of nine warehouses eight of them were empty, and they had surplus grain stored in one warehouse. These communes are typical."

To a silent and shocked hearing room Goodrich continued his presentation with a description of the countryside between Norda, reputed to be the richest of the Volga communes, and Schilling:

> Between that commune [Norda] and the commune of Schilling I saw in one field as I went by grandparents—I judged so by their appearance, and afterwards learned that was true—the grandfather and grandmother and the son and the daughter-in-law and five children, who were on their knees going across their little allotment of land gathering every weed they could get, tying them in bundles, hauling them down to their commune, and there they intended to thrash out the weed seeds and grind them in the communal mill, mix with rye, and try to get along. The straw from the weeds they put in stacks that their stock might eat it to keep them alive until the next harvest. I asked them whether or not the stock would eat it, and they said, "They will not until everything else is gone, but before they will starve to death." I saw children out along the little waterways gathering rose pods, cockle burrs, and things like that in little bags that they would take home to grind in their little communal mills, which they have everywhere. In that commune were 145 people starved to death this year, 65 died from typhus, which is just getting under way there, and 82 from cholera.

Goodrich effectively augmented his statistics with personal vignettes. First he told of the crowded communal hall at Schilling where the farmers told him, "There is not enough to keep us all alive until the next harvest. If we divide up now and do not get help, we will all starve to death. It is better that some shall die in order that others might live." The answer, conceded Goodrich, was not easy for an American to understand "but when you get inside of Russian life and understand the terrific situation that confronts those people you cease to wonder why, knowing that death must overtake them all if they divide, that they choose to preserve their own families."

Cleverly Goodrich aroused the sympathy of the listeners by citing cases in which innocent children were victimized by the catastrophe. He described his impressions upon visiting the local orphanage at Houk, an institution filled to overflowing with abandoned children and orphans:

> We found 145 children in this home. They are first taken into one part of the home, deloused, and given a bath. These children when they come in are dirty, ragged, living skeletons, with a helpless, hungry look in their faces, and take little or no interest in their surroundings. They seem more like an animal that has been shot to death and crawled off in the brush to die. It was a terrific sight for an American to witness. After the children are cleaned up they are given rough cotton clothing, very scant and light, most of them without shoes and stockings, although the thermometer on the day we were there was 28° below zero and the home in which they were quartered not very well heated on account of the shortage of fuel.

Saving the best of his vignettes for last, Goodrich then told of finding in a shed near Houk the two young girls "who probably would have starved to death if we had not found them." Goodrich had himself seen the lightly dressed children emerge from the shed "holding their arms close about them, shivering and crying in the cold, bitter wind blowing the snow across the commune that day." And he told of seeing at Saratov a destitute peasant and his wife who had not eaten for a week and were "lying at the point of death." To Goodrich they said: "There is no hope for us; we are too weak to get out; we shall die but it does not matter."

By the conclusion of his remarks Goodrich had effectively disarmed skeptics on the House Foreign Affairs Committee. Was the proposed $10 million appropriation sufficient to save the starving of Russia? Goodrich replied, "No sir; I do not think it is enough, gentlemen. It ought to be 20,000,000 bushels of corn and 5,000,000 bushels of wheat sent over from this country to save that situation." Actually Goodrich had slightly misspoken because the administration bill provided for an appropriation of dollars, not bushels. With an assist from Hoover, who pointed out that corn was selling 55 to 60 cents a bushel at east coast ports, Goodrich quickly recovered. The sum of $20 million, he suggested, should be adequate to meet the emergency. When asked whether his request was merely a rough estimate improvised on the spur of the moment, Goodrich insisted he had settled on $20 million only after the most thorough investigation. "You would not, and I should regret to see, this country start in and not do the job right because of the lack of two or three million dollars," he testified. Would the $20 million be enough to restore

Russia's agricultural and industrial foundations? That, insisted Goodrich, was an irrelevant question. "If you please," he admonished, "I am addressing myself to what is necessary to do to save human life and people in Russia from starving to death because of lack of food."[19]

Only four days later the House approved the appropriation, now doubled from $10 million to $20 million. According to the House version all food should be purchased in the United States and transported in American ships. Opponents contended it was poor public policy to spend such a large sum abroad when many Americans at home were in want, but they were overwhelmed by a vote of 181 to 71. By a voice vote the Senate concurred but added an additional $600,000—$100,000 to provide relief for the unemployed nationally, and $500,000 to benefit hospitalized veterans in the state of Arizona. Senator Henry W. Ashurst of Arizona, the sponsor of the amendments, was highly displeased when both were dropped in conference. On 23 December President Harding was able to sign the legislation— a last minute Christmas present from capitalistic America to the atheistic regime of Lenin. To acquire the needed grain and speed its distribution through the ARA, Harding appointed a five-member purchasing commission which included Goodrich as one of its members.[20]

Both Hoover and Goodrich were justifiably pleased by their success. Hoover could take credit for having mapped out the overall political strategy for securing the congressional appropriation. But Goodrich had also played a crucial role; his triumphant appearance before the House Foreign Affairs Committee had effectively shamed Congress into a doubling of the Russian relief appropriation. Edgar Rickard, a devoted Hoover loyalist, aptly described the outcome in a letter to Walter Brown: "We have had many examples in this Russian job of his [Hoover's] uncanny ability to anticipate events of the future. As a remarkable instance is his choice of Governor Goodrich to prepare himself on Russian first-hand information for the efforts on Congress. While, of course, the Chief applied the method of attack, Goodrich was responsible for the personal work which carried the Bill through despite the opposition of the Leader of the House, the Speaker of the House, the Chairman of the Appropriations Committee and the Chairman of the Foreign Relations Committee, an array of opposition which is considered to be impregnable and able to definitely block legislation. Hence, we have Goodrich to thank for the chief work in securing this money."[21]

5

Snowbound in Russia

THE events of 1921 gave Goodrich a new lease on life, although not quite in the manner he had anticipated. In January, to his great relief, he had completed his term as governor and was thereby freed to return to his chosen career as a banker and investor. But it was the accident of the Russian famine, rather than his business, that rejuvenated his life. His availability and his connections within the Republican Party led to his being sent for two months to roam throughout Soviet Russia. That trip, Goodrich told an audience of Fort Wayne businessmen, "was the most interesting experience of my life."[1] Having painstakingly completed his survey of the Volga region and reported his findings to Herbert Hoover, Goodrich had played a crucial role in securing a $20 million congressional appropriation for Russian relief. Once the ARA had completed arrangements for transporting American corn and wheat to Russia, Hoover intended to send Goodrich on a second inspection trip.

In the meantime Goodrich had almost two months to recuperate from his journey of the fall and to prepare for his next encounter with Russia's primitive travel conditions. In practice his crowded agenda left him little time for relaxation. One of Goodrich's most time-consuming responsibilities was to attend the weekly meetings of the Purchasing Commission, established by an executive order drafted by Hoover and signed by Harding on 24 December. At the first meeting of the group, held the previous day, Hoover was designated as chairman and Goodrich as vice-chairman. In view of the food crisis in Russia no one, not even attorney Goodrich, questioned whether the commission could legally function before the President formally signed the executive order establishing its existence. On five occasions before leaving on his second trip to Russia, Goodrich served as acting chairman as the commission considered how much corn and other relief supplies should be purchased and at what price. With Goodrich presiding, the commission on 4 January decided to accept bids on two million bushels of corn and to advertise for bids on fifty thousand cases each of condensed milk and evaporated milk, one million bushels of seed grain, and five thousand tons of corn grits. Hoover and Goodrich took the position that the fastest and most economical method for shipping ARA corn and wheat to Russia was in bulk form. At its final destination the grain could be milled locally. As Hoover wrote Goodrich: "It is obvious to me that if we cannot secure transportation of this material in bulk we may as well throw up our hands." With reference to a rumor that Goodrich was about to be sent to Russia as ambassador, Hoover added, "I got no excitement out of the suggestion that you were going to Russia to represent the American government, so do not worry."[2]

Reflecting his near celebrity status, Goodrich found that he was presented with numerous opportunities to speak and write about his Russian views and experiences. Much of his time prior to his second Russian trip was, therefore, occupied with giving interviews and preparing speeches and articles. Goodrich, who himself wrote, typed, and revised his literary efforts, gave careful thought as to what would be the most effective approach for influencing American opinion. As an official of the ARA he appreciated that he had been sent in a nonpolitical capacity to gather information. As he reflected on what he had seen, Goodrich found that many humanitarian and political questions were intertwined. In discussing his impressions of Russia and the challenges facing the ARA he could hardly avoid touching upon political implications. Would famine relief to the starving people of Russia bolster an ideologically repugnant government? Was Communist Russia the final product of the Russian Revolution? And, if it appeared that the Soviets were firmly entrenched, should America abandon nonrecognition and restore United States-Soviet trade? In addressing these questions Goodrich, as a professional politician, selected his words carefully. He was well aware of the dangers in getting too far ahead of public opinion and tried his best to keep open an avenue of retreat. For every favorable statement about the regime of Lenin, therefore, he included a balancing note of criticism.

In launching his modest campaign of public education, Goodrich stressed America's humanitarian duty to alleviate suffering. It would be "a disgrace," he told the Foreign Policy Association at New York's Hotel Astoria, "if the American people do not do everything possible to stay the famine in Russia." Famine relief, he suggested, would pay long term benefits to America in the form of Russian gratitude. "Because we have extended the helping hand in time of direst need," Goodrich wrote in the *Outlook*, "Russia will come back with a traditional friendship for the United States, cemented with new ties of the kind that are not easily severed." One of the most important advantages of the ARA program, Goodrich implied, would be to accelerate the return of capitalism to Russia. Writing in the *Century*, Goodrich contended that "the swing toward individualism and capitalism is increasing." And in an interview with the *New York Times*, he suggested famine relief would hasten the evolution of the Soviet government in a capitalistic direction.[3]

The theme that most appealed to his listeners was Goodrich's repeated insistence that Communism was "an idle dream which cannot be realized in Russia or anywhere else." "I came away with the certain conviction," he said at Fort Wayne, "that however attractive may be the utopian dream of the communist, however logical may be the arguments in favor of its establishment, it has not stood the pragmatic test in Russia and the signs of its failure are abundant on every hand." Goodrich's admiration for the courage and good-natured spirit of the Russian farmers he had met in the Volga region was also well received. "The meetings of the communes," he told the Foreign Policy Association, "reminded me of meetings of American farmers. They are a fine, rugged lot of people, and with good conditions they will develop a civilization rivaling America's." However, with the benefit of perfect hindsight, Goodrich regretted his characterization of the Soviet leaders as "honest, sincere, misguided enthusiasts." Ralph Easly, the secretary of the American Defense Society, assailed Goodrich as a Red and the Fort Wayne *Journal-Gazette* published a critical editorial, a copy of which Goodrich received from his friend Arthur K. Remmel, city editor of the rival *News and Sentinel*. Goodrich did not deny using the characterization "honest, sincere, misguided enthusiasts" with reference to Lenin and Chicherin. But he insisted he was not duped, and that his statement was essentially accurate. "I could not explain their actions and sacrifices on any other ground. I have met these men and talked to them and they impressed me as such." His view, he told Remmel, was that American relief policy should be based upon "what is best for the Russian people" regardless of the individuals heading the Russian government. "I like the Russian people," he concluded, "they are so much like our own folks."[4]

Goodrich was more circumspect regarding the all-important questions of trade and diplomatic recognition. In public he simply refused to be pinned down on such explosive matters. When asked point blank by Representative Tom Connally of Texas his position on trade and recognition, Goodrich discreetly replied, "That, again, is a question I would rather not discuss except in executive session." Privately it is likely Goodrich had already made up his mind on both trade and recognition and was only looking for a suitable opportunity to speak out. There is every reason to believe Goodrich was in agreement with his friend Lincoln Hutchinson who, as early as 9 November 1921, had advised Hoover to break with past American policy. Hutchinson, an economist, suggested that limited American trade with Russia would facilitate the return of the country to capitalism. A "necessary part" of the question, contended Hutchinson, was for the United States to accept the fact that the Soviets were firmly in "the saddle," and to abandon its "holier than thou" policy of moral condemnation and "frankly recognize it as a de facto government."[5]

Goodrich dropped several broad hints that he agreed with Hutchinson when he was introduced to Alexander Gumberg at the Washington hotel room of Will Hays on 19 December. Gumberg, a native Russian, had served during the revolutions of 1917 as translator, advisor, and friend to Colonel Raymond Robins of the American Red Cross. In 1921 Gumberg was working in Washington as a representative of the Far Eastern Republic, a temporary political creation of World War I. His real interest, however, was reestablishing Russian-American trade and diplomatic ties. Following his conversation with Goodrich, Gumberg excitedly wrote Robins, "What he [Goodrich] said is so important and interesting and GOOD that there is only one thing for you to do (provided you know that he is all right)—to me he certainly looked like a REAL person, and that is to use all your influence to back that bill for 20 million for Russian relief." Gumberg was not at liberty to repeat the specifics of what Goodrich had told him. But Gumberg was plainly delighted by what he had heard: "He talked like the most intelligent person, in fact outside of yourself I never heard a foreigner talk with more intelligence or real human sympathy or understanding about Russia. I simply can't believe that I am wrong about the man." In a second meeting with Goodrich on 20 December, Gumberg broached the idea of accompanying the governor on his next trip to Russia as guide and interpreter—the same function he had performed for Robins. "My only ambition," he wrote Goodrich, "is to be useful in this tremendous problem of reconciliation between Russia and the rest of the world, and particularly the United States." At first Goodrich did not encourage Gumberg because "the entire matter of my going to Russia is up in the air."[6] However, neither Goodrich nor Gumberg forgot the idea and a few months later when Goodrich made a third Russian trip he tried hard to have Gumberg sent as his assistant. As their friendship developed, Gumberg kept Goodrich supplied with Russian newspaper clippings and he often urged Goodrich to write letters on behalf of bettering Russian-American relations—to which

Goodrich usually agreed. From his isolated residence at Winchester, Goodrich appreciated Gumberg's many Soviet-American contacts and his ability as a coordinator of political strategy. Despite their personal friendship they did not always agree. Eventually Goodrich disappointed Gumberg by taking the politically practical position that diplomatic recognition of Soviet Russia should be delayed until after the establishment of commercial relations.

On 18 February 1922, Goodrich was again on his way to Russia. Outwardly his trip began on a festive note as he was accompanied by his wife and her friend Marie Moorman, from Winchester. The two women planned to tour Paris and Egypt before eventually meeting the governor at Moscow.[7] Pleasure, however, was not on Goodrich's mind as on the morning of his departure he ended his silence on the question of recognition and began a quiet personal campaign to convince the Harding administration that normal trade and diplomatic relations with Russia were inevitable and justified. Theoretically he could have begun by approaching either the White House or the Department of State. However, Goodrich felt Harding was uninterested in foreign policy and that the rigid mind of Secretary of State Hughes was closed to any modification of policy toward Russia. Secretary of Commerce Hoover, Goodrich's immediate superior, presented the only real avenue of approach, and not too promising a one at that. Presumably Hoover, an advocate of expanding trade abroad, would look favorably upon opening trade ties with Russia and perhaps even reconsider his position on recognition. Goodrich may also have chosen to write Hoover because the Secretary of Commerce was habitually loyal to those who did good work for him, as had Goodrich. And he probably realized that once he reached Russia he would, at least in theory, have to route all letters to Hoover through the ARA's Moscow headquarters. Displeased by Hutchinson's 9 November letter to Hoover advocating American recognition of Russia, Haskell had banned individual communications by ARA personnel. From Goodrich's perspective an approach to Hoover was at least worth a try; besides, it might well be his last opportunity for some time to influence American policy.

The centerpiece of Goodrich's argument was that recognition would lead to the flourishing of trade and would enable America to play a major role in opening the Russian market. Despite the absence of recognition, American firms had managed to export $15.6 million worth of goods to Russia in 1921, more than half of which consisted of shoes. Goodrich, while not opposing the sale of light consumer goods, was more interested in promoting such durable manufactured products as plows, tractors, and railroad equipment. He emphasized to Hoover that increased trade with Russia was favored by a broad spectrum of American industrialists. Just the previous day, Goodrich related, he had attended a luncheon of businessmen at New York where he discussed "the whole Russian situation" with the president of the Westinghouse Company, the president of the Rock Island Railroad, and executives of the Sinclair Oil Company, the J. G. White Engineering Company, and the Russian-American Industrial Syndicate. All the participants displayed intense interest in fostering United States-Russian trade. Westinghouse, for example, was interested in developing a factory for the production of railroad brake shoes. Goodrich stressed that the entire nation, not just the east coast, would benefit from increased Russian trade. That very morning James Oliver of the Oliver Chill Plow Company at South Bend, Indiana, had informed Goodrich, through his son, of his company's interest in opening a Russian factory. All that was needed was the opening of official trade relations. And Goodrich was told there was a real danger German, French, and British companies would receive concessions in the plow manufacturing field unless America acted with dispatch. In view of the urgency of the situation, the Harding administration should seize the initiative and take "positive action with reference to Russia." His idea was that the Soviets could be told informally that if "certain steps" were taken (presumably a debt settlement and the cessation of propaganda) "recognition will follow so as not to drive them in their desperation to make contacts with and concessions to the French and Germans that will place an unnecessary burden upon the Russian people whose interests we desire to serve."

Indirectly Goodrich suggested that he himself would be an ideal choice to conduct high level talks to explore trade and diplomatic recognition. "I intend to go pretty thoroughly into the whole political and economic situation when I am in Moscow. I believe I can get in touch with men at the top. In doing this, I will not in any way embarrass the American Relief Administration." The present, he felt, would be an ideal time for action and Goodrich urged that Hoover, Hughes, and Harding hold a conference "and determine the position of our country." Concluding with an argument previously advanced by Hutchinson, Goodrich contended, "The Revolution is an accomplished fact and we might as well recognize it and, under proper assurances, cooperate in a friendly way in the rebuilding of Russia."[8]

In a private letter, discreetly avoiding the glare of publicity, Goodrich now leaped ahead of public opinion and rejected the anti-Soviet positions of both political parties. He had joined the mere handful of American politicians who regarded Russian recognition as inevitable. The unpredictable Senator William E. Borah of Idaho was the best-known Republican to endorse the exchange of ambassadors. Goodrich, who had little personal contact with the "Lion of Idaho," was the second most prominent Republican to take the leap. Of the Democrats only Maryland Senator Joseph I. France was willing to accept Russia as a legitimate member of the international community. Probably Hoover was not shocked by Goodrich's views, but he remained, despite the efforts of Goodrich, highly skeptical of the Soviet system and leadership. To have expected Hoover to volunteer as leader of a movement to recognize Soviet Russia was asking too much personally and politically. Hoover responded by merely filing Goodrich's letter without comment and declined to enter a discussion about the merits of recognition. The results of Goodrich's letter were, therefore, negligible; no high level meeting or diplomatic revolution was forthcoming. Goodrich, who was retracing his steps to Moscow, probably was not too surprised or disappointed. As an experienced politician he understood that presenting the "facts" about Russia as he saw them would require great persistence, but he could not have guessed that the debate over recognition would persist until 1933.[9]

Immediately after reaching Moscow on 9 March 1922, Goodrich, at the request of Hoover, took up with Colonel Haskell a potentially explosive problem. Goodrich carried with him a confidential note from Hoover to Haskell which began: "This letter will be given to you personally by Governor Goodrich who has become a member of the Executive Committee of the A.R.A. and whose services to the cause are well known to you. I have asked Governor Goodrich to go to Russia again that he may be of such assistance as he can in the administration there and that he may be able to again report to the American people on the situation of our affairs in Russia." But the governor was being sent for another purpose as well. Hoover had been shocked to learn from Professor Coolidge of several heavy drinking bouts on the part of the Moscow staff which had occurred during Haskell's trip to London the previous month. The possible publication of such reports gave Hoover "the utmost anxiety" as he feared public disclosure would "smear the whole reputation of American effort in Russia to a degree I cannot possibly describe." Goodrich was told to get to the bottom of the problem.[10]

Even before his arrival at Moscow, Goodrich had developed substantial evidence of misconduct on the part of several of the army officers brought to Russia by Haskell. At a Berlin hospital he spent a day interviewing Joseph Rosen, an employee of the Joint Distribution Committee, who had just come from Moscow and was recovering from typhus. According to Rosen, it was Colonel Philip Carroll "who ordered the first installment of booze, and who, when that was consumed, immediately entered an order for another large quantity, [and] was drinking heavily all the time." Based on Rosen's account, Goodrich found that Carroll's job performance had been surprisingly unimpaired "as he seemed to be able to carry a heavier load than some of the others." Another leading offender, Goodrich was told, was Major Thomas C. Lonergan, who was "intoxicated off and on" during Haskell's absence and who was also accused of having maintained "illicit relations" with a Russian woman whom he from time to time brought to the Pink House. Rosen further related that he had been present at a reception hosted by Aleksandr Eiduk, the Soviet liaison with the ARA, at which Major Charles Telford, "while badly under the influence of liquor attempted to assault Dr. Coolidge, and was only prevented from doing so by the other ARA men present." A somewhat lesser malefactor was Captain Earl J. Dodge, who was accused of speculating for personal gain in Russian currency.

Worst of all, in Goodrich's opinion, was the conduct of Shelby Saunders of the ARA's Petrograd office. In 1919 Saunders had done good work for Haskell in Romania and for that reason had been placed in charge at Petrograd. From Rosen, Goodrich learned that "Saunders was not only intoxicated from time to time, but that he brought prostitutes to the ARA headquarters."[11] Possibly Goodrich also had access to a similar complaint from a Russian resident of Petrograd, who denounced Saunders for conducting "wild debauches" in the company of "jolly ladies." Confirmation of the reports came from Golder, who substantiated everything Rosen had said: "He [Golder] stated that he had the most positive evidence that Saunders, when he wanted a prostitute at the house, would order the chauffeur driving the American car to go and get one." Saunders, defended by Haskell, emphatically denied the accusations, but Goodrich regarded him as "a bad actor" and urged that he be dismissed forthwith. Goodrich contended that there "ought to be a confoundedly good reason to justify the continuation of that sort of fellow in the services of the ARA." In London, Walter Brown took Goodrich's side and demanded Saunders's resignation, ending that particular episode.[12]

As a result of Goodrich's findings, Haskell carried out a major housecleaning at Moscow. First, he brutally dismissed Carroll "on account of his inability to comprehend the duties and the responsibilities of his position on the staff of the Director in Russia and further, for continued incompetence in the conduct of the Supply Division,

notwithstanding repeated reductions in the scope of its work." Next
to go was Lonergan.[13] Haskell told Goodrich that he had known of
Lonergan's "weakness in that direction" and had warned him he
would be dismissed if he became intoxicated even once. Narrowly
escaping dismissal was John C. Miller, head of the ARA office at
Riga. Goodrich "almost accidentally" discovered that Miller had engaged in "perfectly foolish conduct" by "philandering" with the
wives of the ARA personnel and by making "impossible proposals"
to the wife of a newspaper correspondent. Goodrich asked Brown
to investigate, but he apparently was unable or too preoccupied to
proceed further.

On the recommendation of Goodrich and Hoover, Cyril J. C.
Quinn was named as Haskell's chief assistant. Goodrich spent three
hours interviewing Quinn and found his account agreed with that of
Coolidge: namely, that Haskell had no knowledge of the drinking
bouts carried on in his absence and that everyone had concealed the
facts from Haskell on his return. Quinn stated that he himself "did
not feel like telling" Haskell about the situation because he wished
to avoid recriminations. In Goodrich's opinion Coolidge, who occupied a more prominent position than Quinn, should have informed
Haskell of the drinking bouts in person immediately upon Haskell's
return to Moscow. Yet Goodrich was confident that Quinn "meas-
ured up" and would be able "to swing the job."[14]

Had the episode disillusioned Goodrich concerning the ARA and
its personnel? On the contrary, Goodrich was confident his efforts
had restored the morale of the Moscow office. Moreover, Goodrich
appears to have thoroughly enjoyed being cast in the role of discipli-
narian. M. M. Mitchell, sent by Brown from London to survey the
situation, found Goodrich to be an excellent source. In Mitchell's
words, "The Governor certainly has gathered a lot of 'dope' one
place and another, and knows more about the gossip of this show
than anyone in it! He has told Dodge that he is suspected of speculation and that if he doesn't watch himself he will be tossed out even
further than Saunders, and has told Telford he will go too, unless he
cuts the liquor and gets to work. He has also told me many interesting things about the reactions of the Chief and of New York, which
he undoubtedly told you, and which make welcome listening—he is
as fresh as a spring breeze."[15]

The resolution of the ARA personnel troubles enabled Goodrich
to concentrate once again upon the famine. Goodrich's intention was
to retrace his route of the fall, going by rail to Samara and then
continuing to Orenburg, two hundred miles further to the east. The
entire trip, he hoped, would take no more than two weeks. In high

spirits Goodrich, accompanied by Hutchinson, set off on the evening
of 15 March, "Things are going along nicely," he reported to Brown.
En route to Samara, an elated Goodrich assured Hoover that the
dismissals of Carroll and Lonergan meant that his troubles at Moscow were over. "It stiffened up the morale of the fellows," he reported to Hoover, "and I think it is pretty well understood among
the force here [at Moscow] that anyone who becomes intoxicated,
at least while on duty, will without hesitation be sent back to the
states."[16] His tedious ride to Samara, which required three nights on
the train, finally terminated at 6:00 A.M. 18 March. Just four hours
later Goodrich was at ARA headquarters interviewing Will Shafroth,
a Colorado native and the son of John Franklin Shafroth, a former
Democratic governor of Colorado (1909–1913) and United States
Senator (1913–1919). Even though they were of different parties,
Goodrich and Shafroth presumably found some time to discuss the
vicissitudes of Colorado and Indiana politics. From Shafroth Goodrich learned that the local authorities had often been less than coop-
erative. Five of his Russian employees had been unjustly arrested for
anti-Communist activity and Eiduk's representative had been "penu-
rious and little" in his relations with the ARA. But Shafroth found
that when he filed complaints and threatened to halt operations,
cooperation improved and the employees were released. Intimida-
tion, he found, could work both ways. A steady flow of American
supplies from the Black Sea port of Novorossiysk was arriving daily
at Samara. As a result, Shafroth was able to distribute adult rations in
addition to continuing the existing program of child-feeding. When
Goodrich visited one of the ARA kitchens he observed 200 children
eating a meal of boiled rice, milk, and sugar. Altogether 2,400 children a day were being fed. Most of them were residents of collecting
homes, only three of which were operating, compared with seven
during Goodrich's visit in the fall.[17]

The same day Goodrich called on the president of the State Bank,
who told him that crop prospects were excellent, especially the outlook for rye, which had benefited from heavy fall rains. A subsequent
interview with the commissar of agriculture for Samara province
confirmed the banker's information. He added that the outlook for
wheat was favorable and said the peasants had enough seed to get
by even without help from America. Both officials expressed great
gratitude for the assistance provided by the ARA. Now that the corn
was arriving in quantity, what Samara needed most was American
trade in the form of agricultural implements.

Another favorable development, thought Goodrich, was the abolition of the Cheka and the introduction of a revolutionary tribunal

to conduct public trials in which the accused had the right to counsel
and the right to know in writing all charges against him. That evening
Goodrich attended the trial, held at the Samara opera house, of
forty-nine people accused of banditry. The proceedings appeared
orderly; all hats were removed, all smoking forbidden, and the audience respectfully rose as the judges entered. Goodrich was, however,
taken aback to discover that five of the defendants, who were not
yet eighteen years of age, were being tried as adults. (On his return
to Samara, Goodrich was slightly shocked to learn that all forty-
nine prisoners had been found guilty and that nine, including a
sixteen-year-old boy, had received the death penalty. The remainder received prison terms varying from three years to life. Still Goodrich regarded the new court as an improvement over the old system, under which all forty-nine would likely have been summarily
executed.)[18]
Even the weather cooperated. Cold temperatures and snow replaced a midwinter thaw, facilitating the movement of corn by
sledges over the frozen terrain. At the railroad station Goodrich
observed "a large number" of sledges pulled by Siberian ponies
which were to haul corn back to their villages. While Goodrich
watched, one man, insisting his sacks were underweight, demanded
a certificate stating the exact weight of his load, so he could not be
accused of theft on his arrival at his destination. According to Shafroth, the situation was so improved that actual starvation would be
eliminated in Samara by the first of April. As Goodrich and Shafroth
departed for Orenburg, Goodrich contemplated the future with optimism. Encouraged by the NEP, he predicted that the peasants of
Samara would "go to work this year." By 15 July they would dig
their first potatoes, by 1 August cut their rye, wheat, and barley,
and by the end of the harvest season begin to furnish surpluses to
all of Russia.[19]
Immediately the weather, so favorable at Samara, changed
abruptly, turning Goodrich's effort to visit Orenburg into a frustrating experience. Sixty miles from Orenburg, Goodrich met his first
delay. The train came to an abrupt halt and he was told that a gang
of bandits was blocking the track ahead. An armored railroad car
was sent ahead to investigate, all lights were extinguished, and Goodrich was told the train would not proceed until daylight. Then overnight "a terrific snow storm" blocked the railroad. Supposedly the
tracks to Orenburg would be cleared by the next day. Despite advancing forty bags of ARA flour to pay the wages of three hundred
section hands and snow shovelers, Goodrich learned that the train
would not be able to move eastward for at least several days. Ascer-

taining that he would be unable to reach Orenburg, Goodrich decided to return to Samara and asked to have his car coupled to a freight train.

During a long stop at the city of Sorochinskoye, Goodrich received a vivid account of the suffering in that city of 20,000 from two American Quakers, Homer and Edna Wright. That morning the corpse of a starved child had been discovered lying in the street. Such events were not unusual, as ten to fifteen people were perishing every day from hunger and typhus. Yet relief was in sight, as freight cars of American corn from Samara were expected to arrive imminently. In answer to Goodrich's inquiries, he was told the people of the area "pretty generally" supported the government despite the presence of very few "real communists." According to the Quakers, there was "no indication whatever" of any sentiment to overthrow the government.

Further to the west the freight train chugged slowly into the village of Bogotai, where it became solidly stuck in "an insurmountable drift." Goodrich was told that there would be a one-day delay: instead the line was closed for five days by conditions which, in Goodrich's opinion, would not have tied up traffic in the United States for more than twenty-four hours. Inwardly Goodrich was furious. "The delay here," he recorded, "is due to lack of equipment, absence of executive ability, and utter inefficiency in dealing with a situation of this kind."[20] Under capitalism, thought Goodrich, the railroad man, such a delay could never have occurred. Goodrich, the politician, did his best to conceal his irritation and used the five days to good advantage by exploring his surroundings and interviewing numerous peasants, an English doctor, and several English Quaker relief workers.

From the Quakers he learned that the situation at Bogotai was "terrible," that sanitary conditions were "very bad," and that an average of three persons a day succumbed to typhus or hunger. In March 1921 the village had counted 4,000 inhabitants; only 3,000 remained and all but 500 needed food assistance. The arrival of American corn, in addition to canned beef and flour from England, promised to eliminate further deaths from starvation, provided the food could be shipped to the countryside before the spring thaw made the roads impassable. Throughout his stay Goodrich observed a determined effort being made to distribute the relief supplies. On his final day he counted 139 sledges drawn by thin horses and camels lined up before the warehouse of the Quakers, as the drivers patiently waiting for their food allotments. On some of the sledges he could see "good, clean, bright hay" to feed the animals, but others had

only black famine weeds. The horses, he observed, refused to touch
the weeds, although the camels seemed not to object. From his interviews with the drivers and peasants, Goodrich compiled harrowing
tales of disaster. In one township of 8,000 he was told, 2,000 had
already died, and in another of 21,000, at least 7,000 had perished.
Many more were doomed, he was told, unless additional corn and
seed grain arrived. On his final day at Bogotai he heard gruesome
second-hand reports of cannibalism. In one nearby village, a woman
was alleged to have eaten the body of her daughter and then committed suicide. He was told further that another woman had been executed by the Cheka after offering human flesh for sale in a local
market. Had Goodrich been able to reach Orenburg, where conditions were far worse than in Samara province, he likely could have
added additional horror stories to his catalog.[21]

How, wondered Goodrich, was he to reconcile these tales with
the fairly healthy appearance of the population? The people, while
dirty and dressed in ragged garb, appeared to Goodrich to be "a
pretty happy, good-natured lot of folks." To pass the time of day,
Goodrich assisted a squad of railroad workers shoveling snow into
a railroad car. A woman shoveler told him his pace was too fast and
that the Russians were too weak from hunger to work any quicker.
But, noted Goodrich, "She looked exceptionally strong and rugged,
and her appearance was not at all consistent with her statement."
More than likely the happy dispositions were explained by the fact
that those arriving to pick up corn were about to receive their first
real food in months. Goodrich may not have appreciated that the
weakest of the villagers were left at home and only the hardiest were
able to transport the food or shovel snow. While retaining his optimism that the worst was over, Goodrich did admit to seeing some
at Bogotai who were neither strong nor happy. In one group of
peasants who had traveled twenty-five miles on sledges, he observed
a dour man eating "a very dark greenish bread. We inquired of what
it was made, and he said of camels' dung mixed with grass. The
various peasants who heard him make this statement nodded their
heads in approval."[22]

On the afternoon of the fifth day at Bogotai the tracks were sufficiently cleared for Goodrich and Shafroth to escape their incarcera-
tion and return to Samara. Arriving at 9:00 A.M., Goodrich spent
the day inspecting a child-feeding operation and observing the distribution of corn to adults. To his eye the 150 young people who
appeared for the noon meal of corn gruel and corn bread, while
"dirty and ragged," appeared "a healthy, strong, normal looking lot
of children." Likewise, he found that most of the women lined up

to receive a raw corn ration of 38 pounds each seemed "rather strong and rugged." Goodrich interviewed one recipient and inquired how she planned to make use of the corn. He learned that she intended to grind it by hand for porridge, rather than have it ground at the local mill where the kulak would keep most of it. Both operations seemed to be orderly in function and administration. All the recipients, children and adults, had been certified as eligible by a committee of local citizens and he saw no pushing or other misbehaving on the part of those receiving the ARA aid. The absence of severe undernourishment, he felt, illustrated that the ARA was making real progress against the famine.[23]

Goodrich intended to return as quickly as possible to Moscow on the 5:00 P.M. train. Once again he found that the schedules of Russian railroads could not be relied upon and that the plans of the traveler to Russia were usually made to be broken. Late in the morning "a terrific snow storm began," and the snow was still falling heavily when Goodrich fell asleep on the train at 10:00 P.M. Not until 5:00 A.M., twelve hours late, did the train leave the station. The delay caused by the snow storm he could accept, but in the course of the trip the governor experienced more "inexcusable delays" than he thought humanly possible. At every scheduled stop the passengers were permitted to alight for five to fifteen minutes in order to purchase tea or hot water. At one station, a delay of fifteen minutes was caused by an argument between the engineer and several Russians as to whether it would be permissible for passengers to ride on the engine. Only after the station agent had settled the question in the negative did the train depart. Inwardly furious, but outwardly composed, Goodrich carefully recorded each delay: the loss of four hours at Sysran due to the failure of an engine to arrive; seventy minutes at an unidentified stop for unknown reasons; then a delay of three hours and twenty minutes at Ruzayevka because a freight train blocked the roundhouse. Once the fresh engine was coupled to the train there was a further wait of half an hour for the stationmaster to order the train to depart. The whole experience amounted to "a first class illustration" of the inefficiency of the Russian railroad system and of the ineptitude of Communism. The hardest thing of all to understand was the apparent lack of concern by all involved. Even the passengers accepted the delays with complete resignation. "They fight to get on the train," he noted, "but once on sit down in stolid indifference waiting for the train to move, knowing that if it does not move today it will tomorrow or some other day."[24]

Goodrich arrived at Moscow early on the morning of 29 March well rested and in an optimistic frame of mind. He was pleased that the last segment of his trip had gone much better than the first. A new German locomotive, "a fine looking machine, in first class condition," had efficiently carried the train over the final 140 miles, making up nearly an hour's time. In interviewing the engineer, Goodrich learned that fifty such engines were arriving each week and that the engineer had just come from Riga where he had picked up eighty cars of American seed grain.[25] Railroading was still on Goodrich's mind when he and Golder, with some trepidation, called at the office of Feliks Dzerzhinsky, the newly appointed commissar of railroads. By reputation Dzerzhinsky was well known to his American visitors as head of the dreaded Cheka. In that position, which he continued to hold, Dzerzhinsky had displayed great ruthlessness in crushing opponents of the regime. Goodrich was somewhat taken aback to be introduced to a slightly built man with blue eyes, mustache and goatee, and the general air of an intellectual rather than that of a policeman or the operator of a railroad. "I expected to see a bluebeard," recorded Goodrich. "As it was I met as 'kindly mannered a man as ever scuttled a ship.'" Brazenly Goodrich asked Dzerzhinsky about the work of the Cheka. In reply he received a hearty laugh and the comment, "More lies have been told about the Cheka than any other arm of the Russian Service." According to Dzerzhinsky complete records of the Cheka's activities had been maintained and would be published in due course.

The least informative portion of the interview came when Goodrich asked for railroad statistics. In Goodrich's opinion Dzerzhinsky didn't seem very well informed, although he did confirm that only 6,000 locomotives (a decrease of 2,000 since fall) were in running condition and that the regime had achieved "very little" progress in improving coal production. Despite his accumulated problems, Dzerzhinsky assured Goodrich that the seed sent from the United States would be distributed in time for spring planting and that service would soon be improved by the delivery of 187 locomotives from Germany and Sweden. In answer to a direct question from Goodrich, Dzerzhinsky said that the Soviet transportation department preferred American steam engines produced by the Baldwin Company and had only purchased the German and Swedish models out of necessity. Goodrich came away with the impression that American diplomatic recognition of Russia would be followed by the flowering of trade. In all likelihood Goodrich also found himself in full agreement with Golder's candid assessment of Dzerzhinsky: "He is about as much fitted to run a railroad as I am, but he is better qualified because he is a Communist."[26]

The question of Russian-American trade relations arose again the next evening following a dinner at the Pink House given for Aaron Scheinman, the director of the Russian State Bank. The Americans in attendance were Goodrich, Golder, Hutchinson, and Quinn. Goodrich did not attach any particular importance to the occasion until it developed that Scheinman had been sent to explore the attitude of the Americans toward recognition. Not until afterward did Goodrich learn from Golder that Scheinman had had to request permission from a higher authority to attend. Once the meal was over Scheinman, according to Golder's notes, "lost no time in getting to his points." Scheinman began the discussion by remarking that he could not understand the attitude of America. His government was anxious to make large purchases of wheat and rye in America, but the project was hindered by the absence of direct banking connections. Three New York banks had agreed to open accounts for Scheinman, but later reneged on the offer when the State Department objected (on the ground that Soviet Russia had failed to settle pre-revolutionary debts owed the United States.) Scheinman felt sure that if he were permitted to talk to American bankers in person he could easily convince them to open commercial relations with Russia. He believed the United States government would never issue him a visa or permit the banks freedom of action. And he described two proposed Russian-American business deals—one involving manganese, the other pig bristles—both of which had fallen through due to a lack of banking facilities. Up to this point the Americans, especially Goodrich, had given Scheinman a sympathetic hearing. As Scheinman adopted a polemical tone, the discussion rapidly became contentious and unproductive.

Turning to Goodrich, Scheinman asked him to explain the American attitude. How could America, on the one hand, provide such generous famine relief, while simultaneously forbidding its banks to enter into relations with Russia? In his innocence Goodrich said that, speaking as an individual, he was extremely anxious to see normal business relations established between the two countries. However, he cited several legitimate American grievances against the Soviet government such as the seizure without compensation of the property of the National City Bank of New York, and the repeated insinuations by Trotsky and others that the ARA was operating in Russia for other than humanitarian motives. A further obstacle to recognition, said Goodrich, was the opposition of the great majority of the American people. "Why talk about the people," Scheinman cynically retorted. "They have nothing to do with the matter, it is the government that is against us and not the people." The National City Bank of New York not the people, Scheinman contended, set the foreign policy of the United States. In reply, Goodrich and Golder "gave it to him good and strong" that the main question was not the fate of the bank, but whether the Soviet government would behave honorably. Goodrich recalled that when he spoke before the Foreign Policy Association and almost advocated recognition the press attacked him, saying the Soviet government was unworthy of recognition because it had taken over the bank. Scheinman, in what Golder called "a more or less sneering manner," contended that American newspapers were political tools and that Goodrich had been criticized, not because he favored recognition, but because he was of a different political party than the editors. When Goodrich remarked that America, through the ARA, was operating in Russia merely to feed the hungry without any ulterior purpose or hope of receiving anything in return, "the expression upon his face indicated that he wondered if I was foolish enough to believe that sort of thing."

Subjected to Scheinman's abuse, Goodrich finally lost his temper and burst out, according to Golder, "that so long as the Soviet pursued that kind of a policy, the American Government would never recognize it, that America could get along without Russia, that if in [the] face of the sufferings of the Russian people, the Soviet enjoyed playing such petty politics and such childish games, he was through with them." Golder was especially outraged by the high-handed conduct of Scheinman. "Three months ago Governor Goodrich was in favor of recognition," he noted, "but he has now lost much of his enthusiasm. Six months ago I regarded the Bolo [slang for Bolshevik] leaders as real statesmen, but today I see in them cheap east side politicians and shop keepers." Perhaps his pique was accentuated by the adverse results of the poker game played after Scheinman's departure in which Golder lost 300,000 rubles to Goodrich and Quinn.[27]

After a good night's sleep Goodrich's resentment had largely subsided. The bad manners of one doctrinaire Communist had not, Golder to the contrary, fundamentally shaken his view that America's nonrecognition policy ought to be abandoned. As he prepared for his long trip home he drafted lengthy reports to Harding and Hoover. Goodrich purposely neglected Hughes, whom he considered a lost cause. To each Goodrich purported to present factual information about the famine. In both cases he concluded by offering unambiguous political advice. Apparently he concluded that Haskell's directive requiring advance approval before sending messages to Washington did not apply to him.

His report to Harding represented a major investment of time and

energy. While marooned at Bogotai, Goodrich prepared a first draft
which he revised and enlarged upon reaching Moscow. Seeking to
appeal to Harding's human sympathies, Goodrich represented himself as an honest Republican snowbound in the wilds of Russia.
Tactfully he praised the President for the successes of the ARA in
Russia, even though Harding had played a relatively minor role in
the proceedings. And he emphasized the "very touching" gratitude
of the common man for the help extended by the United States.
"They are a fine, open-faced, honest, industrious sort of people, and
you would like them if you could see them and get in touch with
them as I have during my two trips to Russia." The five days during
which he was snowbound, said Goodrich, had provided him with
an opportunity to re-read and re-think all his previous notes and
reports. Nothing he had seen on his second visit to Russia had caused
him to change his views, which he then laid out for the President's
consideration: Communism had failed and was in the process of
being slowly modified by the NEP; the existing government was
firmly entrenched and faced no visible opposition; and the national
interest of both nations favored the resumption of normal diplomatic
and commercial relations.

He elaborated his themes by contending that nonrecognition had
retarded the economic reconstruction of Russia by preventing the
influx of American trade and investment. "Whatever may have been
the wisdom of the attitude of America in the past," he told Harding,
"I believe the time is near at hand when we should recognize the
Revolution as an accomplished fact, resume relations with Russia,
and give American capital a free opportunity to enter in and assist
in her economic development." The way to produce a more moderate
Russian government was not through isolation and opposition, he
stressed, but by adopting a policy of "free intercourse and friendly
relations." Once the people of Russia became acquainted with the
advantages of the free and democratic system of America they would
"become convinced that such a government is far better than the
utopian dream of the communist and out of the disaster and economic despair that now exist will arise a sound government suited
to the needs of the Russian people." On his return to Washington
Goodrich offered to meet with Harding personally "and talk over
the situation."[28] From Goodrich's perspective as a veteran of Russian
travel the need for a more enlightened American policy was imperative. How to convince his fellow Republicans of that need was a
problem Goodrich never succeeded in mastering.

In reporting to Hoover, Goodrich tried an approach similar to
that he had used in his letter to Harding. First, he submitted factual

information in the form of diary reports he had written in the course of his trip. Only later, after condemning "the imbecility and inefficiency of this whole outfit," did he venture into the realm of politics. As the result of a two-hour conference with Haskell and Quinn, Goodrich assured Hoover that he was encouraged by the course of the ARA work, notwithstanding some lack of cooperation from Eiduk and the fact that the inefficient railroads were "shot to pieces." Perhaps as a result of his encounter with Scheinman, he would concede some doubts about his earlier idea that the Soviet leaders were merely honest idealists who were ignorant of economic principles. Despite the many shortcomings of the existing government, Goodrich could see no possibility of a counterrevolution, which led him back to the view he had expressed in his 18 February letter to Hoover. "I am still of the opinion," he concluded, "that the situation will be solved sooner, and the Russian people be more quickly relieved from this intolerable burden by the recognition of its Government, the setting up of a diplomatic and consular corps, with commercial agents throughout Russia, and the opening up of Russia to the outside world."[29]

Once again Goodrich won no converts. The receipt of his letter to Hoover alarmed ARA officials such as Christian Herter and Edgar Rickard, who were concerned that Goodrich's political views, should they become public, might embarrass the ARA. On 4 April Hoover drafted a telegram to Goodrich stating: "Some of my colleagues here are anxious that you should be guarded upon questions of political recognition of Russia until after conferences here."[30]

6

An Indiana Banker in the "Inner Temple" of the Kremlin

ON 19 April, after an exhausting journey of fifteen days, Goodrich and his wife landed at New York aboard the *Olympic*. At the pier he was met by Alexander Gumberg, but before he could confer with his friend he had to face the press. Remembering vividly that he had once before had his fingers singed by speaking favorably of the Soviet leadership, Goodrich hardly needed Hoover's reminder to be careful in discussing the question of recognition in public. In his remarks to reporters, Goodrich stressed the positive. The ARA, he categorically stated, was winning the battle against the famine and typhus, and he expressed optimism that the coming harvest would leave Russia able to feed itself. On the question of recognition Goodrich avoided direct comment, although he denied having brought a message about the subject from Lenin. He characterized press reports describing trainloads of corpses as an exaggeration, but he readily conceded that it had been a common occurrence in the famine region to find occasional bodies of starvation victims lying in the streets. In holding the press at arm's length Goodrich was reflecting his basic distrust of reporters. As he had explained to Harding, "I do not believe that the American people have ever had the correct picture of the Russian situation, nor do I believe that it has been reflected by the press of our country. Most of the press reports that have come out of Russia have been misleading."[1]

Having survived his encounter with the press, Goodrich, joined by Gumberg, proceeded to the capital. The train trip, Gumberg wrote Robins, "gave me an opportunity to have a good talk with him. I am convinced that he is a good friend of Russia, and Russia of the people and not the Russia of Semenov." Gumberg now began to toy with the idea of accompanying Goodrich to Russia on his next trip. For personal reasons Gumberg was anxious to visit his homeland, but Gumberg also believed he could arrange contacts for Goodrich with the highest Soviet officials. To Robins, Gumberg explained: "I judge from conversation with him that some things he wanted done were not taken care of. I am sure that if I was with him the things he mentioned would have been done. I now feel sorry that I did not go with him, not so much because of myself, but because I could have been very useful in healing the breach between America and Russia." For Gumberg the personal problem was that he had to earn a living either by continuing as an employee of the Far East Republic or by taking a new position—possibly with the All-Russian Textile Syndicate. "It can be mine if I try to get it," Gumberg wrote Robins. "But I would very much prefer to go with Goodrich because I believe it is extremely important that he be taken care of."[2] Yet Gumberg's own ambivalence proved the fatal flaw in his plan to accompany Goodrich to Moscow. Since Goodrich intended to leave again in just a month, there was no time to be lost if Gumberg was to apply for a State Department visa. Not until virtually the last minute did Gumberg finally make up his mind, and by then it was too late.

The next morning (20 April) Goodrich was in Washington having breakfast with "the Chief." During "an extended conference" the two discussed the various supply and personnel problems of the ARA. Their focus was on practical operations; if they touched on political abstractions Goodrich did not consider the outcome sufficiently important to make a record. Hoover congratulated Goodrich and Haskell for having enforced discipline by purging those whose intoxication had embarrassed the ARA. "You will be very gratified to know," Goodrich wrote Haskell, "how fully he endorses your course, even the exact method of your getting rid of Carroll." Much of their conversation dealt with Haskell's personal financial problems. In particular Haskell hoped to win Hoover's support for a favorable military pension bill pending in Congress. Hoover told Goodrich that he would cooperate, but suggested that any lobbying on his part must await the conclusion of the ARA Russian operation. Hoover then asked Goodrich to make a third Russian inspection trip, leaving in about a month, and to this Goodrich readily agreed.[3]

Afterward a glowing statement was given out to the press under Goodrich's name extolling the ARA (and indirectly Hoover) for having broken the back of the famine. In style the "Statement of Governor Goodrich" resembled that of Hoover, perhaps with an assist from George Barr Baker, the public relations director of the ARA. And the statement was decidedly premature in its claim that the famine was "under control." In late April many areas of the Volga were just receiving their first American aid, and ARA operations in the Ukrainian famine districts bordering the Black Sea had not yet begun. Following his meeting with Hoover, Goodrich managed to secure a luncheon invitation at the White House. But to Goodrich's disappointment the occasion was purely of a social nature and he was unable to raise with Harding the subject of American-Soviet relations.[4]

The four-week interlude between Goodrich's second and third Russian trips passed in a blur. By mid-May Goodrich had to exchange the spring flowers and greenery of Indiana for the cold and wet Russian climate. The plan agreed upon was for Goodrich and his wife, in the company of Rickard and Herter, to leave for London on 18 May. After a few days Goodrich would proceed to Moscow with his two colleagues following in a week or two. On his final day in New York, Goodrich discovered that Gumberg was anxious to give up his job with the Far Eastern Republic. He was, therefore, available to return to his homeland as Goodrich's assistant and translator, provided he could be put on the ARA payroll and secure an American visa from the intensely anti-Bolshevik officials of the Department of State.

Goodrich did all he could to secure Gumberg's services. Through George Barr Baker he made arrangements for Hoover to interview Gumberg in Washington. Goodrich, in a phone conversation with Hoover, urged that Gumberg be hired and he wrote Gumberg a letter of recommendation to be presented to Hoover. Goodrich also secured the support of Allan Wardwell of the American Red Cross, who, like Robins and Gumberg, had served in Russia during the revolutions of 1917. In a letter to "Bert" Hoover a day before the interview with Gumberg, Baker noted, "Wardwell is anxious to have you give him [Gumberg] a chance to talk. He thinks Goodrich needs to see higher-ups than he has so far seen, and that Gumberg can help." The Hoover-Gumberg meeting, held two days after Goodrich's departure for London, was partly a job interview and partly a free-for-all debate. Despite their different perspectives and backgrounds, the two men found they liked each other a great deal: Hoover agreed to send Gumberg as assistant to Goodrich and to use his influence to expedite the issuance of a visa. Two weeks later the project fell apart, as the State Department dragged its feet on Gumberg's visa application, forcing him to give up the idea of joining Goodrich and return to his job with the Far Eastern Republic. "Because of the amount of time lost," Gumberg wrote Baker, "it would hardly be possible for me to reach Russia in time to be of any service to Governor Goodrich. . . . Of course I regret very much that because of some, what I believe to be, trivialities, I was prevented from aiding Governor Goodrich in his work in Russia."[5]

In the meantime, the Goodriches had arrived in London after "a very tedious voyage." Waiting for him was a welcome telegram from Haskell stating that encouraging reports were pouring into the ARA's Moscow office from the famine districts concerning food prospects. Before his return to Washington Goodrich had personally prepared blank forms to be sent to ARA district supervisors. They were requested to visit typical communes and collect statistics on crop conditions, livestock, and the number of deaths claimed by disease and starvation. Goodrich's idea was to have this information available by 1 June so that a planning conference of ARA supervisors could be held at Moscow. "If these reports are all in as Haskell indicates," Goodrich reported to Hoover, "it will not take very long to go over the situation and make a reasonably accurate estimate of the situation and agree upon a recommendation as to the future work of the ARA in Russia." In particular Goodrich was encouraged by word that Shafroth, "one of our best men," had reported good news about crop prospects in Samara. If Samara could take care of itself, he reasoned, then it was likely the rest of the famine areas were also on the road to recovery.

Goodrich was also pleased to learn that the famine was ebbing because it would leave him more time for politics. To Hoover he reported, "This [the optimistic crop prospects] will leave me time enough to go into the political situation and ascertain what, if anything, can be done with the outfit at the head of the Russian government." The governor's spirits were further buoyed by the discovery that Golder, the poker playing history professor, was available and eager to accompany Goodrich to Moscow. "The situation at Moscow," Goodrich explained to Hoover, "is so delicate, the need of accurate information so important and the necessity of having someone, in certain cases, who is entirely reliable to act as interpreter that I have asked Brown to send Golder with me and trust it will meet with your approval."[6]

The Goodriches decided to take their time in reaching Moscow, as the governor wanted to gather whatever Russian information was in the possession of the American embassies in Paris, Berlin, and Riga. Soon he came to regret his decision because, in his opinion, the Russian sources of the ARA and the Commerce Department were far superior to those of the Department of State. At Riga, however, Goodrich learned on 5 June of a potential complication. A telegram from Haskell reported that Lenin had suffered a serious stroke and was not expected to live. Goodrich, fretting that the radical Trotsky would be selected as successor to Lenin, hurried to Moscow, arriving there with his wife on 7 June. He found Golder waiting for him with the news that there would be no change of leadership after all, as Lenin was out of danger and in the process of recovering.[7] Under the circumstances, however, it was asking too much to hope for an interview with Lenin himself. To his relief the temporary power vacuum only slightly delayed his plan to sound out the Soviet leaders on the prospects for establishing Soviet-American trade and diplomatic relations. Over the next two weeks Goodrich was able to conduct with high Soviet leaders wide-ranging political discussions. Although the talks did not alter the status quo, they did produce the fullest high level exchange of United States-Soviet views between the breaking of relations in November 1917, and their resumption in November 1933.

The first order of business was for Goodrich to consult with Haskell and Hutchinson to ascertain what progress had been made against the famine during his absence. From all the Americans Goodrich received about the same story. Haskell stated that the famine was "absolutely broken," and Hutchinson reported that there was sufficient food available to carry Russia until the coming harvest. Falling food prices throughout the country suggested that concealed supplies of food were appearing on the market. A similar report from George Repp, who had spent the winter at Balzer, confirmed that the concealed reserves had "come to the surface" and that the Volga Germans would be able to "get along." On 10 June he was able to talk to several of the district supervisors who had already arrived at Moscow for the 17 June ARA conference. They told him that crop prospects in many areas were excellent, as was the condition of cattle, pigs, and poultry.[8] Concluding that the humanitarian aspect of his mission was under control, Goodrich found he had an entire week to pursue political subjects.

Initially Goodrich was stymied by the problem of how to initiate political discussions with the "higher-ups." The purpose of the ARA, after all, was to feed the hungry, and the organization had specifically promised to refrain from political activity. On 8 June, according to Golder's notes, while he and Goodrich were having lunch and "were scheming how to bring about a meeting with [Karl] Radek [secretary of the Third International's Propaganda Bureau] and [Lev B.] Kamenev [chairman of the Soviet Relief Commission] without taking the first steps," an invitation luckily arrived from Radek asking Goodrich to have tea at the unorthodox hour of ten o'clock that evening. Goodrich accepted on condition that Golder could accompany him as translator. That evening the two Americans, escorted by Aleksandr Eiduk, were admitted to the Kremlin's "inner temple." Mrs. Radek received the visitors and telephoned for Radek, who was attending a meeting at which "the high priest Trotsky was preaching."

Within a few minutes Radek arrived and began the discussion on a sour note as he characterized America as the greatest enemy of the Russian nation. According to Radek, America and France had created a hostile coalition to block the recognition of the Soviet government by the rest of the world. Goodrich took issue with Radek, contending that any similarities between American and French foreign policy were coincidental. Much of the meeting consisted of a rambling attack by Radek on Hoover, the Socialist Revolutionary Party of Alexander Kerensky, and the American attitude on debts, trade, and recognition. Goodrich managed to break into the speech several times to say that the people of America genuinely desired to assist Russia and were willing to reach an understanding on recognition, provided Russia restored its moral credit by promising in good faith to acknowledge its debts and to offer compensation for confiscated private property. And Goodrich made Radek smile when he expressed the opinion that the bankers of America and not the Communists of Russia were the true internationalists of the day.

Gradually Radek became more conciliatory in tone. He related that soon after Congress approved Hoover's $20 million appropriation for Russian relief, he had received a phone call from Lenin asking him to explain the motives behind the American action. According to Radek, he had defended Hoover's program as based on a humanitarian impulse and not upon a desire to interfere in Russia's internal affairs. Radek also expressed skepticism regarding a widely publicized tale which blamed Hoover for the failure of the Hungarian Communist revolution in 1919. Goodrich pointed out that at the time of the Peace Conference, Hoover had in principal actually opposed allied intervention anywhere in eastern Europe. Finally, Radek said that he was sure a declaration could be issued stating the willingness of Russia to honor its debts and he suggested that Goodrich should meet with Kamenev and "other important Communists." Eiduk offered to make the arrangements which, noted Golder, "was not part of our plan, but we had to leave it there for the time being."[9]

Getting all the interested parties together proved a more frustrating and time-consuming process than either Goodrich or Golder had anticipated. The immediate problem for the two Americans was how to exclude Eiduk, who wished to be in on everything, from the process. Both Americans regarded Eiduk as suspicious, interfering, crude, and untrustworthy. They were highly displeased when Eiduk appeared the next day (9 June) with the news that he had made an appointment for Goodrich to interview Kamenev two days later.

After thinking the matter through, Goodrich decided to reject the offer. Under the proposed arrangement, Eiduk would have been present and it was the Americans' conviction that "sooner or later Eiduk had to be shaken." Another consideration was that Goodrich was determined to avoid individual time-consuming discussions. Recalling his less than satisfactory interviews with Scheinman and Radek, Goodrich insisted that only a joint meeting of high officials was acceptable to him. Such a forum, he concluded, would be the most fruitful way to discover the real prospects for establishing normal commercial and diplomatic relations.

Two days were required for Golder to get an appointment with Radek at the typically unorthodox hour of 11:00 A.M., Sunday, 11 June. On behalf of Goodrich, Golder explained that it would be improper for anyone connected with the ARA, either Russian or American, "to be mixed up with this." He asked Radek to take charge of the arrangements, which would mean excluding Eiduk. In reply Radek said he had little hope anything could come of the discussions, but said he would consult Grigori Zinoviev (president of the Third International) and Maxim Litvinov (assistant commissar for foreign affairs) to arrange a meeting. For another week the fencing between Goodrich, Golder, and Radek continued. Golder was able to arrange for Goodrich to conduct separate interviews with Kamenev, Litvinov, Leon Trotsky (commissar for war), Aleksii Rykov (assistant to Lenin), Leonid Krassin (commissar of foreign trade), and Grigori Sokolnikov (commissar of finance), but Goodrich held out for a joint meeting. On the morning of 14 June Sokolnikov came to the Pink House to discuss the situation with Goodrich in person. Goodrich used the occasion to point out that a historic opportunity would be forfeited if he returned to America without holding discussions with Sokolnikov and his comrades. Sokolnikov then took it upon himself to arrange the meeting with Kamenev and Goodrich promised to accept an invitation to meet with "the central executive committee" if Sokolnikov were successful.[10]

With the departure of Sokolnikov, Goodrich was temporarily at loose ends as he awaited the outcome of his latest overtures. That afternoon Eiduk, who resolutely refused to be "shaken," appeared and asked Goodrich if he would like to visit a warehouse to look over some of the confiscated government property. "I accepted the invitation and went with him to the storehouse located in one of the former banking buildings," Goodrich noted. "I was under the impression that it was the furs they desired to show me when I accepted the invitation." It quickly developed that Goodrich was mistaken. On his arrival the building superintendent, "who looked

and acted like a typical communist," showed Goodrich an album
containing photographs of jewels which now belonged to the government. A "prominent Moscow jeweler" and two assistants then appeared bringing with them three sealed iron chests. In Goodrich's
presence the seals were broken and the chests opened, revealing the
stunning crown jewels of the Romanov monarchy. "It was a perfectly
marvelous collection," he noted. "The old Czar's crown, the crowns
of the Czarina and the various members of the royal family, with
diamonds varying from one to 200 carats, all of the purest water,
and wonderful color. Crowns of diamonds, of diamonds and pearls,
emeralds, rubies and amethysts, collars, bracelets and necklaces. The
scene beggared description. I never saw anything like it; it didn't
seem possible there were so many jewels in the world." He was told
by the head jeweler that the collection was completely intact and that
he was in the process of cataloging and assessing each piece.

Why, wondered Goodrich, had he been chosen as the recipient of
such an unprecedented private showing? Part of the explanation, he
thought, was to show the world that the Romanov crown jewels
were safe and had not been broken up, as had been widely rumored
outside Russia. Eiduk suggested another purpose when he asked
Goodrich whether he would be willing to discuss with the minister
of finance (Sokolnikov) the possibility of an American loan with the
jewels as collateral. Goodrich put Eiduk off with the same argument
he had used before with Radek, namely that it would be inconsistent
with his status as an official of the ARA to discuss such a proposal.
He did not completely rule out discussing a loan, but stressed that
the invitation for such discussions should come through Sokolnikov
and not through ARA channels. After looking at the jewels until his
"eyes were weary with the blaze of light," Goodrich returned to the
Pink House to await the outcome of his political negotiations.[11]

As before, the chief stumbling block in Goodrich's path remained
his desire for a joint meeting with those at the top. Sokolnikov returned the next day (15 June) with a letter from Kamenev inviting
Goodrich and Golder to meet him at 1:00 P.M. that day in his office
and stating that he, Trotsky, and Krassin (no others were mentioned)
would be willing to hold individual meetings. Goodrich was very
disappointed. He had just finished a letter to Hoover relating that
he had been "standing rather stiff" on the question of a joint meeting
and he saw no reason to back down. According to Golder's synopsis
of events: "The Gov. at first declined to go but when Sokol. asked
it as a personal favor he agreed to make a formal call but not to
discuss politics. At one o'clock we went to see Kamenev and explained to him that if he and the other Commissars really wished to

talk to him as a body he would meet them." Goodrich probably added that separate meetings with minor officials would be repetitious and a waste of everyone's time. As he had written Hoover, "I felt that if any discussion of America's attitude was to be held at all it only should be with those men in authority." He added further, "I am rather expecting it."[12]

While the waiting continued, Goodrich busied himself with preparing for the meeting of ARA district supervisors and executives which began the following afternoon (16 June). In addition to Goodrich, Haskell, Hutchinson, Golder, and Quinn, the conference was attended by two ARA executives from America, Edgar Rickard and Christian Herter, who were accompanied by Walter Brown from London. Since the purpose of the meeting was to hear reports from those working in the field, the role of Goodrich and the other ARA executives was primarily to listen. According to the minutes of the 16 June meeting, Goodrich interjected several questions in regard to the hard hit Orenburg district, which he had tried unsuccessfully to visit in April. Goodrich wondered whether the ARA should stop all its operations in the district on 1 September; or would it be better to halt only the distribution of adult rations in September, but continue child-feeding until 1 January 1923? Walter A. Coleman, the Orenburg supervisor, said that he would advise leaving in September, as the January weather might well make withdrawal at that date impossible. Coleman could not tell Goodrich the exact number of acres planted in rye in his district. However, through a careful survey of average districts and applying the results to the whole of the Orenburg district, Coleman found that his area had a four-month food supply.

Yet when Hutchinson analyzed Coleman's figures, he came to the conclusion that Orenburg actually possessed an eight-month supply. The discrepancy occurred because the people concerned counted only the grain available for local consumption and excluded grain set aside for planting, transportation, and interest. "From the point of view of the people down there," explained Hutchinson, "they have only four months supply but from the point of view of all the people in this whole country they have eight months supply." Hutchinson, seconded by Haskell, submitted that the ARA must consider "the whole supply for the whole country." The purpose of the meeting, Haskell stressed, was to gather objective information so that "the Chief" could "assemble the whole thing" and make a definitive judgment.[13] The generally optimistic mood of the conference confirmed Goodrich's own view that the food situation was dramatically improving. Yet Goodrich, not content to accept the word of others in regard to the fading famine, resolved to inspect the Volga region in person, after he completed his political discussions, which seemed stalled on dead center.

That evening (17 June) about 7:00 P.M. Eiduk appeared at the Pink House just as Goodrich and Golder had finished dinner. The ostensible purpose of his visit was to say good-bye to Cora Goodrich, who was leaving the next day for Japan. Before departing, Eiduk told Goodrich that Kamenev, Rykov, and "others" were planning to meet with him the following day (Sunday, 18 June) in Kamenev's office at 1:00 P.M. All the next morning Golder "tried hard," but without success, to find out who would attend the meeting. The correct answer, it turned out, was no one. Another misunderstanding had occurred and when Goodrich and Golder appeared at Kamenev's office at the appointed time they found only an empty room. That evening Sokolnikov telephoned to say that the meeting would actually be held the following afternoon in Kamenev's office. Only Trotsky was unavailable, but Goodrich could meet with Kamenev, Rykov, Litvinov, and Krassin as well as Sokolnikov.[14]

When Goodrich, accompanied by Golder, arrived for the second time at Kamenev's Kremlin office he felt a sense of vindication. His "stiff" line had paid off handsomely as all the Soviet leaders who had promised to attend were present. By consensus the gathering agreed on ground rules: none of the discussions would be revealed to the press and Goodrich was to be regarded merely as a private individual, not as a representative of the ARA or the United States government. Rykov then welcomed Goodrich and expressed gratitude that the governor had come seeking an understanding between the two nations. Goodrich began the discussions by frankly stating that the Harding administration had asked him informally to discuss the attitude of the American government. His starting point was a statement issued by Secretary of State Hughes on 25 March 1921 listing four principles the Soviets must agree to respect prior to recognition: safety of life, safety of private property, sanctity of contracts, and freedom of labor.

Without disclosing that he disagreed with America's policy of non-recognition, Goodrich took up the points in order. He first questioned the fairness of the Soviet judicial system in respecting the rights of defendants. Judges must always be independent of the executive, Goodrich said, otherwise the executive would be constantly tempted to interfere in the judicial process. Without an independent judiciary there could be no actual safety of life, liberty, or property. "They made no answer to this," he recorded, "and my impression is that they did not agree." In particular Goodrich was thinking of the fate of thirty-four Socialist Revolutionaries who were on trial in Moscow for sedition. Litvinov volunteered that the Soviet criminal code provided more protection for the basic rights of the people than had been true under the czars; he cited recent revisions to the criminal code which limited prison terms to a maximum of five years except in cases of murder or treason. "To this," noted Golder, "the Governor replied that in America every person arrested has the right to know on what charge." Kamenev spoke out admitting that during the revolution and civil war the Cheka had arbitrarily dispensed justice. Now that the Cheka had been abolished, he said, each person arrested had to be informed within two weeks of the charges against him and had to be put on trial within two months' time before a civil court.

With only a few exceptions the general tone of the meeting was conciliatory and businesslike. On the question of recognizing private property, Goodrich was told that private property, with the exception of land and heavy industry, was recognized just as fully in Russia as in any country in the world. Under the NEP, said Kamenev, the nationalization of property had been ended and private ownership of real estate and factory equipment encouraged. Goodrich next discussed whether the government could arbitrarily cancel a contract which was deemed to be disadvantageous. A chorus of denials greeted the question. Goodrich was informed that only contracts made in violation of the law could be set aside and that in this respect Russian practice was no different than in the United States. To clarify the issue, Golder asked Krassin a question: "Suppose a man sold his wheat to another man at 50 cents a bushel, but the next day the price of wheat went up to two dollars, could the seller break the contract on that ground?" All agreed that the contract could not be altered and Krassin pointed out that over the past two years no contracts between the government and foreigners had been broken. On the last of Hughes's points, the right of labor to choose freely in seeking employment, Goodrich was told that as of 1 June they had abolished the requirement that only union labor could be employed in factories. An employer was now free to hire union or nonunion labor. And, in answer to a question from Goodrich, Sokolnikov said there would be no objection to Americans obtaining concessions to operate formerly nationalized factories, nor would there be any serious objection to the opening of branch banks by American firms in Russia.

In the course of the conversation the Indiana banker and his Communist hosts crossed swords several times. One point of dispute arose when Goodrich asked whether the government was orchestrating a public demonstration to demand the death penalty for the Socialist Revolutionaries on trial for sedition. Goodrich was not at all satisfied when Kamenev represented the demonstration as a spontaneous manifestation of public opinion. The government, said Kamenev, had nothing to do with the demonstration and could not help it if the demonstrators carried banners demanding death to the prisoners. Probably Goodrich's expression of disbelief regarding Kamenev's pretensions of Soviet innocence was as pronounced as had been Scheinman's when Goodrich had portrayed the ARA as purely humanitarian in motivation. Goodrich made a mental note to attend the demonstration the next day so as to judge for himself the accuracy of Kamenev's statements.

Litvinov, Kamenev, and Goodrich then clashed when the governor criticized the execution of five orthodox priests by the government. Such incidents made martyrs of the priests and "left a bad impression in America." Kamenev explained that the government had by decree confiscated church treasures to raise funds for famine relief and that the priests had incited riots which had caused the deaths of innocent persons. Litvinov contended that those executed had richly deserved the death penalty. To Goodrich the imposition of capital punishment upon priests defending church treasures from confiscation seemed completely unjustified.

The dispute upon which the most time was spent concerned the repudiation by the Soviets of all debts owed by previous governments. Goodrich, according to Golder's notes, "made it very clear" that the recognition of the debt must come before America extended diplomatic recognition. After all, he pointed out, the money loaned Russia had been raised through liberty bonds sold to millions of ordinary Americans. For Russia to repudiate such an obligation was basically "dishonest" and unless Russia modified its position there was no hope for the resumption of trade, the extension of loans by American bankers, or diplomatic recognition. In reply Kamenev stated that he wanted Goodrich to understand the psychology of the Soviets. All revolutionary parties since the Revolution of 1905 had agreed that the czar's debts must never be paid. Kamenev, joined by Krassin, suggested that the amount of the debt ($187 million) was so small that it should not be difficult to devise a solution, perhaps involving the extension of American credit as part of a general settlement. Kamenev contended that Russia needed a guarantee of American credit in one form or another before it recognized the debt.

According to Golder's notes:

> To this, the Governor replied: "You have no faith in yourself to pay your debts. We, on the other hand, have faith Russia will pay her debts,"

and added: "You are wasting your time with America unless you are ready to recognize the debts, and issue obligations promising to pay in the future." Kamenev said: "Why is it that since Russia owes less to America than England, you are doing business with England and you refuse to have anything to do with us?" The Governor replied: "Because England has not repudiated her debts and you have; that the question of the amount of debt is not as important as the principle."

Goodrich added that under no circumstances would the American government loan the Soviets so much as a dollar; any loan would have to come from private bankers who were currently making huge loans to Europe and South America. If, however, relations were resumed American capital would naturally flow into Russia. After two hours Kamenev concluded the discussion by observing that the Soviets had "a real desire" to improve relations with America, that there was no major obstacle to a settlement of the debt question, and that the next step would be to submit the issues under dispute to persons who were officially empowered to act.[15]

From Goodrich's perspective the meeting had provided a useful exchange of views, but the governor did not deceive himself into thinking that significant new ground had been broken. After his return to the Pink House he decided that his report of the meeting was not important enough to justify the expense of transmitting it to Washington by telegraph instead of by regularly scheduled courier.[16] On the positive side Goodrich was mildly encouraged by the civility displayed by the Soviet leaders and by the discovery that the positions of the two powers were not too far apart. Nothing occurred at the meeting to alter Goodrich's view that the recognition of the Soviet Union was in the best interests of the United States. Nevertheless, the discussions served as a reminder to Goodrich that the men to whom he had spoken were representatives of a violent revolution. As men who had seized power they had no intention of extending western standards of justice to their few remaining opponents. As they sat talking to Goodrich, it is unlikely that Kamenev and Rykov considered that the summary methods they were in the process of using against the Socialist Revolutionaries could be applied to them in the not-so-distant future.

The following day (20 June) Goodrich and Golder, escorted by Sokolnikov, got a first-hand look at Soviet justice when they spent the day attending the trial of the thirty-four Socialist Revolutionaries who were accused of counterrevolutionary activities. Promptly at noon the three judges entered the hall as the audience, with the exception of the prisoners, rose respectfully. The red draped platform

held the judges, two substitute judges, and several Communist officials, the most prominent of whom was Nikolay Bukharin. The
prisoners, guarded by eight soldiers armed with rifles and bayonets,
occupied a space to one side of the court, but seemed to pay no
attention to their trial. Goodrich was plainly fascinated by the revolutionary atmosphere but, above all, he was struck by the absurdity
of the proceedings. As Goodrich watched, a long-haired Communist
seated on the platform lighted a cigarette and leaned back in his chair
against a red curtain which at first glance resembled a partition. As
the curtain gave way the luckless comrade fell to the floor with a
bomblike crash, while the judges and prosecutor dove under tables
and the armed soldiers sprang to attention. Goodrich and Golder
could not help joining with the audience in laughing at the ridicu-
lous spectacle.

Even more incredible, they thought, was the parade held in Red
Square late in the afternoon. From his vantage point Goodrich
watched thousands marching twenty abreast pass in a seemingly endless procession. The good-natured demonstrators bore banners demanding death to the prisoners and predicting the collapse of
capitalism. Golder found out from the marchers that they had been
paid their wages for the day in return for participating. Goodrich
noticed that when the "yell leader" called for a shouted slogan the
marchers opened their mouths but made little or no noise. Golder
felt that most of the demonstrators "had about as much heart in it
as I had." The most spontaneous response in the whole affair came
when the prosecutor asked the crowd, "Shall we inflict the death
penalty on the prisoners?" and the reply, "translated into good
American meant, 'Give them hell. Shoot them!'" Golder also heard
the chief judge tell the crowd that the Socialist Revolutionaries would
receive "all that was coming to them." Later that evening the court
met again and invited the crowd of workers to jam the chamber on
the ground that the government was composed of the masses. For
the next two and a half hours the marchers, some of whom were
intoxicated, verbally abused the prisoners. "Before the mob scat-
tered," noted Golder, "they were photographed and thanked by the
judge for their public spirit and for the valuable evidence presented."
As Goodrich hurried to the train station for a whirlwind tour of the
Volga, he reflected that he had just witnessed a combination of farce
and tragedy. His sentiments were solidly with the lawyer for the
defense who had dramatically intoned, "Woe to the nation that breaks
the laws which it has made."[17]

In the company of Haskell, Herter, Brown, and Rickard, Goodrich made the train trip to Kazan by way of Nizhnii-Novgorod. On

the way the company probably passed the time of day pursuing "the great American game." But they had to proceed without the company of Golder, who had returned to Petrograd in order to complete the purchase of twenty-four boxes of books for the Hoover War History Collection. For Goodrich the trip was not an extended office party. His purpose was to assess the condition of the crops and the people so as to reach an informed opinion about the future of the ARA program. Typically Goodrich did not trust to second-hand information but personally interviewed government officials and ordinary citizens. On the first leg of the journey to Nizhnii-Novgorod he judged the fields of wheat and rye to be "uniformly good." Before he retired for the evening, having traveled 120 miles to the east of Moscow, he estimated that normal quantities of seed had been sown. Approaching Nizhnii-Novgorod the next morning—Goodrich was awake at 5:00 A.M.—he observed "the same situation." Cattle and sheep seemed plentiful and he saw twenty carloads of flax about to be shipped to Moscow. At every station women gathered to sell milk, bread, and cheese and the nearby gardens were filled with radishes, lettuce, onions, and early potatoes.

That a bountiful harvest was in prospect was confirmed by conversations at Novgorod with government officials, including the president of the local government and the commissar of agriculture. On paper, they said, the crop was smaller than in pre-war years, but the peasants had underestimated their planting, seeking to avoid taxes. In reality, Goodrich was told, the crop was about equal to the pre-war period. His hosts were also optimistic about their ability to harvest the forthcoming crop, noting that "plenty" of horses were available. Goodrich had already noticed that the horses in the region were "unusually good," and reflected favorably upon the local breeding farms.[18]

Goodrich and the party of ARA officials now left the train behind and continued to Kazan via river boat. Through binoculars Goodrich studied the fields and cattle along the banks of the Volga. As far as he could see there was evidence of economic activity: fishermen tending nets, heavily laden oil barges en route to Kazan, large herds of sheep and cattle, and crops which appeared to be doing well. "There were no exceptions anywhere," he recorded. Arriving at Kazan at 9:00 A.M. Goodrich spent the day gathering statistics from the commissar of finance and the head of the state bank. They admitted that they had experienced "a great many difficulties" in starting their bank, but claimed to have made a profit and to have available sufficient funds to carry peasant farmers through the season. In what Goodrich considered an imaginative innovation the peasants' loans were pegged to the price of rye; the number of rubles to be repaid was determined by the price of rye at the time of repayment plus 6 percent interest. Prior to meeting Haskell, Hutchinson, Herter, Brown and Rickard for a conference, Goodrich toured the bazaar and found food in abundance, especially potatoes. "I made a second inquiry about potatoes as the price seemed so low at the rate of exchange," he noted. "A bushel of potatoes cost 50 cents American money."

At the meeting with Ivar Wahren, the district supervisor, Goodrich asked if it would be possible to go out into the country so as to examine the canton of Spassk, reputed to have the worst conditions in the Tartar Republic. Goodrich was told there was no direct road connection and that the only way to reach the famine region was to go downstream by boat about fifty miles and then travel by wagon about twenty-five miles to the east. "On inquiry," he recorded, "we learned a boat left Kazan at 2 P.M. and I proposed to leave the rest of the party at Kazan, go down in a boat, drive back into the country and join them at Simbirsk or Samara and that plan was agreed to." In volunteering for the mission to the back country Goodrich certainly understood that he was leaving behind the comforts of home. It is doubtful he expected to lose a night's sleep.[19]

At 4:30 P.M. that day (23 June), Goodrich and a government interpreter set off on a boat which, typically, departed two and a half hours late. By 11:00 P.M. they had reached a boat landing ten miles from Spassk. There they secured two small Russian wagons and began the plodding journey to Spassk, arriving at 3:30 A.M. Despite the early hour Goodrich was in no mood to rest. "At once started a man out to hunt up a team," he recorded. "Thought it advisable to start at once." In the meantime he interviewed a local veterinarian and learned that the population of the region had declined from 270,000 in 1916 to 170,000 in 1922, that 90 percent of the horses, cattle, and hogs had been consumed, and that the area had experienced a total crop failure in 1921. During the current year it had only been possible to plant about 30 percent of the normal amount of wheat and rye. At 4:30 A.M. Goodrich set out for the southern section of the Spassk canton—the region both Wahren and the veterinarian had told him was the worst affected—to see the situation for himself.

With few exceptions Goodrich found that the conditions in the region did not jibe with the pessimistic reports he had received. Ten miles from Spassk Goodrich passed three girls pulling weeds in the field. They told him the crops were "all right" and that no one in their village had died of starvation. Did they have enough food to carry them through the next year? They answered that the result of their labors was entrusted to the hand of God, who alone knew all. But from the number of people he saw hoeing and pulling weeds, Goodrich felt sure that a bountiful harvest was in store. "God still helps those who help themselves," he observed.

Stopping at the village of Bezdona, Goodrich interviewed the town priest and the town shepherd. According to the priest the village had only a third the number of horses, sheep, and cows as the year before and had harvested almost no grain the previous fall. Since the arrival of the American corn in April, he said, no starvation deaths had occurred, but additional aid was required, either from the government or the ARA, to enable the village to survive the winter. Yet when the shepherd appeared with his flock Goodrich counted seventy-six cows and eighty sheep and was told that there were two other herds nearby, one about the same size and the other somewhat larger. At his next stop, the Tartar village of Tatala, he was served tea in a house papered with labels from American condensed milk cans and was told that only 522 of the 1,177 residents of the previous fall remained. Almost 90 percent of the cattle had been consumed, his host said, and unless additional American aid was furnished many more would die of starvation. As he left the village Goodrich observed many abandoned houses and buildings with boarded windows and doors. At the same time the villagers appeared in "good condition." Goodrich came away with the impression that he had been subjected to a dose of "true oriental cunning" and that "mine host" had deliberately understated the flocks and herds as well as the extent of the crops.

At the final village visited, Novaya Tatala, Goodrich listened to the most harrowing tales of all. According to the president of the village council only 248 inhabitants were left of the 488 in 1921. Moreover, the village allegedly had been the scene of cannibalism. Goodrich was told that the corpse of a young girl had been stolen and sold in the local meat market. According to the official, further American aid was essential, as they had only 18 sheep left of the previous year's 200, only 38 cows left of 180, and no hogs at all. Goodrich listened with growing disbelief. To his mind the case of cannibalism did not seem to be well authenticated. And as he toured the village he saw several hogs roaming the streets, while in the distance he observed a herd of cows which appeared to consist of more than 38. Then as he left, a flock of sheep came in from the pasture and Goodrich, as inconspicuously as possible, counted 52 sheep and 47 lambs. He noticed also that in a nearby field of rye the flourishing grain was taller than the horse pulling his wagon. "I do not believe they made a single truthful statement about their livestock and crops," Goodrich noted in his diary. "Their lying about the sheep makes me doubt their entire statement."

Returning to Spassk by a different route Goodrich found the fields generally to be "in excellent condition." Where the crops were not so prosperous, Goodrich placed the blame upon inefficient management, not the weather. At one estate possessing new reapers, mowers, plows, and threshing machines from Germany, Sweden, and Norway, Goodrich interviewed the manager and found he had 105 employees under his direction. "I can take a dozen Americans," Goodrich observed, "and with proper equipment secure better results than he is getting with his hundred." In his judgment the Spassk region had been able to plant 40 to 60 percent of the arable land, not the 25 to 30 percent claimed. "I am quite certain," he wrote in his diary, "that if this canton is the worst in the Tartar Republic it can get along without outside help and even have a surplus."[20]

At Spassk Goodrich took a boat to Simbirsk with the intention of rendezvousing with Haskell's party. Typically, the boat was ten hours late in arriving and Haskell and his companions had already left for Samara when Goodrich finally reached Simbirsk at noon on 25 June. Goodrich then proceeded to Samara without changing boats. When he reached Samara at 3:00 A.M., after a twenty-four-hour journey, he found Haskell waiting up for him. "We spent two hours in going over our mutual experiences," he noted, "and at 5 A.M. went to bed." It was the intention of the Americans to return directly to Moscow. As the result of a bureaucratic snag, no order had been issued to attach Haskell's car to the Moscow train and it was decided to return by way of Saratov, rather than to sit at Samara for two days waiting for the next train to the capital. The side trip to Saratov confirmed Goodrich's earlier impressions. At ARA headquarters Goodrich by chance met George Repp, who reported that the Volga Germans would be able to take care of themselves after the fall harvest. In the German communes, he said, ARA work should be ended. Two other Americans came in while Goodrich was at Saratov, Marshall Tuthill from Novorossiysk and Paul Clapp from the Urals, and both agreed the ARA should "get out after [the] harvest and just as soon as the food now on hand can be distributed."[21]

Goodrich returned to Moscow in a thoroughly optimistic frame of mind. As a result of his investigations and the 17 June conference of ARA supervisors, Goodrich was convinced that the Volga region, even if it was not fully recovered, would be able to get along without large scale American aid during the winter of 1922–1923. "I am absolutely certain that our position will be sustained by future events," Goodrich wrote Hoover on his way to London. "I am not unmindful of the responsibility we take in advising the course outlined in our wire, yet after our trip through the Volga valley I would make the statement stronger rather than weaker! I am sending you the notes I took of the trip not that they will add much to the sum of your information of the famine situation and yet I thought perhaps they might not be uninteresting!" Goodrich also promised Hoover that he would send him additional "political notes." "They are necessarily brief," he stated, "and do not give the picture as I will give it to you when I see you in Washington." Therefore, as had been the case with his two previous trips to Russia, Goodrich did not compile for Hoover a final report. When Hoover was asked by Senator Joseph Frelinghuysen of New Jersey for a copy of Goodrich's report on Russia, he truthfully replied, "Governor Goodrich never submitted any formal report but he did give me a few personal memoranda on various phases connected with his trips."[22]

Yet in a sense Goodrich did submit a final report to Hoover in the guise of a lengthy memorandum entitled "Economic Situation in Russia." Goodrich's previous memoranda to Hoover had consisted of narrative diary accounts of his travels and contacts with Russian officials. These had avoided recommendations in regard to American policy toward Russia; this was decidedly not the case with his memorandum of 25 June 1922. In his survey of the economic situation, Goodrich recited statistics he had gathered through his interviews with Soviet officials illustrating the repeated failures of Communism in railroading, agriculture, industrial productivity, and banking. In his opinion, the Soviet leadership had reached a crossroads. They faced a choice between economic decline to a pastoral society, or the Soviets could continue the NEP, agree to the guarantees required by Hughes, and "extend to foreign capital the opportunity to assist in the restoration of the country." Goodrich freely conceded that Soviet rhetoric stressed that the NEP was only a temporary policy, but in his view the Soviet leaders were faced "by hard, stubborn and irresistible forces from within, forces which are still at work and gathering new power from each concession granted, forces that will compel the continuance of the onward movement toward a sound economic system."

He would send a commission to Russia to examine "the whole economic situation" and report to the President. (No recommendation was offered as to the chairmanship of such a commission, but Goodrich may well have had himself in mind. With the possible exception of Lincoln Hutchinson, Averell Harriman, Armand Hammer, and Herbert Hoover, no one could claim more first-hand acquaintance with the Russian economy than Goodrich.) Assuming the commission report was favorable, Goodrich would "recognize the revolution as an accomplished fact, [and] deal with this government as the only possible government in Russia. . . ." The final step would be the opening of trade relations, assuming the Soviets would recognize the debt to America and offer compensation for confiscated property.

Goodrich's argument was concise, logically presented, and well written, but it was buried on the twenty-seventh page of a twenty-nine-page memorandum. Because the governor's recommendations were similar to those which had been earlier rejected, Hoover may have ignored the commission suggestion as impractical. Or he may simply have stopped reading before he reached Goodrich's conclusion. Goodrich personally regarded his 25 June memorandum as an important summation of his thinking on Russia. When he was preparing a manuscript about his Russian trips in 1923–1924, he removed the memorandum from his papers and, having crossed out the heading "Economic Situation in Russia," inserted the paper as his final chapter with a new title reading "Summary and Conclusions." As was the fate of Goodrich's work on behalf of Soviet-American relations, the manuscript was abandoned unfinished, untitled, and unpublished. The concluding sentence of Goodrich's memorandum, ignored in 1922, had about it a prophetic quality which summed up his Lincolnesque view of the future: "These forces now at work in Russia making for its regeneration will be greatly strengthened and not weakened by every step taken to restore the industrial life of Russia and the opening up of trade relations with the eastern world will hasten the day when the Russian people will thru the orderly process of their rapidly developing system of law and procedure, using even the present soviet system of representation, change the present dictatorship of the communist party to a government of and by and for all the people."[23]

Goodrich's third trip to Russia concluded with his arrival at New York on 15 July. Following a verbal report to Hoover and a brief visit to his home, Goodrich returned to New York for a meeting of ARA directors presided over by Hoover. On the recommendation of Haskell, and with the concurrence of Herter, Rickard, and Goodrich, the directors concluded that adult-feeding should be ended with the new harvest on 1 September and that child-feeding should be continued through existing institutions such as schools and orphanages. The phasing out of the famine relief operation meant that many fewer employees were required.[24] Now the Moscow staff of the ARA would be able to handle the work of inspecting a smaller operation. Thus after three exhausting trips to Russia in only nine months, Goodrich, with the assistance of the ARA, had worked himself out of a job.

7

Goodrich Is Forced to Start Over Again

GOODRICH spent the fall of 1922 at his Winchester home tending to his neglected business affairs and recovering from his strenuous travels. How to resolve the dilemma of Russia was a question that remained high on his priority list and on short notice Goodrich was prepared to return to Russia if his services were needed. Although Goodrich had his bags packed the call never came. Through a regular correspondence with Haskell, Goodrich managed to keep up to date on current Moscow developments, including the shaky state of Lenin's health. But in view of the reduced scope of the relief operation, Haskell felt he could handle the situation without assistance. Haskell's main problem, he told Goodrich, was that the Army had asked him to relieve ten of the fourteen Army officers assigned to the ARA. Only Haskell and three senior officers remained. Haskell was afraid that if the remaining three, such as Dr. Henry Beeuwkes, the medical director, were recalled it would cost the ARA $10,000 for each replacement and seriously disrupt his operation. Goodrich was asked to use his influence to keep the remaining officers on the job. "Governor," wrote Haskell, "you can see the ridiculousness of relieving a man like Beeuwkes carrying nearly $8 million responsibility—we have no man in Russia who could attempt to carry out such a great administrative operation."[1]

Over the fall months Goodrich rethought his Russian tactics as he worked quietly to modify the official nonrecognition policy which bore no relation to the Russia he had seen with his own eyes. Previously he had advocated diplomatic recognition and trade. After his return to America in the summer of 1922, seeing that he was making no progress on recognition, Goodrich began to alter his tactics. When he met Gumberg on 15 July he mildly disappointed his Russian-American friend by taking "a rather hazy" stance on the recognition question. Goodrich would only endorse the sending of an official commission to Russia to gather information for the President. Even more disappointed with Goodrich was Robins, who spent three hours with the governor after he (Robins) spoke at Richmond, Indiana. Goodrich tried to sell Robins on his commission idea. But Robins was offended because Goodrich spoke glowingly of Hoover's desire to "help" Russia. "It was all Hoover from beginning to end," Robins complained to Gumberg. Even worse, concluded Robins, were Goodrich's allusions to the profits that awaited western bankers and businessmen once trade relations were established. From Robins' perspective Goodrich's plan was "impossible" and the governor a predator who regarded Russia as "a rich morsel for the hungry wolves of the capitalist world!" Gumberg's reaction was one of surprise, as he had "not the slightest idea what plan the Governor could have outlined . . . that would be impossible." Gumberg would have preferred outright recognition, but he considered Goodrich's suggestion of a commission as worth pursuing.[2]

And quite unexpectedly the commission idea came close to fruition when it was endorsed in principle by Hoover, Hughes, and Harding. But the commission plan, which might logically have included Goodrich and Golder as members, collapsed in September when the Russians, for reasons of national pride, insisted on simultaneously sending a similar body to the United States. Goodrich later told Golder that he had tried to convince Boris E. Skvirsky, the unofficial Soviet representative in Washington, to cable Moscow urging acceptance of the commission proposal. However, Goodrich could not guarantee who would be selected as members of the commission and Skvirsky, fearing a hostile commission would be appointed, refused to cooperate. In Goodrich's opinion, Hughes had deliberately sabotaged the commission idea by casting the proposal in an offensive manner, thus making rejection certain.[3]

By the winter of 1922–23 Goodrich had refined his strategy for normalizing Soviet-American relations. Now he emphasized establishing business relations as a first step without making any mention of diplomatic ties. Instead of sending a commission, an idea which had floundered previously, Goodrich leaned toward establishing trade contacts through personal diplomacy. Addressing an audience of businessmen on 10 December at New York, Goodrich stressed that inevitable forces were pushing Russia down the path of capitalism. According to Gumberg, who was among the listeners, Goodrich's speech was "quite scientific and he quoted all the prophets (Lenin, Trotsky, Rykov, etc.) very extensively." However, looking about the room, Gumberg felt the governor was speaking to deaf ears. "His trouble," Gumberg reported to Robins, "was that his audience was not intelligent and he had no voice." Nevertheless, Gumberg was pleased by Goodrich's effort. "He is working hard,"

Gumberg noted. "When I see him on the job I am more than ever convinced that 'economic determinism' is not such [an] empty sound as you try to tell me."[4]

Goodrich continued his trade offensive by renewing his efforts to enlist Hoover's support. Writing to Hoover on 18 December, Goodrich noted that he had been receiving weekly information from his own sources in Moscow who were "pretty close to Lenine and his outfit." (This was a reference by Goodrich to his correspondence with the journalist H. L. Rennick and the *New York Times* reporter, Walter Duranty, and possibly Haskell, who regularly forwarded to Goodrich copies of his letters to London and Washington.) "The information I get," said Goodrich, "is to the effect that they are ready to do business on a basis I believe will be satisfactory to our country." It was Goodrich's opinion that "we ought to take steps before long to open up trade relations with Russia," and he volunteered his services to make another trip to Russia with the dual purpose of serving the ARA and exploring trade possibilities. "I presume nothing will arise until after the first of the year," he wrote, "and I will be at liberty almost any time after that date."[5]

A few weeks later, no invitation having arrived, Goodrich renewed his efforts to sway Hoover. Theoretically Goodrich should have directed advice on foreign policy to the State Department of Charles Evans Hughes. In Goodrich's opinion the mind of the secretary of state was completely closed about the subject of Soviet Russia. "I can't talk to Hughes about it," Goodrich complained to Hoover. "He takes the view of a technical lawyer. . . ." Considering Hughes a lost cause, Goodrich used Hoover as a sounding board for his ideas. He pointed out to Hoover that practically all the ARA men with experience in Russia, men such as Haskell, Golder, Hutchinson, and Quinn, agreed that trade relations should be opened with the Soviets. Goodrich would not guarantee that trade would immediately flourish between the two nations. The advantage, as he saw it, was that the opening of trade would hasten the transformation of Russia "into the solid realities of an individualistic and capitalistic government." Seeking to convert Hoover, Goodrich cleverly quoted a letter he had received from Haskell:

> I think a great mistake is being made in not negotiating with the Soviet towards a trade agreement at least. In my mind it is foolish to pay any attention to what is published in their newspapers as to what they will do at some frontier etc. etc. . . . All those things are so insignificant compared to the big show. Furthermore, they would all disappear if friendly relations, i. e. business relations, were inaugurated. Of course,

they are bad in one sense and silly in another but when understood one can get along with them. We are doing business today with worse people.

Using an argument later advanced by Franklin D. Roosevelt, Goodrich maintained that it was unnatural and fraught with danger not to be on speaking terms with the Russians. "I would rather have them in the family circle where we can talk things over with them," Goodrich concluded. "With the departure of the ARA the last point of contact with Russia will be severed." His recommendation was to send to Moscow a commission empowered to open trade relations; diplomatic relations could be postponed indefinitely.[6] Who should head such a commission? Goodrich did not specifically suggest himself, but recommended that the person selected be one who was aware of the shortcomings of the Russian government, but one who was also sympathetic with the struggles of the Russian people toward liberty. Who but James P. Goodrich could have fitted that job description?

In principle Hoover agreed with much of what Goodrich had to say. "On the question of some sort of trade relationship I am, of course, in agreement with you," Hoover replied. As a potential successor to Harding, Hoover apparently felt it would be too risky politically to become identified with the controversial views of his ARA colleague. No doubt Hoover asked himself whether a substantial political constituency existed for opening trade relations with a radical regime. Yet Hoover did not demand political conformity from Goodrich and confided, "You may be interested to know that your leading light from Indiana [Senator James Watson] recently had a conference with the leading light from California [Senator Hiram Johnson] and other aspirants and imposed a self-denial pledge in the matter of competition with the President. I do not know how far he got on but he claims to have some illumination by virtue of some meeting in Indianapolis."[7]

Failing to enlist Hoover's support, Goodrich then turned to Senator Henry Cabot Lodge, the chairman of the Senate Foreign Relations Committee. In a Senate speech on 21 February Lodge, taking his lead from Hughes, described Soviet Russia as a nation that combined anarchy at home with disrespect for treaty obligations abroad. It was Gumberg who alerted Goodrich to Lodge's statements and who discreetly suggested that Goodrich should counterattack. Goodrich then wrote the senator the first of two letters contending that Lodge's information was inaccurate. "I said to him . . . ," Goodrich wrote Gumberg, "that after having traveled all over Russia sometimes alone and after talking to the hundreds of American boys who have been there for a year and a half, I could assure him that the information upon which he relied was entirely false." In his second letter, written two weeks later, Goodrich told Lodge that his talks with Soviet leaders had convinced him that Russia would respect all international agreements including business contracts. Thus, he implied, the time was ripe for opening trade relations.[8]

Once again Goodrich's timing was faulty, as the Soviet government proceeded to discredit itself. First, the ARA developed convincing evidence that the Soviets were exporting grain from the famine areas at Petrograd and Novorossiysk. And the Soviets badly tarnished their image through the execution of Monsignor Constantine Buchavich, the highest ranking Catholic official in Russia for counterrevolutionary activity. "Sometimes," lamented Gumberg, "it does look as they follow the advice of Satan over there." Goodrich agreed, noting "his Satanic Majesty seems to be constantly interfering in Russia. The main difficulty in my opinion is that they don't understand the importance of these things on America."[9] Wisely Goodrich decided to delay an approach to President Harding as he waited for the political dust to settle.

Goodrich's supreme effort to reverse the Harding administration's Russian policy came in a nine-page letter he addressed to the President on 5 June. The letter was the culmination of a campaign orchestrated by Gumberg and Robins to mobilize support for a more enlightened American policy. On 11 May Goodrich met at Senator Borah's Washington home with Gumberg and Robins, and agreed to join in an approach to Harding. Enthusiastically Gumberg reported to Robins, "The Governor so far has been behaving nobly. He is really trying to do something. He should be treated nicely and encouraged in his good work." Robins took this advice to heart and forwarded to Goodrich a memorandum suggesting points which might be covered in a letter to "the big chief."[10] However, Goodrich was perfectly able to do his own composition and, for the most part, relied upon arguments he had previously used in his correspondence with Harding and Hoover.

Goodrich hoped his letter would pave the way for a face-to-face meeting with Harding prior to the President's departure for Alaska in July. He tried to show Harding that America's diplomatic and commercial boycott was an outmoded policy which had been inherited from the discredited Democratic administration of Woodrow Wilson. It was a policy which violated the Republican platform of 1920, which had promised: "We hereby pledge our party to resumption of trade relations with all nations with which we are at peace." The continued boycott had disappointed "many intelligent businessmen," Goodrich among them, and was "one of the few places where the present administration up to this point failed to fulfill the reasonable expectations of the people."

Tactfully avoiding all criticism of Harding, Goodrich implied that Hughes had been the main obstacle to a more enlightened Russian policy. His four conditions for recognition (Russia must guarantee safety of life, private property, sanctity of contract, and the rights of free labor), and his proposal in the fall of 1922 to send a commission to Russia had been presented in so rigid a manner as to guarantee their rejection. Yet, argued Goodrich, "I undertake to say without fear of successful contradiction that the conditions laid down by our State Department have been substantially met." Over the long run the resumption of trade would offer great opportunities for American industrialists; a continuation of the trade boycott would, by default, encourage Germany to dominate Russian economic development. The opening of trade relations would benefit American farmers, too, said Goodrich. Presumably trade contacts would increase American influence in Russia and convince the Soviets to limit their farm exports so as not to depress prices on the world market. Goodrich contended, a bit weakly, that the Soviets were so desperate to reestablish formal relations that they would readily agree to limit grain exports. If Harding was still reading at this point, he could have been excused had he failed to follow Goodrich's logic.

To rectify the errors of the past, Goodrich urged Harding to appoint a commission to consider the resumption of trade relations. "The sooner we have the courage to recognize the solution the sooner will real peace be established and the return of the world to normalcy be accelerated," he concluded. Goodrich, now playing the role of defense attorney for Soviet Russia, had presented the President with a highly polished brief. Omitting any suggestion that the time was ripe for recognition, he sought to show Harding that the resumption of trade would be good for American industry and agriculture and would be good politics besides. Left unstated was Goodrich's availability to head an American trade commission to Russia.[11] Ten days later (15 June) Goodrich was able to follow up his letter when he and Will Hays attended a White House ceremony at which Harding presented several Theodore Roosevelt medals. In passing, Goodrich was able to raise the question of reassessing America's Russian policy. In reply the President told Goodrich he would be unable to give the matter attention until his return from the west coast.[12]

For Goodrich the delay was terribly frustrating because he had information from Haskell suggesting that the present moment was crucial. As one of the last steps in concluding the ARA famine operation Haskell, on 16 June, hosted a testimonial dinner at the Pink

House. In attendance were such high Soviet officials as Kamenev, Dzerzhinsky, Sokolnikov, Litvinov, Chicherin, and Radek. The proceedings featured mutual professions of thanks and goodwill and the offering of numerous toasts to Haskell, Hoover, and the three hundred idealistic young Americans who had served in Russia. Writing to Goodrich, Haskell contended that the after dinner speeches were not made out of politeness, but were "significant of their willingness to go a great distance to establish some kind of relations with the United States." As he told Goodrich, Haskell believed the present was a propitious time for action:

> It is absolutely marvelous the amount of interest and anxiety on the part of the big fellows in the Government to obtain some kind of contact after our departure. I fully believe that they would accept practically our own terms in concluding a trade agreement at the present time, and even include recognition of debts and restoration of private property. It is simply a question of getting down to negotiations. I believe that if negotiations were started, they would conclude an agreement satisfactory to both sides.

Goodrich could not help feeling that a psychologically favorable opportunity had been permitted to slip. At least Goodrich felt he had a promise from Harding to reconsider the entire question of Soviet-American relations. "I am really somewhat hopeful of getting results after the return of the President if nothing happens between now and then to complicate the situation," Goodrich wrote Gumberg. "In the past something has always happened. I hope it won't this time."[13]

But the Harding-Goodrich meeting was never held because the President became ill at San Francisco and died there on 2 August. His successor, Calvin Coolidge of Vermont, was an unknown quantity, but he seemed to be even less informed and less interested in foreign policy than his predecessor. All the plans of Goodrich were suddenly thrown into disarray. "I am shocked by the death of Harding," Goodrich wrote Gumberg. "Coolidge is an entirely different type of man, cold as an icicle. He is without a particle of sentiment in his makeup, which is more like Hughes than Harding. I don't know what the future has in store for Russia."[14] In effect the change in presidential leadership meant that Goodrich had to start all over in seeking to promote a more moderate American policy toward Russia.

For several months Goodrich held forth high hopes that Coolidge could be won over to the cause of establishing trade relations with Russia. Twice Goodrich wrote the new President seeking to demonstrate that American business and press sentiment supported the opening of trade. Primarily he regarded Charles Evans Hughes, not Coolidge, as the main obstacle to a more flexible Russian policy and Goodrich found Hughes's rigidity a source of great frustration. Seeking to convert a skeptical Edgar Rickard to support trade with Russia, Goodrich remarked:

> I am becoming so thoroughly disgusted with the conduct of our State Department with respect to the whole foreign situation that I don't know what to do. I don't even want to talk about it. We are in the world, yet not out of the world. We have set ourselves on a little pedestal apart from all the rest of the world and are assuming the position of the world's schoolmaster, undertaking to tell them all what to do. Occupying the most important position in the world, we are not able to make it effective for bringing about industrial peace and stability and are refusing to do our clear duty as a participant in the war by refusing to aid in liquidating its consequences. The Democrats might not do better. I doubt they would do much worse.

Goodrich told Rickard that he feared the rise of Coolidge could mean the end of Hoover's political ambition.[15] But to Goodrich's relief, Hoover was asked to remain in the cabinet and just a few weeks later the Secretary of Commerce tried to arrange a plan for sending Goodrich on a fourth trip to Russia.

On 31 August Hoover was approached by Dr. George Vincent of the Rockefeller Foundation, who was seeking someone to represent the foundation in Russia. Hoover was probably asked to make a recommendation because he was still the chairman of the ARA and in that capacity had solicited funds from the Rockefeller Foundation to purchase ARA medical supplies for Russia. Hoover immediately suggested Goodrich for the job and arranged for him to go to New York for an interview with Vincent on 11 September. What Hoover did not tell Vincent was that he had in mind a dual role for Goodrich whereby the governor could use the Rockefeller position to explore trade possibilities with his Kremlin contacts. Both Vincent and Goodrich regarded their discussions at New York as successful. Vincent told Hoover he had spent an hour with Goodrich and come away "much impressed by his first-hand knowledge of conditions in Russia and his reasons as to policies which might safely be adopted by American agencies like the Rockefeller Foundation."[16]

For his part Goodrich told Hoover that he had enjoyed a "very pleasant" talk with Vincent. "I of course did not give the slightest intimation of what you had in mind," he noted. "I would be very glad if a situation should develop where the suggestion you made could be carried out." Still there remained one formidable obstacle: Goodrich's nemesis, the State Department of Charles Evans Hughes. "I will discuss with the President at an early date," Hoover replied, "the desirability of establishing at least a temporary contact in Russia and if he and Mr. Hughes are in the notion of it I can undoubtedly secure that the Rockefeller Foundation would make the basis for such an offer." On 17 September Goodrich wrote back expressing the hope that "the matter can be worked out," but nothing more was heard of the idea.[17] Goodrich's papers do not reveal what caused the plan to flounder, but the most likely source of opposition was the State Department.

No sooner had the Rockefeller Foundation project disintegrated than Goodrich found himself preoccupied with a spectacular scandal within the Indiana Republican Party. Temporarily Goodrich was forced to shift his attention to domestic politics and therefore he played little role in the next phase of the struggle for reestablishing trade and diplomatic ties with Russia. In late August 1923 the financial affairs of Warren T. McCray of Kentland, Goodrich's successor as governor of Indiana, unraveled when McCray was compelled to beg his creditors for relief. McCray and Goodrich had been rivals for the governorship in 1916 and Goodrich (by supporting Ed Toner) had tried to block McCray when he successfully sought the Republican nomination in 1920. Although they were not personal friends, Goodrich mounted an abortive rescue effort seeking to minimize the embarrassment to the party.

On 1 October, together with state chairman Clyde A. Walb and Senators Harry New and Jim Watson, Goodrich attended a meeting of the state committee at Indianapolis held to discuss ways and means of containing the damage. Goodrich was incensed when John Moorman, the governor's chief political advisor, implied that Goodrich had conspired with President Coolidge to force McCray from office. Such an accusation, said Goodrich, was "absolutely false" and an effort "to throw dust in the eyes of the people of this state." Goodrich felt compelled to issue a public statement defending himself. "I spent nearly three months in trying to untangle the Governor's affairs," he stated, "and finally raised $350,000 to save him and some of his associates from the most serious personal consequences as the result of his own acts and I deeply resent the efforts of Mr. Moorman or the Governor, or anyone else, to reflect upon the good faith of the men responsible for the conduct of the affairs of the party in this State."[18] To the acute embarrassment of Goodrich, the Bank of Kentland failed two weeks later and the governor was subsequently indicted by a federal grand jury for mail fraud. Not until his conviction and sentence to a ten-year prison term in April 1924 would McCray finally resign.[19] The McCray affair required numerous meetings of the state committee and so monopolized the attention of the Indianapolis press that Goodrich found himself quite out of touch when Coolidge unexpectedly made overtures to Moscow in his 1923 state of the union message.

On 1 December Coolidge invited Raymond Robins to the White House for lunch and a discussion of the entire Russian question. Apparently influenced by Robins' magnetism, Coolidge then included a conciliatory passage in his annual message to Congress suggesting discussions between Washington and Moscow on all major problems. America, said the President, ought to be "the first to go to the economic and moral rescue of Russia," provided compensation was paid for confiscated property and repudiated debts. Coolidge also insisted on an end to revolutionary propaganda, and concluded: "We have every desire to help and no desire to injure. We hope that the time is near when we can act." Chicherin replied in a conciliatory tone expressing a "complete readiness" to discuss all outstanding problems. But the Soviet reply fell short of unconditional surrender in that Chicherin spoke of basing the negotiations upon reciprocity and nonintervention in the internal affairs of others. The legalistic Hughes, strangely without protest from Coolidge, then decisively intervened and rejected any thought of negotiations until Moscow abandoned its propaganda for the violent overthrow of the American government. According to Hughes, the Soviet government should restore repudiated property and recognize the validity of the debt prior to negotiations.[20]

Back in Winchester Goodrich was besieged by frantic telegrams and letters from Gumberg and Borah asking for a counterattack against the willful Hughes. Preoccupied by the McCray affair and lacking even the text of the various notes, Goodrich felt he was living in a vacuum. "I am so sore and disappointed over the situation," Goodrich wrote Gumberg, "I don't know what to do. I don't even have possession of the facts, nor have I seen Chicherin's communication, nor can I understand why it was given out to the papers without having been submitted to Senator Borah and friends here." Not until 27 December did Goodrich receive a letter from Gumberg containing relevant newspaper clippings and excerpts from the *Congressional Record*. Undertaking a postmortem, Goodrich felt that Chicherin had made a tactical error (and given Hughes an opening) by failing to state that he would be willing to negotiate on the basis outlined in Coolidge's message: namely, the payment of debts and the restoration of repudiated property. To Goodrich the misunderstanding demonstrated "the difficulty of dealing with this situation by cable with the utter lack of appreciation on the part of the Russian officials of conditions essential to any discussion of relations with America." In Goodrich's opinion face-to-face oral discussion, such as he had conducted with Kamenev and his colleagues in June 1922, was the only method that promised a resolution of the impasse.[21]

Two years later, during his final Russian visit, Goodrich had an opportunity to meet with Chicherin and discuss with him Hughes's note. According to Chicherin, he had been "very greatly surprised by the tone" of Hughes's reply, which he characterized as "insulting in the extreme." So long as the State Department continued its attitude of intransigence, said Chicherin, "it would be useless to discuss the question [of recognition] at all." Tactfully Goodrich refrained from stating his opinion that Chicherin had blundered by insisting on negotiations based on reciprocity and by failing to mention either debts or confiscated property.[22] The Christmas 1923 debacle made it clear to Goodrich that his arguments and those of his friends had fallen on deaf ears and that immediate prospects for any trade agreement—much less the restoration of diplomatic relations—had evaporated. The start of the 1924 presidential campaign and the breaking of the Harding scandals further pushed the question of Russian policy into the background. Not until after his fourth Russian trip in 1925 did Goodrich consider the atmosphere sufficiently favorable for again approaching the Coolidge administration.

In the interim Goodrich became involved in promoting a new cause which was much closer to home: the welfare of Wabash College at Crawfordsville, Indiana, the alma mater of Pierre Goodrich. Since 1904 Goodrich had been a member of the college's board of trustees and in 1924, as Goodrich marked his sixtieth birthday, he became the board's chairman. In this position Goodrich provided frequent investment advice to the college treasurer and solicited money for the endowment fund. Seeking a contribution from John D. Rockefeller, Goodrich wrote that Wabash College sought to achieve, in the midwest, a position comparable to that of Amherst, Bowdoin, and Williams colleges in the east. Increasingly it was Goodrich who became the financial guardian angel of the college. He personally assumed the cost of remodelling the president's home and repairing its furnace, and in 1919 he pledged the substantial sum of $50,000 to the Wabash College endowment fund.[23]

During this time the Russian question seldom left his mind and he spent considerable effort assembling and proofreading his manuscript about his Russian travels. Strangely, he omitted any mention of his political contacts and confined his account almost entirely to a description of Russian travel and social conditions. Perhaps he was seeking, consciously or subconsciously, to emulate the travelogue aspects of George Kennan's narrative *Siberia and the Exile System*. In the fall of 1925 Goodrich unexpectedly received an opportunity to add to his Russian experiences when he and Haskell received invitations to attend a meeting of the Soviet Academy of Sciences. As had been his practice on his previous trips, Goodrich kept a copious diary which he probably intended to add as a final chapter to his book manuscript. On his return he decided to abandon the entire project as futile, possibly because he found his enthusiasm for the new Russia still had no ready or receptive audience in America.

8

Goodrich's Final Trip to Russia

On his fourth Russian trip (1 September–5 October 1925) Goodrich was accompanied by his wife, Haskell, and Golder. Starting at Leningrad they traveled to Moscow and, after Haskell's return to America, the Goodriches and Golder visited Nezhnii-Novgorod and finally Goodrich made a solo trip to the Volga. Attending meetings of the Academy of Sciences—their official purpose—was the least attractive aspect of the journey, as Goodrich and Haskell anticipated being subjected to a propaganda barrage. At least the visit presented an opportunity for the gathering of current economic information, for sightseeing, and for renewing old friendships, an activity which probably required numerous games of poker.

From the moment he crossed the Finnish border near Leningrad on a chilly, grey afternoon Goodrich was generally impressed by the contrast between the conditions of 1921–22 and those of 1925. To be sure, the condition of the countryside appeared careless and disordered after the neatness and cleanliness of Finnish Karelia, but the Russian train was clean, the right of way free of weeds, and the roadbed "trimmed up and in good condition." Soviet customs officials at the border were "kind and courteous," and at Leningrad his party was met by a reception committee bedecked with ribbons. From the station they were conveyed in "somewhat dilapidated" automobiles to the luxurious Hotel Europe and provided a fine suite of rooms. "The hotel was clean, the service excellent," he recorded.[1]

Goodrich was not ignorant of the fact that he was the recipient of a red-carpet guided tour which was designed to produce the most favorable impression possible. Many of the people who called on him seemed to have been sent to spread Soviet propaganda. Likewise he and the other delegates were treated to highly laudatory guided tours of the Putilov Iron Works and the Winter Palace. Afterward a military parade was held for their benefit in the large square in front of the Winter Palace. Colonel Haskell, who accompanied Goodrich, expressed the opinion that the soldiers would not last very long in combat with a modern army.[2]

On 5 September Goodrich's celebrity status was confirmed when he received a private tour of a palace built for Catherine the Great, located sixteen miles from the city. His guide was Maxim Litvinov, an official with whom Goodrich was already acquainted and who in 1933 negotiated the agreement with President Roosevelt which established diplomatic relations between the two countries. Litvinov, who spoke flawless English, proved an amiable and knowledgeable host. He asked not to discuss foreign relations until the next week when they agreed to meet again in Moscow. But he gave the impression that the government was in the process of returning by a circuitous path to the NEP. "Our progress," he reassuringly told Goodrich, "will necessarily be something of a zigzag course going as far as we can to the right and perhaps having to make some concession to the left, but each time going a little further in the right direction."

Goodrich was impressed by his guide's intelligence and his curiosity about the conditions and political influence of American workers. As was the case with many of the Russians Goodrich met, Litvinov inquired about the recently concluded Scopes "monkey trial" in Tennessee and about auto manufacturer Henry Ford, whom he considered "the greatest and most typical American." As they returned to Leningrad, Litvinov described the broad boulevard on which they traveled as "November Seventh" and then confused Goodrich by expressing the opinion that the Nevski Prospect was the most beautiful street in the world. In his diary Goodrich noted: "I replied, 'Will you not drive over to the Nevski, I would like to see it?' 'Why,' he said, 'You are on the Nevski now.' 'Pardon me,' I said, 'but I thought this was the November Seventh.' 'Ah!' he said, 'it is still the Nevski to a Russian.'"[3] To Goodrich the exchange suggested that Litvinov, like many of the Soviet leaders, was as much a Russian nationalist as an international Communist.

In between tours Goodrich found numerous opportunities to take stock of conditions for himself. Walking from his hotel Goodrich was able to examine the plentiful food and merchandise for sale in stores and markets. Despite the high cost of meat, shoes, and clothing, the population "seemed well fed, comfortably dressed, and with every appearance of content." Several of his guests and the people he called upon voiced criticisms of the government, which helped to put matters in perspective. One of the most outspoken critics was Dr. Ivan Pavlov, the experimental psychologist, whom Goodrich and Golder visited for an hour. Pavlov emphatically denounced the government for neglecting the school system and insisted the entire Communist experiment should be abandoned. During a two-hour sightseeing ride in a droshky, Goodrich was told by the driver that the government was to blame for high taxes and for a general breakdown in respect for law and order.[4]

In the course of the tour Goodrich observed extensive new construction and repair work under way. But he was puzzled because the workers employed in new construction seemed energetic and efficient, while those engaged in repair work "seemed to be loafing on the job." The apparent explanation, he discovered, was that the efficient laborers were employed by labor artels which had contracted to undertake projects in hope of a profit, whereas the lazy workers were paid only a low wage and had no incentive to put forth more than the minimum effort. In Goodrich's opinion the most convincing evidence of the follies of Communism came during his tour of the Putilov Iron Works when he was proudly told that the plant had just produced one hundred exact replicas of Ford tractors. On inquiry Goodrich found that the cost in labor and material, with no allowance for interest or depreciation, was twice that of importing the same tractor from America.[5]

The meetings of the Academy of Sciences, as Goodrich had anticipated, consisted more of propaganda and spectacle than of substance. The opening meeting was preceded by a three-hour parade in which "tens of thousands" participated, either as marchers or as sidewalk observers. Then as Goodrich mounted the forty steps leading into Philharmonic Hall he passed an impressive honor guard of soldiers standing at attention presenting rifles with fixed bayonets. Lengthy speeches followed, the longest being made by Mikhail Kalinin, the President of the Russian Soviet. All the speakers stressed that cooperation between science and labor was essential to achieve a progressive society. But the greatest applause of all was reserved for the composer, Aleksandr Glazunov, who conducted the orchestra in one of his own works and in the ninth symphony of Beethoven. Afterward Goodrich, Golder, and Haskell attended a banquet that featured ten courses, more speeches, and numerous champagne toasts. The festivities were still in full swing when the tipsy Americans retired at 1:30 A.M. to a chorus of "For he is a jolly good fellow." The following day Goodrich "put in the afternoon at the market," and attended a performance of *Ruslan and Lyudmila* by Glinka before taking the night train to Moscow with Haskell.[6] It was his intention to make a quick side trip to Nizhnii-Novgorod before the Academy of Sciences held its next meeting in the capital.

For once Goodrich was able to record that a Russian train was clean and on time, the road bed seemed "fine," and the countryside appeared "rather prosperous," with workers busily harvesting rye and oats. "Saw men on the threshing floors of the farms along the railroad," he noted, "flailing out grains and winnowing it just as they did three thousand years ago." One unexpected development was the discovery that Litvinov was on the Moscow train. Goodrich thought Litvinov's presence was coincidental, but could not be sure. Nevertheless, the two men seized the opportunity to spend two hours discussing "the American situation." Litvinov told Goodrich that he was personally "very anxious" to secure American recognition and agreed that a Russian-American commission of "fair-minded men" could quickly resolve all outstanding questions. Hughes, who had "grossly insulted" the Soviets, appeared the main obstacle to an agreement, said Litvinov, and the two agreed to continue the discussion at the conclusion of the Moscow session of the Academy of Sciences. Arriving in Moscow, Goodrich had trouble recognizing the city after having been away for three years. It appeared that "Aladdin's lamp" had been rubbed, because the station, streets, and nearby buildings were clean and well maintained. He and Haskell registered and had dinner at the Hotel Savoy before leaving on the night train for Nizhnii-Novgorod.[7]

Their guided tour of the city began on a sour note, as the first hotel to which they were taken they rejected as "filthy"; an alternative room with "good clean military beds" in the local Soviet was then located. Despite a disagreeable chilly rain the two Americans received an extensive tour of the local bazaar where Goodrich observed for sale a Ford tractor equipped with an Oliver plow from Indiana. The tour also included a peasants' rooming home, which was established for the use of people from distant villages wishing to sell or buy goods in the local market. Goodrich was shown one room filled with agricultural implements and instructional matter and a nearby room known as "Lenin's Corner" which contained books and pamphlets promoting Communism. Goodrich observed that the agricultural room was filled with curious peasants, while "Lenin's Corner" was entirely vacant. The lesson, thought Goodrich, was that the people of Russia were more interested in the problems of everyday life than in the study of Marxist-Leninist ideology. In the evening Goodrich and Haskell were invited to attend a performance by a traveling light opera company. The musical experience was satisfactory enough, but Goodrich felt that he and Haskell had erred in their selection of seats. "Colonel Haskell and I," Goodrich recorded, "very foolishly paid three rubles a piece for our seats and found that we occupied the orchestra part alone except for two jews and a few private traders. The Proletarians took the 20 kopek seats in the galleries. I wanted to be with the Proletarians."[8]

The final day in Nizhnii-Novgorod was devoted to a tour of a new workers' housing project equipped with nurseries, street car service, and a fire department—that conducted a practice drill for the American visitors in the cold rain. Goodrich was less impressed with the local steel plant, as he calculated the cost of producing wire, nails, and bolts was nearly three times the cost in America. Finally he visited the hospital and found it transformed from his earlier tour in 1921. Then Goodrich had found it "indescribably dirty" and without medical supplies or equipment. On this occasion the place was clean and well supplied and the doctor in charge said he had been promised a substantial increase in his budget.[9] That evening Goodrich and Haskell took the night sleeper to Moscow. Immediately they became suspicious that they had been cheated, because they were assigned to a second class compartment even though they had paid for first class. "The difference was only $5.52," noted Goodrich. "We were perfectly comfortable, just as comfortable as we would have been in first class, but we were mad over the loss of $5.52." It was the principle of the thing that mattered, thought Goodrich, and he had the conductor write out a statement testifying that they had not received the accommodations they had paid for. "I sent the affidavit down to Novgorod," he wrote in his diary, "and in three days had the money back, which was not bad at all."

On his arrival at Moscow Goodrich was cheated for a second time, but again found the new Russia dispensed justice, this time of the drumhead variety. Carelessly Goodrich put down his briefcase while haggling with a droshky driver over the fare to his hotel and when he turned to retrieve his property found it was gone. Colonel Haskell advised Goodrich "to forget it." Promptly a young army officer found out from bystanders who was responsible and within a few minutes Goodrich's briefcase was returned with its lock broken minus only a fountain pen and pencil. As for the thief, Goodrich saw the officer grab him by the coat collar, jerk him off his feet, and place him under arrest. The malefactor, Goodrich was told, was a member of a gang of thieves who infested the depot.

Goodrich used his six days in Moscow to good advantage, as he toured as widely as possible and made numerous contacts with Soviet officials. He never forgot that his official purpose was to attend the meetings of the Academy of Sciences, but he found the gathering of information a more productive activity. On his first afternoon in the city (11 September) Goodrich and Haskell toured the largest textile mill in the region. Interviewing the superintendent Goodrich found that no new machinery had been installed for over twenty years and that negotiations were currently under way with English manufac-

turers of textile machinery. Nearby he observed a new power plant
of the most modern design being constructed. According to the superintendent, German manufacturers had received the contract.[10]
Two days later Goodrich called on an English speaking coal engineer
named Karchevsky, who told him that coal production in the Donetz
basin had almost doubled since the revolution despite the lack of
modern machinery. What was needed, he said, was to purchase Sullivan mining machinery in the United States so that Russia might
compete with English, French, and Italian producers.[11]

In an interview with the assistant commissar of agriculture, neces-
sitated because his superior was on vacation—"Great people the Russians, for vacations," commented Goodrich—he learned that the
current grain crop was the largest in Russian history, with the possible exception of 1914. What the peasant needed most, Goodrich
was told, was modern farm machinery—an area in which America
excelled. In a final series of interviews Goodrich called upon the
new commissar of railroads and the head of the textile trust. From
the former he learned that the government had made considerable
progress in overhauling its decrepit railroad equipment, but that foreign capital was essential to create an adequate transportation system.
And the latter official showed Goodrich a contract he had just signed
with an English manufacturer of textile machinery and said he hoped
within a year to purchase fifty million rubles worth of textile machinery abroad. Goodrich felt the various officials were not in collusion
and had spoken to him candidly and honestly. Here, felt Goodrich,
was concrete proof that a substantial market existed in Russia for the
products of American industry.[12]

As had been the case during his stay in Leningrad, the official
meetings of the Academy of Sciences were largely a waste of time.
Goodrich and Haskell attended the opening session in the newly
redecorated Conservatory of Music, but they felt the proceedings
were staged and lacked spontaneity. The same was true of a meeting
of the Moscow Soviet, held at the Bolshoi Theater, to which Goodrich, Golder, and Haskell were invited. "It was propaganda from
start to finish," recorded Goodrich. To great applause the names of
the various delegates were announced, and when it was the turn of
Goodrich and Haskell to be recognized "the entire theatre stood up
as one person and cheered again and again until we too were compelled to go to the front and cries of 'America' arose from all over
the great building." The only discordant note was struck by Kamenev who, in an hour-long address, bitterly attacked the United
States, Britain, and France for having supported the cause of the
Whites through military intervention and economic blockade. In

Goodrich's opinion: "The speech left a bad taste in the mouths of the delegates from Western Europe and had better not been uttered."[13]

Having survived another banquet which lasted until the early morning hours, Goodrich spent the remaining day of the conference attending a session on economic policy. One of the speakers was John Maynard Keynes, who criticized both Leninism and the gold standard and advocated a new paper monetary standard. As a respectable Indiana banker, Goodrich's sympathies were solidly with those members of the audience who "jumped on to Keynes" and defended the gold standard. The occasion did provide an opportunity for Goodrich to renew his acquaintance with Sokolnikov, the commissar of finance. In answer to Goodrich's query, Sokolnikov contended that Russia was in no condition to settle the American debt. Russia, he said, was better off to use its resources for internal reconstruction than to commit itself to recognizing "old debts." It was one of the few occasions on Goodrich's trip when he was not told what he wanted to hear. Afterward Goodrich and Haskell spent the evening "talking over old times" before Haskell departed for America on the night train.[14]

With his official duties behind him, Goodrich determined to take an extensive tour of the Volga to assess the extent of that region's recovery from the famine. To his irritation the Foreign Office took two days longer than expected to locate a translator, so Goodrich, with time on his hands, was forced to spend the time talking and playing cards with Golder. Also to his dismay the train to Tambov had no sleeping cars or blankets; therefore, "I was condemned to make the trip sleeping on a seat with my clothes on." As a veteran Russian traveler Goodrich survived the experience despite "a rather restless night" and he spent the next day (19 September) observing the land and its people. Already the winter wheat was well established and Goodrich forecast an excellent crop for 1926. The peasants, unlike the land, were little changed from his previous visits. "Men and women," he noted, "while strong and rugged physically are miserably dressed and have a pathetic, sad appearance as they stand along the railway in the little Communes through which we passed." Compared to his previous visit three years before, the stations and roadbed were in excellent condition and the train was clean and on time to the minute. At Tambov the train was boarded by a prosperous, well dressed crowd. Goodrich shared his compartment with a well-to-do private trader, one of the so-called "Nepmen," who was going to Samara to purchase wool for his business. The trader claimed he had no difficulty competing with state produced woolen products because he provided a better product and better service. Faced with such vigorous private competition, thought Goodrich, the future of Communism appeared bleak indeed.[15]

From Samara Goodrich proceeded by boat to tour the German colonies. Once on board Goodrich found that only three passengers, including himself and his interpreter, were traveling first class. Perhaps it was just as well because the second and third class accommodations and the deck were "literally crowded with men, women, and children most miserably dressed from an American viewpoint." Schilling, a scene of desolation when Goodrich and Repp had visited four years before, was the boat's first stop and Goodrich carefully recorded the contrast:

> The boat had a great deal of freight to unload and I got off and went up on the bluff where a large number of peasant women were gathered selling their milk and butter and cheese and eggs and various food stuffs to the travellers on the boat. The same women [were] going up and down the high bluff carrying water hung at either end of a yoke over their shoulders. It all had a familiar look and yet so different from four years ago. Then death stalked the land. Then every day people were dying of cholera, typhus or starvation, then gloom and despair was on every face, for death faced the whole Commune, with only the ARA to stay its hand. Now strong, sturdy men and women were there to sell to the passengers of the boat their melons, bread, meat and pastries, while round faced happy children played on the sandy shore or with curious faces studied the crowd that went from stand to stand, bargaining to the last kopek before they purchased.
>
> I stepped up to a peasant woman who was operating a stand to inquire about the price of her wares, told her who I was in my broken Russian. She cried and threw her arms around my neck and kissed me on either cheek and told me that I saved her children from starvation. Soon a crowd of people were gathered around me and I saw several faces whom I recognized among those whom I met [four] years ago. It was a wholesome looking lot of folks gathered around there, ignorant so far as the ordinary education goes, but with a world of good, hard common sense and of great industry, educated and given a fair chance in life they will give a good account of themselves.

Although his friends grumbled about the low prices they received for their grain and about a shortage of teachers, they told Goodrich their warehouses contained a surplus reserved for the next famine. And in four years the number of sheep and horses had more than doubled so that they had all the animals they could care for on their pastures. "They welcomed me with a heartiness that left no doubt as to its sincerity and bid me Godspeed with a regret that was plainly stamped on their faces," he noted.[16]

Stalingrad, better known to his fellow travelers by its traditional
name Tsaritzen, was his next destination. What seemed to interest
his companions was not Communism, but capitalism. At each stop
he observed the same loading and unloading of freight, the same
exodus of passengers, "the same haggling, bargaining and sharpening
of wits and the petty trading that took place. At the ringing of the
bell, the same cries, rush and crowding to get on the boat for fear
it might leave them." On a lower deck a speaker presented a well
attended illustrated talk on modern agriculture, not on Communist
ideology. His interpreter then told him a story about a well-to-do
young man who sought admission to the Communist Party and
which seemed to demonstrate that even Communists possessed normal human characteristics. According to Goodrich the candidate was
asked: "'In what class did your parents belong?' His family were of
the nobility and he answered: 'Same as Lenin.' 'When did you become a Communist?' The answer was: 'The same time as Trotsky.'
Trotsky having been a Menshevik until after the 1917 Revolution.
'Do you use intoxicating liquor?' He answered: 'No more than Rykov.' Rykov is known to be addicted to the excessive use of intoxicating liquor." Without exception his fellow passengers displayed great
curiosity about American life. How much grain could an American
farmer raise, who is Ford, and what was the "Dayton Monkey
Trial?" he was repeatedly asked.

Stalingrad proved a disappointment, as Goodrich found the city
to be "dirty, out of repair, the worst place I have yet seen in Russia."
Contributing to his irritation was a rude porter who demanded an
entire ruble to carry Goodrich's bag from the boat up a nearby
hill. Convinced he was being cheated Goodrich noted: "Mad clear
through I carried my own bag to the top of the hill only to learn
afterward that the fee fixed was the maximum fee and that I could
have bargained for much less." One consolation was the discovery
that the lower Volga was "wonderful melon country" and soon
Goodrich had purchased the best melons he had ever tasted.[17] The
next morning (21 September) his guided tour resumed, as Goodrich
departed by train for Rostov-on-Don, Kharkov, and the Donetz coal
basin. Not until mid-afternoon did Goodrich discover he was on the
wrong train, but he adopted the attitude "it doesn't matter." Instead
of fretting, he decided to enjoy the roundabout trip through the state
of Kuban, noting that "no place in the world can excel the fertility
of the soil" and that the grain produced was "as good wheat as I
ever saw."

Time did not permit Goodrich to tour a Russian coal mine, but
at Rostov-on-Don, he interviewed a "very bright" coal engineer who

furnished statistics showing that coal was being produced for only
$8.00 a ton and that production had improved by five to six times
compared with 1921. American mining equipment, which the Soviets
hoped to purchase, would increase production even further. And
Goodrich learned from an American representative (a Mr. Church)
of a company producing dock loading machinery that the Soviets
were interested in purchasing American conveyer equipment provided his bankers could be convinced "that these fellows would pay."
After twelve hours Goodrich was off on the midnight train for Kharkov.[18] Entering the Ukraine Goodrich was up at 5:00 A.M. (23 September) to observe "wonderful fields stretching as far away as I could
see, either level or generally rolling." From the train he observed
barefooted women working side by side in the fields with men. He
saw winter wheat being sown by hand "as we did in Indiana fifty
years ago when I was a boy on the farm." In another field he alertly
counted thirty-five men cutting grass with scythes, assisted by a
single Ford tractor.

At Kharkov he also received a whirlwind twelve-hour tour and
much of that time was taken up with waiting in line to check his
baggage and in conducting a rambling interview with the president
of the Ukraine, Grigori I. Petrovsky. Perhaps inevitably he was
asked again about the Scopes trial and the prospects for recognition.
Goodrich tried to explain that the "monkey trial" involved only a
state, not a federal, law and that recognition required assurances on
propaganda, debts, and confiscated property. "If that is all, it could
be settled any time," was his host's reaction. He also found time to
collect statistics on coal quality and production from the "most excellent mining engineer in charge of the coal office here." According to
the engineer the labor cost of mining Donetz coal had been reduced
from $9.00 a ton to $3.00 as a result of the introduction of the
piecework system, and the quality was equal to that of the best
English coal. Following his interviews Goodrich ate dinner in a local
restaurant where he discovered "a new custom" which he succinctly
described: "I went in and gave an order for dinner. The waiter kept
standing after the order was given. I finally told him as best I could
in Russian to go and bring the meal. He told me I had to pay first,
that they never served the dinner until it was paid for and so I paid
in advance and got a very good dinner afterwards."[19]

Goodrich spent the final ten days of his fourth Russian trip in
Moscow. Some of the time was occupied with social and sightseeing
activities with his wife, but Goodrich was more interested in a series
of meetings he had scheduled with Soviet economic and political
leaders. First he spent an entire afternoon (25 September) with Litvi-

nov discussing the obstacles to diplomatic recognition. Goodrich
stressed that Coolidge regarded a debt settlement and compensation
for nationalized property as essential conditions. Only payment of
debts acquired under the Provisional Government, not czarist debts,
was insisted upon. "You owe no Kerensky debts to any other country
except America," said Goodrich. But Litvinov contended that Britain and France would demand payment of czarist debts should the
Soviets agree to pay Kerensky debts to the United States. On the
topic of propaganda Goodrich said his own opinion was that "it
amounted to nothing." But he argued that revolutionary propaganda
by the Third International greatly embarrassed those in America,
like himself, who were sympathetic to extending diplomatic recognition. Goodrich ridiculed Litvinov's contention that no connection
existed between the Soviet government and the Third International,
insisting the relationship was "as close as hands and feet." For Russia
to shelter an organization committed to revolutionary violence
amounted, said Goodrich, to an unneighborly act: "If you are my
neighbor and are sheltering in your house one who constantly threat-
ens to blow up my house, we cannot be good neighbors as long as
you shelter him and he holds to the avowed purpose of destroying
my home, neither can you set up any good relationship with other
countries so long as you tolerate that."[20]

Two days later Goodrich and Litvinov continued their discussion
during an elaborate luncheon hosted by Litvinov and his wife Fay.
Karl Radek and his wife were also in attendance as was a foreign
office official in charge of publicity and the editor of Pravda. After
a distinctly nonproletarian meal the company retired into the library
and for two hours engaged in a spirited discussion. Goodrich came
away with the impression that Radek, the publicist, and the editor
had been invited to support Litvinov's incredible argument that the
Soviet government had no connection with anticapitalist propaganda
efforts. "They did this with a sincerity that staggered my judgment
to the contrary," noted Goodrich. "They all said that since 1923 the
Soviet Government had not given a single kopek to its support [the
Third International]." Litvinov did most of the talking, but Radek,
his hair askew and with chin whiskers looking like Goodrich's
memories of his grandfather, occasionally joined in. All the partici-
pants, including Fay Litvinov—who impressed Goodrich with her
command of international affairs—argued that the Soviets were anxious to settle the American debts, but could not afford to sign an
agreement which the French and British could cite as a precedent.
Not under even the best of circumstances, they said, could they
consider interest payments to France and Britain on the debts of the

czar's government. To restore American nationalized property would likewise set an undesirable precedent vis-à-vis the property of others. Goodrich recorded that "all together I spent a very interesting afternoon," yet he had to admit that the discussion had ended at about the same point it had begun.[21]

Always alert for business opportunities, Goodrich called on several Soviet trade representatives. The head of Amtorg, the corporation set up in 1924 to conduct limited trade with the United States, proudly reported that he had purchased $2.5 million worth of Ford tractors, each equipped with an Oliver plow. Their current needs included typewriters made by the Remington Company and all kinds of American agricultural equipment, but the negotiations had stalled due to a lack of credit. Krassin, the trade commissar, told Goodrich much the same story: "He gave it as his opinion that Russia needs above all else American credits to purchase machinery, farm implements and the things they need; that the general conditions of the two countries are so similar. Then he added: 'We can trust America. They have no unfriendly designs upon our country.'"[22] The need for American credit was again emphasized when Goodrich called at the office of the textile syndicate and was told that the Russian textile industry, producing at 80 percent of the prewar rate, "was very anxious to buy American equipment." British, French, and German manufacturers of textile machinery had extended generous terms on the basis of 25 percent interest.[23] Leon Trotsky, with whom Goodrich spent an hour, likewise "frankly admitted that Russia could not restore its enterprises without the aid of outside capital." In particular Trotsky said the government was so desperate for foreign investment to build workers' apartment buildings it was willing to guarantee investors a profit. Goodrich's reaction was: "It sounds good but it is rotten economics."[24]

On the afternoon of 29 September Goodrich called on Joseph Stalin, who impressed him as "a man of rare common sense, sound judgment, and in my opinion is easily the most powerful factor in Russia." To Goodrich Stalin seemed sensible and moderate. He downplayed the importance of revolutionary rhetoric saying: "We have neither time nor money to devote to propaganda in your country. We have not done it and don't intend to do it regardless of whether you recognize us or not, but we have our own situation to take care of and cannot move with too great rapidity in changing our policies." Russia needed time to develop internally, he said. "A man may be a good Communist," stated Stalin, "well acquainted with Marxian ideology and yet make a bad factory superintendent. We can only succeed as we build up the economy of Russia."

Much of their conversation dealt with a discussion of the obstacles to recognition and again Stalin seemed more like a practical business-man than a fanatic. He expressed confidence that a solution would be found to the problems of debts and confiscated property once talks were held. The chief difficulty, said Stalin, was that the Soviets were unable as a matter of politics to repeal the decrees repudiating the debts of previous governments. Goodrich quoted Stalin as reas-suringly stating: "The other governments tell you they will pay, but don't and won't. Russia, while it may not be willing at this time to withdraw the disavowance of its debts, will find a way to liquidate them." Stalin, with the silent concurrence of Goodrich, placed much of the blame for the diplomatic impasse at the door of Hughes. According to Stalin, relations would have been established soon after Coolidge's message of December 1923 "had it not been for the tenor of Hughes's reply to Chicherin's note." In conclusion Stalin told Goodrich "that the Russian people liked the Americans and preferred closer cooperation with them to any other country in the world."[25]

For five weeks Goodrich had been permitted to roam about Russia looking at anything he wanted to see and interviewing ordinary citi-zens and officials ranging from lowly bureaucrats to the highest members of the politburo. Most of the time he was accompanied only by a young Moscow University student as his translator. Prob-ably such latitude was permitted because Goodrich was a known favorable quantity, which Goodrich himself readily conceded. As he typed his diary of his trip he began with the comment, "It may be at times I become a bit enthusiastic over the remarkable progress made."[26] In some respects Goodrich permitted his enthusiasm to run away with him. He still held to his faith that inexorable economic forces would "soon bring about the surrender of the last vestige of Communism and give free field for the exercise of the abilities and energies of the Russian people."[27] As a short-range forecaster Good-rich could be spectacularly wrong. His belief that the Soviets would soon be compelled to restore confiscated property and settle debts in return for recognition and bank credits was mistaken. Nor did he appreciate the intensity of the power struggle then in progress among the Soviet leadership. One clue that could have made a greater im-pression on Goodrich came during his interview with Stalin when the subject arose of Kamenev's anti-western speech to the Academy of Sciences. Stalin's angry reaction was dismissed by Goodrich as mere disappointment. In a colossal understatement Goodrich noted of Kamenev, "I don't think he helped himself in Russia."[28]

In a larger sense, however, Goodrich had a knack for seeing the overall picture with greater clarity than those Americans who remained at home. His travels reinforced his conviction that the revolution was permanent and that there existed no organized opposition. From Golder he found that the professor's "White friends" in Leningrad and Moscow were "resigned to the situation."[29] His trip reinforced his impression that American businessmen were needlessly sacrificing a substantial opportunity for trade to European competitors. For his part Goodrich found it no more difficult to transact business in Russia than in Indiana. In Leningrad Golder found some rare books he wished to purchase for the Hoover War Library. Goodrich, therefore, cabled New York in the afternoon for one thousand dollars and at 9:00 A.M. the next day the funds were credited to his account.[30]

On his return to the United States on 20 October, Goodrich was in a quandary. More than ever he was convinced that the Soviets were a permanent fixture in world politics. As usual the stumbling block was how to convince the administration that it was in America's best interests to break with past policy. One possibility was to work through the State Department, now headed by former Minnesota Senator Frank B. Kellogg. When Hughes had departed in January 1925, Goodrich at first had high hopes that Kellogg would "simplify the problem" and would "not take the legalistic view." Soon Goodrich was disillusioned and convinced that Kellogg had adopted the intensely anti-Bolshevik viewpoint of Assistant Secretary of State Robert F. Kelley.[31] Concluding that the State Department presented an unpromising avenue of attack, Goodrich decided his only hope was to start at the top and seek an interview with Coolidge himself.

At Goodrich's request, Hoover wrote Coolidge's secretary asking whether the President would schedule a time to meet with Goodrich so as "to discuss his observations in Russia." Hoover added, "I think it might be valuable for the President to learn from Governor Goodrich what the real economic and political situation is in Russia." Presently Coolidge, through his secretary, confirmed that he "would be glad to see Governor Goodrich." Soon after his return, Goodrich spent a thankless day in Washington seeking to convert the State Department and the White House. Goodrich left no record of what transpired, but in a letter a few months later to Fay Litvinov he alluded to his less than successful experience. First he was received by Secretary of State Kellogg who shocked Goodrich by opposing recognition as dogmatically as Hughes. Kellogg expressed himself as being especially angry over continued revolutionary propaganda in America on the part of the Third International. His interview with the President was inconclusive. Goodrich came away with the impression that "the President does not attach as much importance to propaganda as does his Secretary of State." Coolidge, cautious as ever, made no commitments and urged Goodrich to summarize his views on paper.[32]

Back in Winchester Goodrich felt more isolated and frustrated than ever. After four Russian trips, having seen and heard what no other American had experienced, Goodrich decided there was no turning back and on 24 November dispatched a final political manifesto to President Coolidge. His sense of futility was reflected in a rather weak opening: "It is with some hesitation that I write you concerning the Russian situation. Yet I venture to do so." His theme was that Russia was steadily moving to the right and was building a western-style industrial society. "It is safe to say today," he contended, "that the working classes of Russia are in better condition and better satisfied than they were under the Tsar." He described his conversations with the highest Soviet leaders and noted their interest in American machinery of all kinds as well as their intense desire for loans and recognition. "My judgment," he stated, "is that whenever the Governments of Russia and America get together to discuss the questions at issue a program will be agreed on consistent with your message to Congress." Goodrich conceded that he had so far refrained from publicly endorsing Soviet recognition. However, the conciliatory attitude of Stalin and other Soviet leaders convinced him that there was no time like the present. Coolidge was about to present to Congress his annual state of the union message and Goodrich suggested that it would make a perfect vehicle for reopening the Russian question. Recognition, advised Goodrich, would advance world stability, strengthen American business ties with Russia, and "accelerate rather than retard the march now going on from communism to capitalism." Even the persistent Goodrich must have been disappointed when the only response from Coolidge was a bland two-sentence note thanking him for his "very interesting letter on the situation in Russia. I am always glad to have your views and am obliged to you for writing me so fully."[33]

Goodrich was, therefore, disappointed but not shocked when Coolidge's state of the union message was entirely silent on the topic of Russia. As Goodrich wrote Fay Litvinov, he had greatly hoped the President "would again open the way for Russia as he did in 1923." The main obstacle, thought Goodrich, was the lack of widespread American public support for recognition. In fact, Goodrich told Mrs. Litvinov, "The ignorance of the American people concerning the real Russian situation is most discouraging." Coolidge, noted Goodrich, was by nature cautious and reluctant to take controversial actions. "In the absence of any general demand by the American people for the recognition of Russia," he concluded, "it is not likely he will be in any hurry to open the question." The only way Goodrich could see for reestablishing Soviet-American relations was for Moscow to approach Washington via diplomatic channels, preferably through Ambassador Alanson Houghton in London. The formula recommended by Goodrich was remarkably similar to the agreement Maxim Litvinov and President Franklin D. Roosevelt reached in 1933: in return for American recognition, the USSR would acknowledge its debt to the United States after adjustments were made for Soviet claims stemming from the allied intervention of 1918–1919. Finally the parties would promise to desist from propaganda. Maxim Litvinov, apparently under the impression that Goodrich's overture was officially inspired, eagerly responded through the Soviet representative in Paris. But from the perspective of Goodrich and Litvinov the results were just as disappointing as ever since the Coolidge administration showed no inclination to alter the status quo.[34] The debacle meant that Goodrich's personal crusade had reached an abrupt dead end. As he retired from the field, American recognition of Soviet Russia appeared to be no closer than at the time of Goodrich's first Russian encounter four years before.

9

"A Vote for Hoover is a Vote for Jim Goodrich"

In the final fifteen years of his life Goodrich remained active in business and Republican politics. Quietly he continued to favor American recognition of Russia. Since, for all practical purposes, public discussion of the question had ceased, he was frankly baffled as to what more he could do. Privately he kept open his Russian contacts, but was not able to offer much encouragement that a reversal of American policy was imminent. Writing to Fay Litvinov in January, 1927, Goodrich admitted he was "discouraged at times." Thoughtful Americans, such as himself, he said, were tired of having every world problem attributed to the machinations of the Kremlin. "Whether it is trouble in China, a Revolution in Mexico, a coup d'etat in Central America, a strike among the underpaid textile workers in New Jersey or whatever happens anywhere under the sun it is the Bolsheviks alone that are responsible for it all," he lamented. "Now I have a very great admiration for your great country and a genuine affection for the Russian people, but I do not believe even so great a country as yours has the power to set in motion forces throughout the world." Goodrich intended, he said, to pay a visit to Russia within a few months to visit Karelia. However, the trip failed to materialize when the Goodriches decided to remain at home due to the temporary illness of their son Pierre.[1]

Not only was Goodrich unable to make progress on recognition, but he twice failed—in 1928 and 1929—to convince the State Department to issue a visa to V. V. Ossinsky, the Vice Chairman of the Supreme Economic Council, who wished to tour American automobile plants and exhibitions. Goodrich was pleased that Soviet exports from the United States soared under the Five Year Plan, but was disappointed that the increased trade appeared to bring normal relations no closer. During an overnight stay at the White House (in the Lincoln suite) in February 1932, Goodrich raised with Hoover the possible recognition of Soviet Russia. Burdened with depression worries and the forthcoming presidential campaign, Hoover took the position: "No occasion to recognize Russia, no sentiment in country for it."[2]

Unable to make headway on Russia, Goodrich returned to his first love of Republican politics. Looking ahead to the presidential campaign of 1928, Goodrich foresaw the likely retirement of Calvin Coolidge and did all in his power to promote Herbert Hoover as his successor. "I think he is the one outstanding figure in this National Administration, the best bet and the greatest hope the Republican Party has," Goodrich wrote George Lockwood. "I think he is the greatest constructive power in America today and he has with it a vision and an idealism that prevents him from going to seed." His main disagreement with the Republican administration in Washington was over Treasury Secretary Andrew W. Mellon's "excessive reduction" of the progressive income tax. To Goodrich, who had proposed higher state taxes on the wealthy during his governorship, it was "pure moonshine" to claim that lower taxes on the rich would promote increased capital investment. Presumably a Hoover administration would correct such "silly" economic fallacies. "My fear has always been," wrote Goodrich, "that the hide-bound, narrow ultra-conservative politicians [he was probably thinking of Senator Jim Watson] would not follow his leadership."[3]

Goodrich's dreams became reality when President Coolidge announced his retirement in August, 1927. By the spring of 1928 Hoover had emerged as by far the strongest Republican candidate. But in Indiana Hoover ran athwart the ambition of Senator Watson, who desired to head Indiana's delegation as a favorite son. Watson's insistence on entering the primary against Hoover struck Goodrich as a self-centered decision which threatened to destroy party unity. "I have known him all his life," Goodrich wrote Representative Will Wood, "you are perfectly at liberty to tell him all I have said in this letter. There has never been a time and I can cite you to numerous occasions where the interest of the party conflicted with Jim's desires, when he didn't sacrifice the party. . . . I only have sympathy and pity for him. It is discouraging to see him with his really unusual ability betraying the great trust the people have committed into his hands, for the simple reason that he has no moral foundation on which to build. I say this not in anger but rather in sorrow." Goodrich was also embarrassed because Hoover's state campaign manager, Oscar Foellinger of Fort Wayne, pointedly asked him "to keep in the background." Goodrich felt Foellinger had displayed poor judgment, but felt he could not object on so personal a matter. "I have been and am so much for you," Goodrich wrote Hoover, "that I am willing to do, or not do whatever may seem best to advance your cause in this campaign." Temporarily Watson, who defeated Hoover in the Indiana primary election by 25,000 votes, carried the day. But Goodrich and Hoover had the last laugh as Hoover easily captured the presidential nomination at the Kansas City convention.[4]

In the fall election, with Goodrich again on the sidelines, Hoover carried Indiana and the nation over Governor Alfred E. Smith of New York. According to Goodrich, the Democrats of Indiana became so desperate in the final stages of the campaign as to distribute, through the "Independent Farmer's Organization," a broadside stating "A vote for Hoover is a vote for Jim Goodrich." The result, said Goodrich, "was to disgust all decent people and it hurt rather than helped them. It revealed the depth to which the opposition was willing to descend to accomplish their purpose." Nothing in his entire life, said Goodrich, had brought him "half the genuine satisfaction" as Hoover's election.[5]

Two weeks before Hoover began his administration Goodrich, just returned from a month's vacation in Panama, turned sixty-five years of age. Although he was in vigorous good health, Goodrich had no interest in serving Hoover in any official capacity and was content to remain on the periphery. Yet he and Hoover kept in contact through occasional correspondence and Goodrich's frequent business trips to Washington. Hoover first consulted Goodrich about the controversial case of former Indiana Governor Warren T. McCray, Goodrich's Republican successor in the state house. Personally Goodrich had no use whatsoever for McCray, who had been forced to resign in disgrace as governor of Indiana following his 1924 conviction on charges of mail fraud. No sooner had Hoover taken office than Representative Will Wood began strongly pressing for McCray's pardon and the President asked Goodrich what course of action he should follow. Goodrich's frank opinion was to reject the plea for clemency because "a public official who betrays his trust ought to be held to a stricter accountability than the average fellow." The sympathy for McCray, claimed Goodrich, was simply based on "an erroneous understanding of the facts." In an outspoken letter to Wood, which he enclosed to Hoover, Goodrich was even more explicit, calling McCray "a detestable scoundrel" and said he was "disgusted with a lot of the maudlin sympathy that has been wasted on him." Nevertheless, Goodrich predicted that Hoover would probably not be criticized in the event he decided to act as "McCray's friends and the great majority of the people who don't think things through, will approve his pardon." Apparently Hoover found Goodrich's arguments persuasive, as he declined to take immediate action on the clemency request. Shrewdly Hoover delayed until the psychologically favorable moment of Christmas Eve 1930 before granting the pardon.[6]

In the fall of 1929 Goodrich accepted Hoover's appointment to the Commission on Conservation and Management of the Public Domain. His decision to serve proved unwise, however, as Goodrich was philosophically at odds with the majority of the commission. As a former state governor Goodrich took the extreme position that all federal land should be surrendered to the states with the exception of sites for interstate power and flood control projects, national parks, and federal wetlands used by migratory birds. The states, he was positive, could better administer such land than Washington. In Goodrich's opinion the final report of the commission took steps that were "pitiably small" in relinquishing federal control and with "great reluctance" he agreed to sign a document he did not believe in. "My position is so diametrically opposite to that of the rest of the Commission that I wonder why I was put on it," he wrote James R. Garfield, the commission chairman. "I should have resigned when the report first came in."[7]

The Wall Street Crash and the economic collapse which rapidly followed caught Goodrich and most of his fellow Americans completely by surprise. It was luck, therefore, not clairvoyance, which led him to recommend to the ARA that it sell, in mid-August 1929, bonds of the Eastern Indiana Telephone Company, which had been purchased through Goodrich. In the initial stages of the depression Goodrich, in common with most Republicans, seriously underestimated the extent of the catastrophe. At first he claimed to see a silver lining and believed a temporary retrenchment would establish the foundation for an extended period of economic growth during the final two years of Hoover's term. The purchasing power produced by increased savings and repayment of debts would soon produce "a steady and sure improvement," he wrote on New Year's Day 1930. "I shall be greatly surprised," he stated, "if 1932 does not prove to be an unusually good year."[8]

As Goodrich's predictions failed to materialize he became more and more apprehensive about the prospects for Hoover's reelection. He applauded Hoover's proposal for a one-year moratorium on all intergovernmental debts (20 June 1931), but worried about the continued economic slump. A further concern was that the party might become "tangled up on the prohibition question." If only the long-awaited business recovery would begin, he wrote to Lincoln Hutchinson, Hoover's reelection would be assured. But by the fall of 1931 Goodrich, "burdened with cares as I have never been before," was losing his optimism. "Do you think things have finally reached bottom?" he wrote George Barr Baker. "It rather occurs to me that if we have not arrived at that point that we are very close to it."[9]

As a self-made man Goodrich opposed in principle government intervention on behalf of farmers, businessmen, or the destitute. Twice before in his lifetime, in the 1870s and the 1890s, America had recovered from depressions without resorting to radical demands for unlimited paper money or free silver. Philosophically Goodrich agreed with Grover Cleveland's view, "It is the duty of the people to support the government, not the duty of the government to support the people." From the beginning of Hoover's administration, therefore, Goodrich had opposed the creation of a farm board to purchase surpluses. Goodrich did not care that the Republican platform of 1928 had endorsed federal aid to the farmer. He was sure that the solution to agricultural surpluses lay not in Washington, but back on the farm. "All about me in our county," he wrote George Lockwood, "I see farmers going about their business, making money and saving it. Such people have no faith in the promises of bills settled and others who are receiving high salaries for telling the farmer they are only one step ahead of the sheriff and that it is the patriotic duty of the government to help them out."[10]

Balancing the federal budget, Goodrich believed, was "of imperative necessity" to the restoration of prosperity. He repeatedly urged Indiana's senators to cut government expenses to the absolute minimum by eliminating useless officials and cutting excessive salaries. "In every business that I know of, when faced with a deficit, the first thing done is to cut expenses," he wrote Watson. In particular Goodrich was incensed by the extravagant budget of the post office, which employed "girls and boys who could not to save their souls go out in private life and make anything like $1000.00 a year who are getting $2100.00 to $2400.00 a year with vacation, thirty day sick leave and a pension." Not only would cutting salaries and employees be good economics it would also be good politics. Goodrich recounted that Representative Wood had, "without my consent," read during a House debate a Goodrich letter urging a slash in federal salaries. "I was amazed," he noted, "at the number of letters and telegrams received from all over the State, commending me for my courage." In his opinion it was "a deplorable thing" that Congress had failed to retrench sufficiently while at the same time increasing taxes and thereby making the recovery more difficult.[11]

To Goodrich's consternation his prediction that 1932 would be a banner year proved ludicrous. On the eve of the presidential campaign the one-time optimist conceded "the immediate future does not look one bit good." Still, he regarded the Republican cause as by no means hopeless. By fall, just in time for the election, Goodrich looked for an improvement in business and employment. Furthermore, in the person of Hoover the Republicans had a candidate who was "gaining in strength every day." Another favorable factor, thought Goodrich, was the Democrats' nomination of Franklin D. Roosevelt, a candidate who was "extremely vulnerable." Goodrich advised Hoover not only to defend his record, but to go on the attack. He would assail Roosevelt's radicalism in regard to the issues of public electrical power and government planning of the economy. He also advised that Hoover emphasize "the well known condition of Mr. Roosevelt's health" and the danger that John Nance Garner, the Democratic vice presidential candidate, might succeed to the presidency. "I was greatly discouraged a few weeks ago over the outlook," he wrote Hoover on 12 July. "The result is yet by no means certain, but I believe that with an intelligent and vigorous campaign, such as you know how to inaugurate and carry on, we can carry this State with the National ticket and you can be re-elected." A month later Goodrich, having listened to Hoover's acceptance speech on the radio, was still hopeful. He told Hoover his speech "will rank as one of the great state papers of our country," and predicted that many Democrats would support the Republican ticket.[12]

For all his brave posturing Goodrich, the political veteran, was not surprised when the voters sent Hoover to an early retirement. In his diary Goodrich noted: "His election has been impossible from the beginning. Tragedy of it is that Hoover in order to meet emergencies growing out of depression has surrendered convictions of a lifetime. I hope that he never again will be a candidate for any public office but will retire gracefully."[13] Almost immediately, however, Goodrich backed away from his own election day recriminations. As he contemplated the programs of the new Democratic administration and the lack of leadership in the Republican party, Goodrich, during the remaining eight years of his life, made repeated efforts to draft Hoover for another contest with Roosevelt.

From its very beginning Goodrich regarded Roosevelt's New Deal as a calamity for the nation. Writing to Hoover just six months after the inauguration, Goodrich painted a dismal picture. Businessmen were being coerced by the National Recovery Administration (Goodrich himself was so busy "trying to dodge or comply" with NRA codes that he had no time for anything else), and farmers were "distinctly worse off than they have been for the last two years." The average man had lost purchasing power due to inflation and the national debt had soared, which meant "high taxes for another generation at least." Essentially Goodrich believed the New Deal was unnecessary: "Had we been permitted to go on without Government interference, while we might have had the wage increase that follows every recovery, yet with increasing employment and accelerated demand for goods and a gradual improvement in farm prices already under way, our situation would have been vastly better, in my opinion, than it is at this time." Looking ahead to the 1934 elections, Goodrich predicted a major Republican resurgence. In Indiana the party would win a Senate seat and nine of the twelve congressmen "just as certain as the election day comes and nothing can prevent it."[14]

Two months after Goodrich wrote that bitter critique, Roosevelt surprised and pleased Goodrich by taking the first steps toward the recognition of the Soviet Union. Roosevelt addressed a letter to President Michail Kalinin suggesting the start of negotiations and in return Maxim Litvinov agreed to come to Washington for discussions with the President. Goodrich used the occasion to offer Roosevelt support and advice:

> I have delayed writing you relative to the recognition of Russia. Although I am not of your political faith, as you know, I want to congratulate you upon the invitation extended to Russia to send someone here to discuss the matter of the resumption of relations between America and Russia.
>
> I am glad to know Mr. Litvinov is coming over. I got quite well acquainted with him on my four trips to Russia. He is a man of undoubted ability, sensible and realistic in his dealings.
>
> I trust that you will see your way clear to extend recognition without any strings tied to it and then sit down as equals and discuss the question of just how the situation is to be handled.
>
> Experience and observation have taught me that Russia can be depended upon to meet her obligations, her record in that respect is at least as good as that of any of our "associates" in the World War.
>
> I shall not hesitate publicly and otherwise to support you in this matter.

In return Goodrich received a note of appreciation from Roosevelt thanking him for his support.[15]

With the exception of Roosevelt's recognition of the Soviet Union on 17 November 1933, Goodrich continued to be steadfastly opposed to the "crazy program at Washington." To Senator Arthur Robinson, Goodrich exploded: "Oh the folly of this AAA." His outburst was triggered by the decision of the Agricultural Adjustment Administration to compensate dust bowl wheat farmers, at taxpayers' expense, for their ruined crops. "This will be 'peaches and cream,'" he protested, "for the drought stricken areas where the wheat crop has already been ruined and they could never harvest it anyway." In Indiana, he predicted, public indignation against New Deal waste would elect six Republican congressmen (down from the nine he had predicted the year before). Goodrich's ability as a prophet was sadly tarnished when the Democrats retained all twelve House seats and defeated Senator Robinson.[16]

Following the 1934 debacle Goodrich turned his sights to the 1936 presidential campaign. Believing "this administration has been wrong from the beginning and is getting worse all the time," he began casting about for a dynamic candidate to head the ticket against Roosevelt. Herbert Hoover was by far his first choice to challenge the New Deal. "No one," Goodrich wrote Hoover, "is so well qualified as you to do the job and as time goes on, to no one will the people listen as they will to you." Hoover owed the country a patriotic duty to run again, contended Goodrich. And he would benefit from the fact that each day some Democrat or Republican who had voted for Roosevelt regretted the decision. Goodrich had hoped to visit Hoover at his Palo Alto home to press his cause in person, but was unable to make the trip due to the demands of his business. By letter, therefore, Goodrich tried to remind Hoover of his duty to the party and the nation. He recalled that Cleveland had announced he would not run for the presidency in 1892, yet was nominated and elected. "History has a habit of repeating itself," noted Goodrich. "That might happen in this case. For your own comfort and peace of mind, I hope it won't happen, but looking at it from the point of view of the whole country, one is compelled to reach a different conclusion."[17]

As late as January, 1936, Goodrich was still advocating Hoover as Roosevelt's opponent in the fall election. "Hoover," he wrote Frank Litschert, "is furnishing the only leadership of any kind in the Republican Party." With Hoover at the helm the Republicans would carry the country. "This whole New Deal," he believed, "is bound to go to smash. . . . Roosevelt and the whole outfit are mad, charging everyone who fails to agree with them, with bad faith." By spring Goodrich was finally convinced that Hoover had no intention of entering the race, and he turned to Kansas Governor Alf Landon.[18]

Goodrich attended the Cleveland convention and, as a member of the platform committee, fought a bitter losing battle for the endorsement of the gold standard. His respect for Landon was greatly increased when the candidate dramatically restored the gold plank, thereby vindicating Goodrich. His sole reservation about Landon was his endorsement of an "unsound" platform provision promising to pay subsidies to farmers on all crops which were produced in surplus. "I like Landon," he concluded. "I think he is honest, clean and courageous, but he has about him many advisors whose opinions are influenced by an aggressive farm leadership and have misled him as to the real situation." Through the summer Goodrich remained hopeful that Landon would attract a coalition of Republican and Democratic farmers and businessmen. Roosevelt's landslide margin of victory came as an unpleasant, but not wholly unexpected, surprise. The trouble, thought Goodrich, had not been so much Landon, but the platform written by conservative eastern Republicans. "If the Republican Party is to be a conservative party, I am not interested in it," he wrote his friend Richard Scandrett, Jr. "My natural place is with the liberals, but not the kind of liberals that have infested Washington for the past four years."[19]

Despite his immersion in Republican politics, Goodrich continued to monitor developments in Russia. In November, 1935 he wrote Maxim Litvinov inquiring about making a fifth Russian tour and perhaps bringing with him an automobile. "I am very glad to learn that you have not lost interest in my country and are contemplating revisiting it," replied Litvinov. His advice was for Goodrich to leave his car in America and to rely upon the Russian railroads for transportation. Probably it was the demands of the 1936 campaign which caused Goodrich to shelve the idea for a year. Early in 1937 Goodrich made new inquiries through John L. Van Zant, a correspondent for the *Moscow News*. His idea was to visit "some of the best of their state farms," the Donetz coal basin, and a number of unspecified industries. "From translations which reach me every week from the Russian papers . . . ," he noted, "the inefficiency in the coal mines and the management of their farms must be very bad. I wanted to check it. Outside of such an investigation, I would only want to spend a few days in Moscow to see the changes that are taking place."[20] Whether such a trip (which coincided with the brutal purging of Kamenev, Radek, Rykov, and others) would have caused him to reappraise his opinion of Stalin is unknown because Goodrich was forced to cancel the trip when he suffered a serious heart attack in June, 1937.

The illness brought Goodrich, now seventy-three years old, even closer to death than had his typhoid fever attack in 1917. On the recommendation of his physician, he spent ten weeks at Johns Hopkins Hospital in Baltimore for an evaluation of his condition. His doctors, he related to his wife, made him sit up each day one hour longer than the day before, and they were "also requiring me to walk a little more each day until I am tired, then quit." Goodrich used his recuperation to get his financial affairs in order; his son Pierre was asked to draw up deeds to the family farm and a block of office buildings, to sell a lot in Union City, and to disconnect the garage phone since "I am quite sure I will not need it again." Possibly it was at this time that Goodrich began telling visitors how much he would regret missing out on all the money to be made in the coming years. He endured his two-month stay at Johns Hopkins accepting "just day after day of the same thing." "All this," he wrote a friend, "attempting to patch up my heart for a longer life of one who has about lived out his time. I am very cheerful about everything." In reality Goodrich was for a time quite discouraged, as his son pointed out to his cardiologist. In response Dr. Lewis Hammond advised Goodrich that his condition was by no means hopeless and that he might, assuming a good recovery, be able to regain his active life.[21]

Spending the winter of 1937–38 at Fort Lauderdale, Florida enabled Goodrich to make progress both physically and mentally. Slowly regaining strength, he turned his attention to reducing his estate for the benefit of Wabash College. While still at Johns Hopkins he established a trust for the college of $220,000, which permitted the construction of the Goodrich Hall of Physical Sciences, a building which was dedicated on 5 June 1938. "I am greatly interested in the development of Wabash," Goodrich wrote Professor John Cass, "and if my life is spared until spring, shall do something substantial in addition to what I have already done." What he had in mind was the establishment of another trust fund of $100,000 to support graduate education. Altogether he contributed more than $380,000 to Wabash College, a total which did not include anonymous gifts made in his capacity as the college's "financial angel." Hanover College at Hanover, Indiana was another recipient of Goodrich's largesse, receiving over $92,000. On 14 June 1938 Goodrich was well enough to travel to Hanover to receive a doctor of laws degree, an honor which appears not to have occurred to the trustees of Wabash College.[22]

One advantage of his weakened physical condition was that Goodrich was able to find ample time for reading. With "a great deal of care" he read Adolph Hitler's *Mein Kampf*. His reading, combined with Hitler's absorption of Austria and Czechoslovakia, and the Nazi assault on Poland in September 1939, convinced Goodrich that the "fool neutrality law" of 1937 should be repealed. That statute, "which never should have been passed," forbade American loans or the sale of arms to either side in the event of another conflict. By denying the Allies access to American munitions, pointed out Goodrich, the law "decidedly favored Hitler." For one of the few times in his life, therefore, Goodrich found himself on the side of Franklin D. Roosevelt, who proposed the repeal of the arms embargo. Over bitter Republican resistance, including that of Goodrich's congressman, Raymond Springer, Roosevelt finally got his way. "I think those who argued against the law [the repeal of the arms embargo] failed to deal with the realities," Goodrich wrote Springer. "I think it is fortunate for America, for civilization, and especially important for you fellows who voted against the law that it was finally enacted."[23] Had he lived, Goodrich would have been a likely candidate for membership in William Allen White's Committee to Defend America by Aiding the Allies.

In the spring of 1940 Goodrich was seriously ill with pneumonia and was confined to bed and briefly hospitalized during March and April. At first it appeared he would be unable to attend the Republican convention at Philadelphia. By the middle of May he had sufficiently recovered to consider making the trip. His first choice for the nomination was New York District Attorney Thomas E. Dewey and his second choice was Senator Robert A. Taft of Ohio; philosophically he preferred Herbert Hoover most of all. Wendell Willkie of Indiana, whom Goodrich heard address the state Republican Committee on 15 May, impressed Goodrich as a fine orator, but he dismissed Willkie as an outsider and a political lightweight. As he wrote Dewey, "There is nothing to his candidacy. If I continue to recover my strength I shall be able to attend the convention and will be either a delegate at large or from my district whichever my choice may be. I want to go if possible and will if my health permits." He could not resist a parting shot at Jim Watson, who intended to be a Dewey delegate: "Your friends hope he will remain of that opinion until the national convention meets." However, Goodrich probably agreed with Watson's characterization of Willkie, a one-time Democrat, as a reformed prostitute who wanted to lead the choir immediately after joining the church.[24] Elected as a delegate from the tenth Indiana district, Goodrich thoroughly enjoyed the Philadelphia convention and accepted philosophically its choice of Willkie for the Republican nomination.

On his return to Winchester, Goodrich experienced a reoccurrence of a "nervous heart" and spent the first week of August confined to his home. The setback did not prevent him from offering Willkie encouragement and political advice. As the result of his own "special investigation," Goodrich wrote Willkie on 10 August, "there is no doubt in my mind but that you will carry Indiana by a very large majority." He congratulated the candidate for his decision that the

Republican National Committee would not place any speakers on its payroll. Goodrich recalled his years as Indiana state chairman when he had been "pestered to death" by Republicans seeking pay for their oratorical efforts. "It was seldom," he noted, "that any of these could do the party any good." He advised Willkie to concentrate his efforts upon winning the votes of Indiana's industrial workers; among farmers he detected "a decided trend" to the Republican cause. "I do not believe any President has ever, on his inauguration, faced as serious a situation as you will confront next January," he concluded. As for himself Goodrich said he intended, as soon as he was able, to make a second trip to John Hopkins "to get straightened out." As noted by Pierre Goodrich in a telegram to Willkie, Goodrich's letter of 10 August was the last he wrote to anyone. The next day he suffered a stroke and died four days later at the Randolph County Hospital of an apparent heart attack.[25]

At the time of his death at age seventy-six, Jim Goodrich had been out of office for so long that his was no longer a household name in his home state. Almost twenty years had elapsed since Goodrich had completed his single unhappy term as governor of Indiana, and it had been almost fifteen years since the last of his trips to Russia—an activity that had generated little publicity or political results. Historically he has attracted little attention either; he is seldom mentioned in histories of progressivism or Soviet-American relations. Part of the explanation may be that his governorship coincided with the very end of the progressive era and was overshadowed by the nation's participation in World War I. Even his efforts on behalf of Soviet Russia have been ignored, partly because Goodrich's public role was so ambiguous. Tactfully he had avoided association with radical causes. Not once did Goodrich in public, although he often did in private, explicitly advocate American recognition of the Soviet Union.

In Indiana he was remembered as much for his role as a power behind the scenes in the Republican Party as for his governorship. Lacking a commanding voice and oratorical flamboyance, Goodrich found his niche as Republican state chairman. He was in his element constructing a political machine starting at the precinct level and exchanging gossip and sharing male conviviality with "the boys," both old and young, of the party. All the while he pragmatically sought to balance the competing interests of conservatives and progressives. Goodrich always regarded himself as a progressive Republican, as assessment which was accurate enough from an Indiana, if not a national, perspective. Many of his difficulties as governor he blamed on the reactionary wing of his own party. Reflecting on his four years as Indiana's wartime governor, Goodrich tended to remember only such traumatic experiences as the rejection of his tax plan by traitorous Republicans, his life-threatening bout with typhoid fever, and his crippling automobile accident. In his own mind he equated personal distress with failure. In reality, Goodrich had achieved a solid record as a businesslike administrator who eliminated useless state positions while promoting such progressive programs as tax reform and conservation of natural resources. Woman suffrage was the only major progressive idea unacceptable to Goodrich, but as a practical politician he had the good sense to conceal his views on the subject.

After leaving the governorship he remained an influential member of the party and did not regret the "unhorsing" of the Watson faction. But Goodrich would not acknowledge the assistance rendered by Franklin D. Roosevelt in Watson's demise since, like many self-made businessmen, he was shocked by the Democrats' "crazy" expenditures on public works, relief, agricultural price supports, and by Roosevelt's experiments in public power and social security. For the party to fight the New Deal, he believed, was as basic and necessary a cause as the Republicans' opposition to agrarian radicalism in the 1870s and 1890s. All about him he saw examples of boondoggling waste—in paying farmers to reduce acreage while they increased production on their remaining land, or (as described in a favorite Goodrich story) in sending ten Works Progress Administration men to construct a privy "that one hatchet and saw carpenter could have done in a day without the slightest difficulty," or in "helping the farmer" by handing out payments for rotating crops "which every intelligent farmer in my State has been doing for fifty years." "If we are ever going to balance the budget," he wrote New York Senator Royal S. Copeland, "this sort of thing, and along with it the P.W.A. and matters of that kind, must cease."[26]

Yet Goodrich did not permit his ideological distaste for the New Deal to become personal. In 1939 he sent a heartfelt message of congratulation to Eleanor Roosevelt for having criticized the Daughters of the American Revolution because the group denied the black singer Marian Anderson the use of Constitution Hall. "It was so stupid of them to do this and so fine and brave and generous for you to condemn their actions. You have forgotten me long since, but I met you at the conference of Governors, French Lick Springs, something over ten years ago."[27]

Notwithstanding his immersion in Republican politics, the cause that most appealed to Goodrich, and the one that occupied the bulk of his writings and papers, was normalizing Soviet-American relations. At age fifty-seven, mainly because of his political connections and availability, he was asked to tour the Volga famine district on behalf of Herbert Hoover and the American Relief Administration. Speaking "straight from the shoulder" Goodrich told the 1925 ARA reunion, "It was a great work, and a great privilege to be in it, and I count it really as the most distinguished honor that ever came to me to have had some part in the work of the ARA."[28] Entering Russia almost completely without information, Goodrich approached his task using the same methods that had worked for him in business and politics: he rolled up his sleeves and went to work by riding trains, river boats, and wagons, sometimes through the night, seeking to assemble the "brass-tack facts" about Russia. In the process he demonstrated toughness, youthful vigor, and open-mindedness. And Goodrich came to admire the courage and character of the Russian people, who reminded him of "the folks at home."

As a prophet his vision was imperfect and too optimistic. He was handicapped by his lack of information about the revolution and its background, which contributed to his failure to see that Lenin's New Economic Policy was only a temporary retreat. Viewing the Bolsheviks as honest but ignorant idealists, he had difficulty appreciating the deep ideological commitment of the Soviet leaders to establishing socialism. He was also mistaken in thinking that the Soviets were so desperate for American trade, loans, and recognition that they would restore confiscated property and settle debts. Moreover, despite his four trips to Russia and his contacts in the Republican party of America and the Communist Party of the Soviet Union, he made little progress in moderating American policy. Seemingly he had failed. Paradoxically, however, it was the pragmatic views of Goodrich that ultimately found acceptance in America, and not the rigid, moralistic, and legalistic views of his opponents. Yet establishing harmonious United States-Soviet relations proved a far more formidable, complicated, and time-consuming process than envisaged by Goodrich.

If he was not always right on the details, Goodrich frequently saw the overall picture more clearly than the so-called "experts" who confidently expected the Soviets to collapse. His assessment of the "plain facts" about Russia led him to conclude that the revolution was an accomplished fact, that the Soviets had the support of the vast majority of the Russian people, that they were capable of maintaining law and order, and that they faced no visible opposition. His travels and contacts with the highest Soviet leaders led him to the conclusion that the United States should extend diplomatic recognition, encourage trade, and accept Soviet Russia as a legitimate factor in world politics. At the same time he saw no reason to retreat from his conviction that Communism was but an idle dream, applicable only to a land of lotus eaters, not to the real world. Demonstrating a remarkable degree of intellectual independence and political courage, Goodrich refused to be stampeded by the conventional wisdom of the day and made up his mind on the basis of the evidence before him. His pragmatic approach to Soviet-American relations was vividly illustrated by an early morning incident on the Volga when he recorded:

19 October [1921]. My cup of bitterness and dissatisfaction is now full and running over. At exactly 4:00 A.M. the secretary to the governor came thundering at our door telling us to hurry to make the boat as it would soon sail. In fifteen minutes we were ready and after much trouble a Cadillac car turned over to Deniken and captured by the Soviets conveyed us to the dock. No boat in sight and finally we were told it would not sail until the next day. I was mad enough to swear, but what was the use; they wouldn't understand English so I laughed instead and made up my mind not to hem and haw, but to take Russia as it is and not as I would have it.[29]

Notes

Preface

1. Herter to Hoover, 1 June 1922, quoted in Terence Emmons and Bertrand M. Patenaude, *War, Revolution, and Peace in Russia: The Passages of Frank Golder, 1914–1927* (Stanford, Calif.: Hoover Institution Press, 1992), 181 (n).
2. Herbert Hoover, *The Cabinet and the Presidency*, vol. 2, *The Memoirs of Herbert Hoover* (New York: The Macmillan Company, 1952), 23, 191, 239.
3. James K. Libbey, *Alexander Gumberg and Soviet-American Relations, 1917–1933* (Lexington: University Press of Kentucky, 1977), 79–81.
4. William E. Wilson, *Indiana: A History* (Bloomington: Indiana University Press, 1966), 104.

Chapter 1. "A Country Lawyer from Over at Winchester"

1. Muncie *Evening Press*, 16 August 1940, Winchester *Journal-Herald*, 16 August 1940, Indianapolis *News*, 16 August 1940, *New York Times*, 17 August 1940, Box 4, James P. Goodrich Papers (Herbert Hoover Presidential Library, West Branch, Iowa); Goodrich to Arthur K. Remmel, 24 January 1922, Box 15, Goodrich Papers. Goodrich's role in the Russian operations of the American Relief Administration is briefly traced in Harold H. Fisher, *The Famine in Soviet Russia, 1919–1923: The Operations of the American Relief Administration* (New York: Macmillan, 1927), 143–50; Frank Alfred Golder and Lincoln Hutchinson, *On the Trail of the Russian Famine* (Stanford, Calif.: Stanford University Press, 1927), 75–89; and Benjamin M. Weissman, *Herbert Hoover and Famine Relief to Soviet Russia, 1921–1923* (Stanford, Calif.: Hoover Institution Press, 1974), 97, 109, 130, 136–38, 180–81.
2. Indianapolis *News*, 24 June 1950, Winchester *Journal-Herald*, 16 August 1940, Box 4, Goodrich Papers.
3. Autobiography of James P. Goodrich, 3–6, Box 4, Goodrich Papers.
4. Ibid., 7–19, Box 4, Goodrich Papers.
5. Ibid., 19, 29, Box 4, Goodrich Papers.
6. Ibid., 30–31, 22–23, Box 4, Goodrich Papers.
7. Ibid., 23–24, 26–27, Box 4, Goodrich Papers.
8. Ibid., 27–29, Box 4, Goodrich Papers.
9. Ibid., 24–26, Box 4, Goodrich Papers.
10. Ibid., 28–29, 66, 106, 89–91, Box 4, Goodrich Papers. Watson, in his memoir *As I Knew Them* (Indianapolis, Ind.: Bobbs-Merrill, 1936), makes no mention of Goodrich.
11. Goodrich Autobiography, 38–39, Box 4, Goodrich Papers.
12. Ibid., 41–43, Box 4, Goodrich Papers.
13. Ibid., 44–45, Box 4, Goodrich Papers.
14. Ibid., 47–51, Box 4, Goodrich Papers.

15. Ibid., 51–54, Box 4, Goodrich Papers.
16. Ibid., 53–64, Box 4, Goodrich Papers; Clifton J. Phillips, *Indiana in Transition: The Emergence of an Industrial Commonwealth, 1880–1920* (Indianapolis: Indiana Historical Bureau and Indiana Historical Society, 1968), 92.
17. Goodrich Autobiography, 69–75, Box 4, Goodrich Papers.
18. Ibid. 78–83, Box 4, Goodrich Papers; Phillips, *Indiana in Transition*, 100–101, 106.
19. Ibid., 82–84, Box 4, Goodrich Papers.
20. Ibid., 86, 109, 111, Box 4, Goodrich Papers.
21. Ibid., 86–88, Box 4, Goodrich Papers.
22. Ibid., 92–97, Box 4, Goodrich Papers; Phillips, *Indiana in Transition*, 117–18.
23. Ibid., 98, Box 4, Goodrich Papers; Phillips, *Indiana in Transition*, 119.
24. Ibid., 99–100, Box 4, Goodrich Papers; Phillips, *Indiana in Transition*, 121.
25. Ibid., 100–106, Box 4, Goodrich Papers.
26. Ibid., 110–11, Box 4, Goodrich Papers.
27. Will H. Hays, *The Memoirs of Will H. Hays* (Garden City, New York: Doubleday, 1955), 108.
28. Goodrich Autobiography, 112–13, Box 4, Goodrich Papers; James H. Madison, *The Indiana Way: A State History* (Bloomington: Indiana University Press, 1986), 225.
29. Goodrich Autobiography, 112–13, Box 4, Goodrich Papers; Hays, *Memoirs*, 106–7. Hays's skillful organization of the 1916 campaign is treated in James O. Robertson, "Progressives Elect Will H. Hays Republican National Chairman, 1918," *Indiana Magazine of History*, 64; (September, 1968): 173–90.

Chapter 2. A Hoosier Caesar?

1. Goodrich Autobiography, 117–20. Goodrich's term as governor is briefly treated in Madison, *The Indiana Way*, 221–22; Phillips, *Indiana in Transition*, 126–27, 611–12; Philip R. VanderMeer, *The Hoosier Politician: Officeholding and Political Culture in Indiana, 1896–1920* (Urbana: University of Illinois Press, 1985), 19, 65, 196–97; Hays, *Memoirs*, 106–38; and Charles F. Remy, "Governor Goodrich and Indiana Tax Legislation," *Indiana Magazine of History* 43 (March, 1947): 41–56.
2. Indianapolis *Daily Times*, January 10, 23, 1917; Indianapolis *News*, 17, 18 January 1917; Goodrich Autobiography, 128, Box 4, Goodrich Papers.
3. Goodrich Autobiography, 107, 121–26, Box 4, Goodrich Papers; Indianapolis *News*, 23 February, 5 March, 1917.
4. Phillips, *Indiana in Transition*, 596–97; Goodrich Autobiography, 128–33, Box 4, Goodrich Papers; Indianapolis *Star*, 22 August 1917; John D. Barnhart and Donald F. Carmony, *Indiana: From Frontier to Commonwealth* (New York: Lewis Historical Publishing Company, 1954), 2, 381.
5. Litschert to Goodrich, 15 September 1939, Box 4, Goodrich Papers; Goodrich to Dr. C. S. Wood, 22 October 1917, Box 6, Goodrich Papers; Indianapolis *Star*, 21 October 1917; Goodrich Autobiography, 136–37, Box 4, Goodrich Papers; Goodrich to Randolph G. Leeds, 5 November 1917, Box 6, Goodrich Papers.
6. Goodrich Autobiography, 139–42, Box 4, Goodrich Papers.
7. Indianapolis *Star*, 17 May 1918; Goodrich Autobiography, 147–51, Box 4, Goodrich Papers.
8. Goodrich Autobiography, 151–52, Box 4, Goodrich Papers; Goodrich to

Emma and Mary Hunt, 31 August 1918, and Goodrich to Charles M. Kimbrough, 9 September 1918, Box 6, Goodrich Papers; Indianapolis *News,* 29 August 1918.

9. Goodrich to A. C. Richardt, 15 January 1919, Box 6, Goodrich Papers; Beveridge to Goodrich, 5 April 1919, Box 1, Goodrich Papers; Goodrich to Fred Buggie, 10 June 1919, Box 1, Goodrich Papers; Goodrich to Mahlon M. Garland, 17 October 1919, Box 3, Goodrich Papers.

10. Goodrich Autobiography, 153–56, Box 4, Goodrich Papers.

11. Indianapolis *Star,* 2, 12 March 1919; Indianapolis *News,* 11 March 1919; Goodrich Autobiography, 157–59, Box 4, Goodrich Papers.

12. Goodrich Autobiography, 157–63, Box 4, Goodrich Papers; Indianapolis *News,* 5 April 1919.

13. Goodrich Autobiography, 161, 186, Box 4, Goodrich Papers.

14. Ibid., 155–56, 168, Box 4, Goodrich Papers.

15. Ibid., 168, 171–73, 179, Box 4, Goodrich Papers; Indianapolis *Star,* 2 May 1919.

16. Goodrich Autobiography, 177, Box 4, Goodrich Papers; F. C. Ball to Goodrich, 26 May 1919, Box 25, Goodrich Papers; Indianapolis *Star,* 5 July, 3 August, 15 October 1919; Indianapolis *News,* 10 September 1919; T. E. Myers to Goodrich, 26 May 1919, Box 25, Goodrich Papers; George Patterson to Goodrich, 26, May 1919, Box 25, Goodrich Papers.

17. Goodrich Autobiography, 180, Box 4, Goodrich Papers; Goodrich to Hays, 24 January 1920, Box 11, Goodrich Papers.

18. Goodrich Autobiography, 180, 183–85, Box 4, Goodrich Papers; Indianapolis *Star,* 6 May 1920.

19. Goodrich to New, 3 April 1920, Box 13, Goodrich Papers; Indianapolis *Star,* 13 July, 11 October 1919; Indianapolis *News,* 13 July, 26 August, 1919.

20. Indianapolis *News,* 1 November 1920; Goodrich to Harding, 14 September 1920, Box 10, Goodrich Papers.

21. Indianapolis *Star,* 4 November 1920; Indianapolis *News,* 10 January 1921.

22. Remarks of Goodrich delivered at the inauguration of Warren T. McCray, 10 January 1921, Box 26, Goodrich Papers.

23. Goodrich to Watson, 15 January 1917, Box 28, Goodrich Papers; Indianapolis *Star,* 12 November 1920.

Chapter 3. A Short Retirement

1. Goodrich to Harding, 14 September 1920, Box 10, Goodrich Papers; Marion, Indiana, *Leader-Tribune,* 5 July 1919, Box 25, Goodrich Papers; Goodrich speech 1 March 1920 (enclosed in Goodrich to Haley Fiske), 5 March 1920, Box 26, Goodrich Papers.

2. For the New Economic Policy see Edward Hallett Carr, *A History of Soviet Russia,* Vol. 2, *The Bolshevik Revolution, 1917–1923* (London: Macmillan, 1952), 280–383; Georg von Rauch, *A History of Soviet Russia* (New York: Praeger, 1967), 124–31; and Adam B. Ulam, *A History of Soviet Russia* (New York: Praeger, 1967), 59–87.

3. Maxim Gorky's appeal to the American people, 23 July 1921, *Documents of the American Relief Administration, 1921–1923,* ed. H. H. Fisher and Suda L. Bane (10 typed volumes, Stanford University, Calif., 1931), 1, 1–2. See also Harold J. Goldberg, ed., *Intervention, Famine Relief, International Affairs, 1917–1933,* vol.

1, *Documents of Soviet-American Relations* (Gulf Breeze, Florida: Academic International Press, 1993), 198–99.

4. Fisher, *Famine in Soviet Russia*, 65–67, 160–62, 457–68; Weissman, *Hoover and Famine Relief*, 85, 96–101; League of Nations, *Report on Economic Conditions in Russia with Special Reference to the Famine of 1921–1922 and the State of Agriculture* (Nancy, France, 1922), 26–56.

5. Data sheet of William H. Haskell, Box 1-A/259, ARA Personnel Records, Hoover Presidential Library; Hoover to Hays, 22 August 1922, Box 276, Records of the American Relief Administration, Russian Operations, 1921–1923 (Archives of the Hoover Institution on War, Revolution and Peace, Stanford, California). This collection is hereafter cited as ARA Records.

6. Goodrich to Hays, 21 August 1921, Box 276, ARA Records.

7. Hoover to Goodrich, 23 August 1921, Box 276, ARA Records; Goodrich to Hoover, 24 August 1921, Box 276, ARA Records.

8. *ARA Association Review*, vol. 1, no. 1 (1 April 1925), 13; Goodrich, "Manuscript on Various Trips to Russia, 1921–1922," Introductory Chapter, 7, Box 16, Goodrich Papers; Goodrich to Hoover, 30 August 1921, Box 276, ARA Records; Hoover to Goodrich 1 September 1921, Box 276, ARA Records.

9. Goodrich, "Manuscript on Various Trips to Russia," Introductory Chapter, 6–7, Box 16, Goodrich Papers.

10. Galpin to Christian A. Herter, 20 September 1921, Box 276, ARA Records.

11. Herter to Galpin, 21 September 1921, Box 276, ARA Records.

12. "Report from Geo. Repp," *Newsletter of the Volga Relief Society*, 3 October 1922, Box 276, ARA Records.

13. James P. Goodrich diary, 27, 28 September 1921, Box 17, Goodrich Papers.

14. Goodrich diary, 29 September 1921, Box 17, Goodrich Papers.

15. Ibid., 1 October 1921, Box 17, Goodrich Papers.

16. Ibid., 3 October 1921, Box 17, Goodrich Papers.

17. Goodrich, "Manuscript on Various Trips to Russia," Chapter "A," 4, Box 16, Goodrich Papers.

18. Goodrich diary, 3 October 1921, Box 17, Goodrich Papers.

19. Ibid., 4 October 1921, Box 17, Goodrich Papers.

20. Ibid., 5 October 1921, Box 17, Goodrich Papers.

21. Ibid., 6 October 1921, Box 17, Goodrich Papers.

22. Goodrich, "Manuscript on Various Trips to Russia," Chapter "A," 9–10, Box 16, Goodrich Papers.

23. Goodrich diary, 8 October 1921, Box 17, Goodrich Papers; Goodrich, "Manuscript on Various Trips to Russia," Chapter "B," 2, Box 16, Goodrich Papers.

24. Goodrich, "Manuscript on Various Trips to Russia," Chapter "B," 4, Box 16, Goodrich Papers. For sympathetic portraits of Golder see Alain Dubie, *Frank A. Golder: An Adventure of a Historian in Quest of Russian History* (Boulder, Colo.: East European Monographs, 1989), 268; and Terence Emmons and Bertrand M. Patenaude, eds., *War, Revolution, and Peace in Russia: The Passages of Frank Golder, 1914–1917* (Stanford, Calif.: Hoover Institution Press, 1992).

25. Goodrich, "Manuscript on Various Trips to Russia," Chapter "B," 3–4, Box 16, Goodrich Papers; Goodrich diary, 9, 14 October 1921, Box 17, Goodrich Papers.

26. Goodrich diary, 9 October 1921, Box 17, Goodrich Papers; Goodrich, "Manuscript on Various Trips to Russia," Chapter "B," 10, Box 16, Goodrich Papers.

27. Goodrich diary, 9 October 1921, Box 17, Goodrich Papers; Goodrich, "Manuscript on Various Trips to Russia," Chapter "D," 3–4, Box 16, Goodrich Papers; Golder and Hutchinson, *On the Trail of the Russian Famine*, 91.

28. Goodrich diary, 9 October 1921, Box 17, Goodrich Papers; Goodrich, "Manuscript on Various Trips to Russia," Chapter "B," 8, Box 16, Goodrich Papers.

29. Goodrich diary, 10 October 1921, Box 17, Goodrich Papers; "Governor Goodrich's Preliminary Report on Russia," 1 November 1921, *Documents of the ARA*, 3, 399–401.

30. Goodrich diary, 13 October 1921, Box 17, Goodrich Papers.

31. Goodrich, "Manuscript on Various Trips to Russia," Chapter "C," 1–8, Box 16, Goodrich Papers; Goodrich diary, 12 October 1921, Box 17, Goodrich Papers.

32. Goodrich diary, 13 October 1921, Box 17, Goodrich Papers; Goodrich, "Manuscript on Various Trips to Russia," Chapter "D," 3–4; Golder and Hutchinson, *On the Trail of the Russian Famine*, 82.

33. Goodrich diary, 16 October 1921, Box 17, Goodrich Papers; Golder and Hutchinson, *On the Trail of the Russian Famine*, 82.

34. Goodrich diary, 17 October 1921, Box 17, Goodrich Papers; Golder and Hutchinson, *On the Trail of the Russian Famine*, 83.

35. Golder and Hutchinson, *On the Trail of the Russian Famine*, 83; Goodrich, "Manuscript on Various Trips to Russia," Chapter "E," 3, Box 16, Goodrich Papers.

36. Goodrich diary, 17 October 1921, Box 17, Goodrich Papers; Goodrich, "Manuscript on Various Trips to Russia," Chapter "E," 3, 7–8, Box 16, Goodrich Papers.

37. Goodrich diary, 18 October 1921, Box 17, Goodrich Papers; Goodrich, "Manuscript on Various Trips to Russia," Chapter "E," 5, Box 16, Goodrich Papers.

38. Goodrich diary, 19 October 1921, Box 17, Goodrich Papers; Goodrich, "Manuscript on Various Trips to Russia," Chapter "E," 7, Box 16, Goodrich Papers.

39. Goodrich diary, 19, 20 October 1921, Box 17, Goodrich Papers; Goodrich, "Manuscript on Various Trips to Russia," Chapter "F," 1, Box 16, Goodrich Papers.

40. Goodrich diary, 20 October 1921, Box 17, Goodrich Papers; United States Congress, House Committee on Foreign Affairs, *Russian Relief: Hearings before the Committee on Foreign Affairs*, 67 Cong., 2 Sess., 13, 14 December 1921, 6; Goodrich, "Manuscript on Various Trips to Russia," Chapter "F," 2, Box 16, Goodrich Papers.

41. Golder and Hutchinson, *On the Trail of the Russian Famine*, 88–89; Goodrich diary, 20 October 1921, Box 17, Goodrich Papers.

42. Goodrich, "Manuscript on Various Trips to Russia," Chapter "F," 6–8, Box 16, Goodrich Papers; Goodrich diary, 20 October 1921, Box 17, Goodrich Papers.

43. Goodrich, "Manuscript on Various Trips to Russia," Chapter "F," 8–9, Chapter "G," 1, Box 16, Goodrich Papers; Goodrich diary, 22 October 1921, Box 17, Goodrich Papers.

44. Goodrich, "Manuscript on Various Trips to Russia," Chapter "G," 2–3, Box 16, Goodrich Papers; Goodrich diary, 22 October 1921, Box 17, Goodrich Papers.

45. Goodrich, "Manuscript on Various Trips to Russia," Chapter "G," 5–6, Box 16, Goodrich Papers; Goodrich diary, 22 October 1921, Box 17, Goodrich Papers.

46. Goodrich, "Manuscript on Various Trips to Russia," Chapter "G," 5–6, Box 16, Goodrich Papers.

47. Ibid., 7–9, Box 16, Goodrich Papers.
48. Ibid., 10–11, Box 16, Goodrich Papers.
49. Ibid., Chapter "H" 1–2, Box 16, Goodrich Papers.
50. Ibid., 3–10, Box 16, Goodrich Papers.

Chapter 4. Goodrich Converts Congress

1. Goodrich diary, 31 October 1921, Box 17, Goodrich Papers.
2. Goodrich to Hughes, 2 November 1921, Box 24, Goodrich Papers.
3. "Governor Goodrich's Preliminary Report on Russia," 1 November 1921, *Documents of the ARA*, 3, 398–410.
4. Goodrich, "Manuscript on Various Trips to Russia," Chapter "H," 1–8, Box 16, Goodrich Papers.
5. Goodrich diary, 2 November 1921, Box 17, Goodrich Papers.
6. Goodrich diary, 2 November 1921, Box 17, Goodrich Papers; Goodrich, "Manuscript on Various Trips to Russia," Chapter "Eye," 2, Box 16, Goodrich Papers; Goodrich to Hoover, 2 November 1921, Box 24, Goodrich Papers.
7. Goodrich diary, 5, 7 November 1921, Box 17, Goodrich Papers; Goodrich, "Manuscript on Various Trips to Russia," Chapter "J," 3–4, Box 16, Goodrich Papers.
8. Goodrich diary, 8, 9 November 1921, Box 17, Goodrich Papers; Goodrich, "Manuscript on Various Trips to Russia," Chapter "J," 4, Box 16, Goodrich Papers.
9. Goodrich diary, 10 November 1921, Box 17, Goodrich Papers; Goodrich "Manuscript on Various Trips to Russia," Chapter "J," 6–7, Box 16, Goodrich Papers.
10. Goodrich diary, 12 November 1921, Box 17, Goodrich Papers.
11. Ibid., 13 November 1921, Box 17, Goodrich Papers; Goodrich, "Manuscript on Various Trips to Russia," Chapter "J," 8, Box 16, Goodrich Papers.
12. Goodrich diary, 15, 17, 18 November 1921, Box 17, Goodrich Papers.
13. Ibid., 20, 21, 23 November 1921, Box 17, Goodrich Papers.
14. Ibid., 23, 24 November 1921, Box 17, Goodrich Papers.
15. Ibid., 1 December 1921, Box 17, Goodrich Papers.
16. Haskell, "Memorandum for Governor Goodrich on matters to be taken up with Mr. Hoover," 14 November 1921, Box 276, ARA Records; Rickard to Walter L. Brown, 31 March 1922, Box 1A/237, ARA Personnel Records.
17. Weissman, *Hoover and Famine Relief*, 29–34, 199–200; John M. Thompson, *Russia, Bolshevism, and the Versailles Peace* (Princeton: Princeton University Press, 1966), 257–59; Hoover to George Barr Baker, 19 November 1925, Box 240, Commerce Papers, Hoover Presidential Library.
18. *New York Times*, 7 December 1921.
19. U. S. Congress, *Russian Relief Hearing*, 3–13.
20. *New York Times*, 18, 24 December 1921.
21. Rickard to Brown, 30 December 1921, Box 1A/236, ARA Personnel Records.

Chapter 5. Snowbound in Russia

1. Undated Goodrich speech, Box 16, Goodrich Papers.
2. Minutes of the Purchasing Commission, 23 December 1921, 4, 11, 16, 25 January and 17 February 1922, Warren G. Harding Papers, Ohio Historical Society

(microfilm edition, roll 182); Hoover to Goodrich, 27 December 1921, Box 16, Goodrich Papers.

3. *New York Times*, 22 January 1922; James P. Goodrich, "Can Russia Come Back?", *Outlook* 130, no. 9 (1 March 1922), 341–44; James P. Goodrich, "Impressions of the Bolshevik Regime," *Century* 104 (May, 1922), 55–56; *New York Times*, 29 January 1922.

4. *New York Times*, 29 January 1922; Undated Goodrich speech, Box 16, Goodrich Papers; *New York Times*, 22 January 1922; Goodrich to Remmel, 24 January 1922, Box 15, Goodrich Papers.

5. Hutchinson to Walter L. Brown, 9 November 1921, Box 85, ARA Records. ("I am enclosing two carbons," noted Hutchinson. "One for New York and one for the Chief.")

6. Gumberg to Robins, 19 December 1921, Box 2, Alexander Gumberg Papers (State Historical Society of Wisconsin); Gumberg to Goodrich, 26 December 1921, Box 2, Gumberg Papers.

7. *New York Times*, 19 February 1922.

8. Goodrich to Hoover, 18 February 1922, Box 24, Goodrich Papers; Christine A. White, *British and American Commercial Relations with Soviet Russia, 1918–1924* (Chapel Hill: University of North Carolina Press, 1992), 218–23.

9. The struggle for recognition, emphasizing the role of Borah, Robins, and Gumberg, is surveyed in Edward M. Bennett, *Recognition of Russia: An American Foreign Policy Dilemma* (Waltham, Massachusetts: Blaisdell Publishing Company, 1970), 60–65; Peter G. Filene, *Americans and the Soviet Experiment, 1917–1933* (Cambridge: Harvard University Press, 1967), 87–92; Claudius O. Johnson, *Borah of Idaho* (New York: Longmans, Green and Company, 1936), 354–68; James K. Libbey, *Alexander Gumberg and Soviet-American Relations, 1917–1933* (Lexington: University Press of Kentucky, 1977), 102–18; Robert J. Maddox, *William E. Borah and American Foreign Policy* (Baton Rouge: Louisiana State University Press, 1969), 183–214; Robert K. Murray, *The Harding Administration: Warren G. Harding and his Administration* (Minneapolis: University of Minnesota Press, 1969), 348–54; Joan Hoff Wilson, *Ideology and Economics: U. S. Relations with the Soviet Union, 1918–1933* (Columbia: University of Missouri Press, 1974), 71–89; William Appleman Williams, *American-Russian Relations, 1781–1947* (New York: Rinehart & Company, 1952), 178–79, 201–10. The fullest treatment of Goodrich is in Libbey (79–84). Goodrich is mentioned in Bennett (61, f.n. 28), Maddox, (201), Wilson (77), and Williams (202, 204, 206).

10. Hoover to Haskell, 16 February 1922, Box 19, Goodrich Papers.

11. Goodrich to Hoover, 6 March 1922, Box 24, Goodrich Papers.

12. Michel Spiridov to Director American Relief Administration, no date, Box 1-A/290, ARA Personnel Records; Goodrich to Brown, 16 March 1922, Box 16, Goodrich Papers; Haskell to Brown, 13 January 1922, and 6 February 1922, Box 1-A/290, ARA Personnel Records.

13. Haskell, Special Memorandum, 3 March 1922, Box 1-A/239, ARA Personnel Records.

14. Goodrich to Brown, 10 March 1922, Box 16, Goodrich Papers.

15. Mitchell to Brown, 11 March 1922, Box 21, ARA Records.

16. Goodrich to Brown, 15, 16 March 1922, Box 16, Goodrich Papers.

17. Goodrich diary, 18 March 1922, Box 18, Goodrich Papers.

18. Ibid., Goodrich Papers.

19. Goodrich to Hoover, 16 March 1922, Box 24, Goodrich Papers; Goodrich diary, 18 March 1922, Box 18, Goodrich Papers.

20. Goodrich diary, 22, 25 March 1922, Box 18, Goodrich Papers.
21. Goodrich, "Manuscript on Various Trips to Russia," Chapter "L," 3, Box 16, Goodrich Papers; Goodrich diary, 23 March 1922, Box 18, Goodrich Papers.
22. Goodrich diary, 25 March 1922, Box 18, Goodrich Papers.
23. Ibid., 27 March 1922, Box 18, Goodrich Papers.
24. Ibid., 28 March 1922, Box 18, Goodrich Papers.
25. Ibid., 31 March 1922, Box 18, Goodrich Papers.
26. Ibid., 1 April 1922, Box 18, Goodrich Papers; Golder to Professor E. D. Adams, 1 April 1922, Emmons and Patenaude, *Passages of Frank Golder*, 153–158.
27. Goodrich diary, 2 April 1922, Box 18, Goodrich Papers; Golder to Adams, 1 April 1922, Emmons and Patenaude, *Passages of Frank Golder*, 153–158.
28. Goodrich to Harding, 24 March 1922, Box 24, Goodrich Papers.
29. Ibid., 29 March 1922, 3 April 1922, Box 24, Goodrich Papers.
30. Hoover memorandum, 14 April 1922, Box 276, ARA Records.

Chapter 6. An Indiana Banker in the "Inner Temple" of the Kremlin

1. *New York Times*, 19, 20 April 1922; Gumberg to Robins, 21 April 1922, Box 2, Gumberg Papers; Goodrich to Harding, 24 March 1922, Box 24, Goodrich Papers.
2. Gumberg to Robins, 21 April 1922, Box 2, Gumberg Papers. General Grigori Semenov, the White Russian successor to Admiral Kolchak, had been actively seeking support in Washington for counterrevolution against the Soviets. See Williams, *American-Russian Relations*, 182.
3. Goodrich to Haskell, 20 April 1922, Box 19, Goodrich Papers.
4. "Statement of Governor Goodrich," 20 April 1922, Box 19, ARA Records.
5. Libbey, *Alexander Gumberg*, 82–86; Baker to Hoover, 19 May 1922, Box 276, ARA Records; Gumberg to Baker, 7 June 1922, Box 2, Gumberg Papers.
6. Goodrich to Hoover, 28 May 1922, Box 24, Goodrich Papers.
7. Goodrich diary, 2, 5 June 1922, Box 18, Goodrich Papers; Goodrich to Hoover, 10 June 1922, Box 24, Goodrich Papers; Dubie, *Frank A. Golder*, 144–45.
8. Goodrich diary, undated memorandum, Box 18, Goodrich Papers; Goodrich to Hoover, 10 June 1922, Box 24, Goodrich Papers.
9. Memorandum by Golder, 8 June 1922, Emmons and Patenaude, *Passages of Frank Golder*, 162–66.
10. Undated memorandum by Golder, "History of the Conversations between Governor Goodrich and Members of the Soviet," Box 19, Goodrich Papers; Golder to E. D. Adams, 11 June 1922, Emmons and Patenaude, *Passages of Frank Golder*, 172–73.
11. Goodrich diary, 14 June 1922, Box 19, Goodrich Papers.
12. Golder, undated "History," Box 19, Goodrich Papers; Goodrich to Hoover, 15 June 1922, Box 24, Goodrich Papers.
13. "Minutes of Conference of District Supervisors at Moscow Headquarters Offices," 17 June 1922, Box 16, Goodrich Papers.
14. Golder, undated "History," Box 19, Goodrich Papers.
15. Goodrich diary, 19 June 1922, Box 18, Goodrich Papers; Golder, "Conference between Governor Goodrich and Representatives of the Soviet Government," 19 June 1922, Emmons and Patenaude, *Passages of Frank Golder*, 347–52; Dubie, *Frank A. Golder*, 146–47.

16. Goodrich to Hoover, 19 June 1922, Box 276, ARA Records.

17. Goodrich diary, 21 June 1922, Box 18, Goodrich Papers; Golder to E. D. Adams, 24 June 1922, Emmons and Patenaude, *Passages of Frank Golder,* 173–79. According to Emmons and Pauenaude (167n) the trial of the Socialist Revolutionary leaders began on 8 June. On 7 August most of the defendants were found guilty of terrorism and counterrevolutionary activity; fifteen were sentenced to death but the sentences were commuted.

18. Goodrich diary, 21, 22 June 1922, Box 18, Goodrich Papers.

19. Ibid., 23 June 1922, Box 18, Goodrich Papers.

20. Ibid., 24 June 1922, Box 18, Goodrich Papers.

21. Ibid., 26 June 1922, Box 18, Goodrich Papers.

22. Goodrich to Hoover, 2 July 1922, Box 276, ARA Records; Hoover to Frelinghuysen, 23 August 1922, Box 276, ARA Records.

23. Goodrich, "Manuscript on Various Trips to Russia," Chapter "Y," 1–29, Box 16, Goodrich Papers.

24. *New York Times,* 15, 31 July, 1 August 1922; Fisher, *Famine in Soviet Russia,* 297–307.

Chapter 7. Goodrich Is Forced to Start Over Again

1. Haskell to Goodrich, 28 September 1922, Box 19, Goodrich Papers; Haskell to Goodrich, 9 October 1922, Box 19, Goodrich Papers.

2. Gumberg to Robins, 16 July, Box 2, Gumberg Papers; Robins to Gumberg, 18 August 1922, Box 2, Gumberg Papers; Gumberg to Robins, 21 August 1922, Box 2, Gumberg Papers.

3. Hoover to Hughes, 14 July 1922, *Papers Relating to the Foreign Relations of the United States, 1922* (Washington, D.C., 1928), 2, 825–26 (hereafter cited as FRUS); Hughes to Hoover, 15 July 1922, FRUS, 1922, 2, 826–27; Alanson B. Houghton to William Phillips, 16 September 1922, FRUS, 1922, 2, 832–34; Golder diary, 6 September 1925, Emmons and Patenaude, *Passages of Frank Golder,* 309–10.

4. Gumberg to Robins, 13 December 1922, Box 2, Gumberg Papers.

5. Goodrich to Hoover, 18 December 1922, Box 261, ARA Records.

6. Goodrich to Hoover, 30 January 1923, Box 240, Commerce Papers (Hoover Presidential Library).

7. Hoover to Goodrich, 1 February 1923, Box 240, Commerce Papers.

8. Libbey, *Alexander Gumberg,* 107–8; Gumberg to Goodrich, 1 March 1923, Box 3, Gumberg Papers; Goodrich to Gumberg, 7 March 1923, Box 3, Gumberg Papers; Goodrich to Gumberg, 16 March 1923, Box 3, Gumberg Papers.

9. H. H. Fisher, "Memorandum for Gov. Goodrich," 15 February 1923, Box 81, ARA Records; Filene, *Americans and the Soviet Experiment,* 82–86; Gumberg to Goodrich, 1 April 1923, Box 3, Gumberg Papers; Goodrich to Gumberg, 3 April 1923, Box 3, Gumberg Papers.

10. Gumberg to Goodrich, 10 May 1923, Box 3, Gumberg Papers; Gumberg to Robins, 24 May 1923, Box 3, Gumberg Papers; Robins to Goodrich, 31 May 1923, Box 3, Gumberg Papers.

11. Goodrich to Harding, 5 June 1923, Box 31, Papers of Frank A. Golder (Archives of the Hoover Institution on War, Revolution and Peace, Stanford, California). For unknown reasons Goodrich either misplaced, misfiled, or lost his letter to Harding.

12. Goodrich to Gumberg, 18 June 1923, Box 3, Gumberg Papers; Goodrich to Gumberg, 21 June 1923, Box 3, Gumberg Papers.

13. "Digest of Speeches at a Dinner Given by the ARA to the Council of Commissars of the USSR," 16 June 1923, Box 16, Goodrich Papers; Haskell to Goodrich, 19 June 1923, Box 20, Goodrich Papers; Goodrich to Gumberg, 25 June 1923, Box 3, Gumberg Papers.

14. Goodrich to Gumberg, 3 August 1923, Box 3, Gumberg Papers.

15. Libbey, *Alexander Gumberg,* 113–14; Goodrich to Rickard, 9 August 1923, Box 288, ARA Records.

16. Hoover to Vincent, 31 August 1923, Box 261, ARA Records; Vincent to Hoover, 11 September 1923, Box 261, ARA Records.

17. Goodrich to Hoover, 11 September 1923, Box 261, ARA Records; Hoover to Goodrich, 12 September 1923, Box 261, ARA Records; Goodrich to Hoover, 17 September 1923, Box 261, ARA Records.

18. Indianapolis *News,* 1, 3 October 1923; *New York Times,* 3 October 1923.

19. *New York Times,* 14 October 1923, 6 February, 29, 30, April 1924.

20. Coolidge, State of the Union Message, 6 December 1923, FRUS, 1923, 1, 8–9; Chicherin to Coolidge, 16 December 1923, FRUS, 1923, 2, 787; Hughes to United States Counsel at Reval, 18 December 1923, FRUS, 1923, 2, 788; Libbey, *Alexander Gumberg,* 115–17; Williams, *American-Russian Relations,* 204–7. See also L. Ethan Ellis, *Republican Foreign Policy, 1921–1933* (New Brunswick, NJ: Rutgers University Press, 1968), 75–78, Robert P. Browder, *The Origins of Soviet-American Diplomacy* (Princeton: Princeton University Press, 1953), 18–19, and Foster Rhea Dulles, *The Road to Teheran* (Princeton: Princeton University Press, 1944), 174–75.

21. Gumberg to Goodrich, 19 December 1923, Box 3, Gumberg Papers; Goodrich to Gumberg, 22 December 1923, Box 3, Gumberg Papers; Goodrich to Gumberg, 28 December 1923, Box 3, Gumberg Papers.

22. Goodrich diary, 4 October 1925, Box 18, Goodrich Papers.

23. *The Wabash Bulletin,* October 1940, 11–12, Box 3, Goodrich Papers; Goodrich to Treasurer O. E. Gregg, 30 June 1920, Box 3, Goodrich Papers; Goodrich to John D. Rockefeller, 21 June 1920, Box 2, Goodrich Papers; Goodrich to Dr. George L. McIntosh, 16 September 1919, Box 2, Goodrich Papers.

Chapter 8. Goodrich's Final Trip to Russia

1. Goodrich diary, 1 September 1925, Box 18, Goodrich Papers.

2. Ibid., 2, 4 September 1925, Box 18, Goodrich Papers.

3. Ibid., 5 September 1925, Box 18, Goodrich Papers.

4. Ibid., 1, 2, 4 September 1925, Box 18, Goodrich Papers.

5. Ibid., 2 September 1925, Box 18, Goodrich Papers; "Russia at the Princeton Club: The Return of Governor Goodrich," *ARA Association Review,* vol. 1, no. 7 (October, 1925), 16.

6. Goodrich diary, 6 September 1925, Box 18, Goodrich Papers.

7. Ibid., 7 September 1925, Box 18, Goodrich Papers.

8. Ibid., 8 September 1925, Box 18, Goodrich Papers.

9. Ibid., 10 September 1925, Box 18, Goodrich Papers.

10. Ibid., 11 September 1925, Box 18, Goodrich Papers.

11. Ibid., 13 September 1925, Box 18, Goodrich Papers.

12. Ibid., 14, 15 September 1925, Box 18, Goodrich Papers.

NOTES TO CHAPTER 9

13. Ibid., 14 September 1925, Box 18, Goodrich Papers; Golder diary, 14 September 1925, Emmons and Patenaude, *Passages of Frank Golder*, 314–15.

14. Goodrich diary, 15 September 1925, Box 18, Goodrich Papers; Golder diary, 15 September 1925, Emmons and Patenaude, *Passages of Frank Golder*, 315–16.

15. Goodrich diary, 18, 19 September 1925, Box 18, Goodrich Papers.

16. Ibid., 20 September 1925, Box 18, Goodrich Papers.

17. Ibid., 21 September 1925, Box 18, Goodrich Papers.

18. Ibid., 22 September 1925, Box 18, Goodrich Papers.

19. Ibid., 23 September 1925, Box 18, Goodrich Papers.

20. Ibid., 25 September 1925, Box 18, Goodrich Papers.

21. Ibid., 27 September 1925, Box 18, Goodrich Papers.

22. Ibid., 28 September 1925, Box 18, Goodrich Papers.

23. Ibid., 29 September 1925, Box 18, Goodrich Papers.

24. Ibid., 1 October 1925, Box 18, Goodrich Papers.

25. Ibid., 29 September 1925, Box 18, Goodrich Papers.

26. Ibid., 1 September 1925, Box 18, Goodrich Papers.

27. Ibid., 4 October 1925, Box 18, Goodrich Papers.

28. Ibid., 14 September 1925, Box 18, Goodrich Papers.

29. Ibid., 16 September 1925, Box 18, Goodrich Papers.

30. Ibid., 7 September 1925, Box 18, Goodrich Papers.

31. Goodrich to Lincoln Hutchinson, 14 January 1925, Box 24, Goodrich Papers. For the anti-Communism of Kelley see Frederic L. Propas, "Creating a Hard Line Toward Russia: The Training of State Department Soviet Experts, 1927–1937," *Diplomatic History*, 8, no. 3 (Summer, 1984): 209–26.

32. Hoover to Everett Sanders, 12 October 1925, Calvin Coolidge Papers, Library of Congress (microfilm edition, roll 85); Sanders to Hoover, 15 October 1925, roll 85, Coolidge Papers; Goodrich to Fay Litvinov, 2 January 1926, Box 20, Goodrich Papers.

33. Goodrich to Coolidge, 24 November 1925, Box 3, Goodrich Papers; Coolidge to Goodrich, 2 December 1925, Box 3, Goodrich Papers.

34. Goodrich to Fay Litvinov, 2 January 1926, Box 20, Goodrich Papers. See also Hugh D. Phillips, *Between the Revolution and the West: A Political Biography of Maxim M. Litvinov* (Boulder, Colo.: Westview Press, 1992), 83–84.

Chapter 9. "A Vote for Hoover is a Vote for Jim Goodrich"

1. Goodrich to Fay Litvinov, 18 January 1927, Box 20, Goodrich Papers; Fay Litvinov to Cora Goodrich, 20 October 1927, Box 20, Goodrich Papers. In the latter letter Mrs. Litvinov expressed thanks for the gift of "a sweet, silken garment." A note attached to the letter by "HS" suggests that the term "silken garment" was "supposed to be some sort of code." However, the meaning of the phrase, if it had a double meaning, was obscure to the note writer and remains so today.

2. Ossinsky to Goodrich, 16 November 1927, Box 20, Goodrich Papers; Goodrich to Joseph P. Cotton, 10 December 1929, Box 20, Goodrich Papers; Cotton to Goodrich, 27 December 1929, Box 20, Goodrich Papers; Goodrich diary, 2 February 1932, Box 3, Goodrich Papers.

3. Goodrich to Lockwood, 10 November 1925, Box 13, Goodrich Papers.

4. Goodrich to Wood, 13 March 1928, Box 1, Goodrich Papers; Goodrich to Hoover, 5 May 1928, Box 11, Goodrich Papers; Indianapolis *News*, 9 May 1928.

5. Goodrich to Hoover, 7 November 1928, Box 11, Goodrich Papers.

6. Hoover to Goodrich, 27 June 1929, Box 11, Goodrich Papers; Goodrich to Hoover, 30 June 1929 (Goodrich to Wood, 28 June 1929 enclosed), Box 11, Goodrich Papers; *New York Times,* 24 December 1930.

7. Hoover to Goodrich, 16 October 1929, Box 3, Goodrich Papers; Goodrich to Hoover, 16 October 1929, Box 3, Goodrich Papers; Goodrich to Garfield, 25 January 1931, Box 3, Goodrich Papers. Herbert Hoover, *The Memoirs of Herbert Hoover,* 2, 239–41, lists Goodrich as a member of the commission, but does not mention his dissenting views.

8. Rickard to Goodrich, 13 August 1929, Box 1, Goodrich Papers; Goodrich to Rickard, 1 December 1930, Box 1, Goodrich Papers.

9. Goodrich to Hutchinson, 5 October 1931, Box 11, Goodrich Papers; Goodrich to Baker, 16 December 1931, Box 1, Goodrich Papers.

10. Goodrich to Lockwood, 19 May 1929, Box 11, Goodrich Papers.

11. Goodrich to Watson, 29 December 1931, Box 28, Goodrich Papers; Goodrich to Watson, 29 March 1931, Box 28, Goodrich Papers; Goodrich to Senator Arthur Robinson, 16 May 1932, Box 15, Goodrich Papers.

12. Goodrich to Watson, 10 June 1932, Box 28, Goodrich Papers; Goodrich to Hoover, 12 July 1932, Box 11, Goodrich Papers; Goodrich to Hoover, 13 August 1932, Box 11, Goodrich Papers.

13. Goodrich diary, 8 November 1932, Box 3, Goodrich Papers.

14. Goodrich to Hoover, 9 September 1933, Box 11, Goodrich Papers.

15. Goodrich to Roosevelt, 6 November 1933, Box 23, Goodrich Papers; Louis McHenry Howe to Goodrich, 10 November 1933, Box 23, Goodrich Papers.

16. Goodrich to Hoover, 14 June 1934, Box 11, Goodrich Papers; Goodrich to Robinson, 7 May 1934, Box 15, Goodrich Papers.

17. Goodrich to Hoover, 5 March 1935, Box 11, Goodrich Papers; Goodrich to Hoover, 1 July 1935, Box 11, Goodrich Papers.

18. Goodrich to Litschert, 17 January 1936, Box 13, Goodrich Papers; Goodrich to Henry J. Allen, 11 April 1936, Box 2, Goodrich Papers.

19. Goodrich to Hoover, 13 June 1936, Box 11, Goodrich Papers; Goodrich to Kenneth C. Hogate, 13 June 1936, Box 11, Goodrich Papers; Goodrich to Allen, 17 August 1936, Box 2, Goodrich Papers; Goodrich to Scandrett, 20 November 1936, Box 2, Goodrich Papers.

20. Litvinov to Goodrich, 1 November 1935, Box 20, Goodrich Papers; Goodrich to Van Zant, 26 March 1937, Box 25, Goodrich Papers.

21. Goodrich to Cora Goodrich, no date, Box 4, Goodrich Papers; Goodrich to I. C. Elson, 4 August 1937, Box 2, Goodrich Papers; Pierre Goodrich to Dr. Louis Hammond, 14 September 1937, Box 4, Goodrich Papers; Hammond to Pierre Goodrich, 16 September 1937, Box 6, Goodrich Papers. According to Dr. Hammond: "Although there is evidence of definite disease to the heart muscle, still it is true that under such circumstances patients often live on for many active years. I shall of course do everything I can to encourage him. He himself seems to be quite happy and contented. He did have another flurry of the fibrillation on Sunday but by Monday morning the attack had disappeared and he has been comfortable since then."

22. Goodrich to Cass, 10 January 1938, Box 3, Goodrich Papers; Goodrich to O. P. Welborn, 16 June 1938, Box 3, Goodrich Papers; "Report of the President of Hanover College, Hanover, Indiana for the Year 1940–1941," Box 2, Goodrich Papers.

23. Goodrich to Springer, 7 November 1939, Box 25, Goodrich Papers.

24. Goodrich to Dewey, 16 May 1940, Box 3, Goodrich Papers; Hugh Ross,

"Was the Nomination of Wendell Willkie a Political Miracle?," *Indiana Magazine of History*, 58 (June, 1962): 88.

25. Goodrich to Willkie, 10 August 1940, Box 28, Goodrich Papers; Pierre Goodrich to Willkie, 16 August 1940, Box 28, Goodrich Papers.

26. Goodrich to Hoover, 9 September 1933, Box 11, Goodrich Papers; Goodrich to Representative Louis Ludlow, 13 March 1935, Box 13, Goodrich Papers; Goodrich to Copeland, 22 May 1937, Box 3, Goodrich Papers.

27. Goodrich to Eleanor Roosevelt, 22 April 1939, Box 15, Goodrich Papers.

28. *ARA Association Review*, vol. 1, no. 1 (1 April 1925), 14.

29. Goodrich diary, 19 October 1921, Box 17, Goodrich Papers.

Bibliography

Manuscripts

The following collections were consulted in the preparation of this work:
Herbert Hoover Presidential Library:
   James P. Goodrich Papers
   American Relief Administration Personnel Records
   American Relief Administration. *Documents of the American Relief Administration, Russian Operations, 1921–1923.* H. H. Fisher and Suda L. Bane, editors. Stanford, Calif., 1931. 10 typed volumes
Hoover Institution on War, Revolution and Peace:
   Records of the American Relief Administration, Russian Operations, 1921–1923
   Frank A. Golder Papers
Library of Congress:
   Calvin Coolidge Papers, microfilm edition
Ohio Historical Society:
   Warren G. Harding Papers, microfilm edition
State Historical Society of Wisconsin:
   Alexander Gumberg Papers

Public Documents

League of Nations. *Report on Economic Conditions in Russia with Special Reference to the Famine of 1921–1922 and the State of Agriculture.* Nancy, France, 1922.
U. S. Department of State. *Papers Relating to the Foreign Relations of the United States, 1922.* 2 vols., Washington, D. C., 1938.
————. *Papers Relating to the Foreign Relations of the United States, 1923.* 2 vols., Washington, D. C., 1938.

Newspapers

Indianapolis *Daily Times,* 1916–1921
Indianapolis *News,* 1916–1921
Indianapolis *Star,* 1916–1921
New York Times, 1916–1940

Periodical Literature

ARA Association Review, 1921–1925
Goodrich, James P. "Can Russia Come Back?" *Outlook* 130 (1 March 1922):341–44.

———. "Impressions of the Bolshevik Regime." *Century* 104 (May 1922):55–65.

Propas, Frederic L. "Creating a Hard Line Toward Russia: The Training of State Department Soviet Experts, 1927–1937." *Diplomatic History* 8(Summer, 1984):209–26.

Remy, Charles F. "Governor Goodrich and Indiana Tax Legislation." *Indiana Magazine of History* 43(March, 1947):41–56.

Robertson, James O. "Progressives Elect Will H. Hays Republican National Chairman, 1918." *Indiana Magazine of History* 64(September, 1968):173–90.

Ross, Hugh. "Was the Nomination of Wendell Willkie a Political Miracle?" *Indiana Magazine of History* 58 (June, 1962):85–95.

Books

Barnhart, John D., and Donald F. Carmony. *Indiana: From Frontier to Commonwealth*. Vol. 2. New York: Lewis Historical Publishing Company, 1954.

Bennett, Edward. *Recognition of Russia: An American Foreign Policy Dilemma*. Waltham, Mass.: Blaisdell Publishing Company, 1970.

Browder, Robert P. *The Origins of Soviet-American Diplomacy*. Princeton: Princeton University Press, 1953.

Carr, Edward Hallett. *The Bolshevik Revolution, 1917–1923*. Vol. 2 of *A History of Soviet Russia*. London: Macmillan, 1952.

Dubie, Alain. *Frank A. Golder: An Adventure of a Historian in Quest of Russian History*. Boulder, Colo.: East European Monographs, 1989.

Dulles, Foster Rhea. *The Road to Teheran*. Princeton: Princeton University Press, 1944.

Ellis, L. Ethan. *Republican Foreign Policy, 1921–1933*. New Brunswick, N.J.: Rutgers University Press, 1968.

Emmons, Terence, and Bertrand M. Patenaude, eds. *War, Revolution, and Peace in Russia: The Passages of Frank Golder, 1914–1917*. Stanford, Calif.: Hoover Institution Press, 1992.

Filene, Peter G. *Americans and the Soviet Experiment, 1917–1933*. Cambridge: Harvard University Press, 1967.

Fisher, Harold H. *The Famine in Soviet Russia, 1919–1923: The Operations of the American Relief Administration*. New York: Macmillan, 1927.

Gaddis, John Lewis. *Russia, the Soviet Union and the United States: An Interpretive History*. New York: John Wiley and Sons, 1978.

Goldberg, Harold J., ed. *Intervention, Famine Relief, International Affairs, 1917–1933*. Vol. 1 of *Documents of Soviet-American Relations*. Gulf Breeze, Fl.: Academic International Press, 1993.

Golder, Frank Alfred, and Lincoln Hutchinson. *On the Trail of the Russian Famine*. Stanford, Calif.: Stanford University Press, 1927.

Hays, Will H. *The Memoirs of Will H. Hays*. Garden City, N.Y.: Doubleday, 1955.

Hoover, Herbert. *The Cabinet and the Presidency, 1920–1933*. Vol. 2 of *The Memoirs of Herbert Hoover*. New York: Macmillan, 1952.

Johnson, Claudius O. *Borah of Idaho*. New York: Longmans, Green and Company, 1936.

Libbey, James K. *Alexander Gumberg and Soviet-American Relations, 1917–1933*. Lexington: University Press of Kentucky, 1977.

Maddox, Robert J. *William E. Borah and American Foreign Policy*. Baton Rouge: Louisiana State University Press, 1969.

Madison, James H. *The Indiana Way: A State History*. Bloomington: Indiana University Press, 1986.

Murray, Robert K. *The Harding Era: Warren G. Harding and His Administration*. Minneapolis: University of Minnesota Press, 1969.

Phillips, Clifton J. *Indiana in Transition: The Emergence of an Industrial Commonwealth, 1880–1920*. Indianapolis: Indiana Historical Bureau and Indiana Historical Society, 1968.

Thompson, John M. *Russia, Bolshevism, and the Versailles Peace*. Princeton: Princeton University Press, 1966.

Ulam, Adam. *A History of Soviet Russia*. New York: Praeger, 1976.

VanderMeer, Philip R. *The Hoosier Politician: Officeholding and Political Culture in Indiana, 1896–1920*. Urbana: University of Illinois Press, 1985.

Von Rauch, Georg. *A History of Soviet Russia*. New York: Praeger, 1967.

Weissman, Benjamin M. *Herbert Hoover and Famine Relief to Soviet Russia, 1921–1923*. Stanford, Calif.: Hoover Institution Press, 1974.

White, Christine A. *British and American Commercial Relations with Soviet Russia, 1918–1924*. Chapel Hill: University of North Carolina Press, 1992.

Williams, William Appleman. *American-Russian Relations, 1781–1947*. New York: Rinehart and Company, 1952.

Wilson, Joan Hoff. *Ideology and Economics: United States Relations with the Soviet Union, 1918–1933*. Columbia: University of Missouri Press, 1974.

Wilson, William E. *Indiana: A History*. Bloomington: Indiana University Press, 1966.

Index

Adair, John A. M., 27–29
Anderson, Albert B., 24
Anderson, Marian, 168
Ashurst, Henry W., 87

Baker, George Barr, 108–9, 160
Beeuwkes, Dr. Henry, 128
Beigler, Warren, 21
Beveridge, Albert: 16; relations with Goodrich, 20–24, 35
Borah, William E.: 9; advocates recognition of Soviet Russia, 94, 132, 137
Bowers, Claude A., 37
Brown, Walter L.: 87, 110; signs Riga pact with Litvinov, 46–47; worried by reports of friction with Soviets, 80; demands resignation of Saunders, 95; sends Mowat M. Mitchell to inspect Russian operation, 96; inspects famine program, 115, 120, 122
Bryan, William J., 23
Buchavich, Constantine, 132
Bush, Edgar: 31; clashes with Goodrich, 33, 36, 40

Carroll, Col. Philip, 95–97
Cass, John, 165
Chicherin, Grigori: 134, 152; says NEP a temporary retreat, 79; conditionally agrees to discuss United States-Soviet relations, 137–38
Clapp, Paul, 124
Coleman, Walter A., 115
Commons, John R., 16
Connally, Tom, 90
Coolidge, Archibald: greets Goodrich at Moscow, 57; clashes with Col. Haskell, 83; reports misconduct by Moscow ARA employees, 94–96
Coolidge, Calvin: 8; selected as running mate of Warren G. Harding, 40–41; assumes presidency, 134–35; makes abortive overture to Moscow, 135–36; rejects recommendations of Goodrich, 153–55; announces retirement, 157
Copeland, Royal S., 168
Cox, James, 41
Cromer, George, 20–21

Dewey, Thomas E., 14, 166
Dodge, Captain Earl J., 95–96
Duranty, Walter, 130
Dzerzhinsky, Feliks: 13, 102; interviewed by Goodrich, 102

Easly, Ralph, 90
Edwards, John, 23
Eiduk, Aleksandr: 95; assists in arranging Kremlin meeting, 111–16
Ellis, Dr. Horace, 34
Ellis, Howell, 34
Engle, Jim, 17

Fairbanks, Charles: 28, 33; relations with Goodrich, 20–22
Famine in Soviet Russia: appeal by Gorky, 46; Hoover's response, 46–50; Goodrich sent to investigate, 51–81; Russian relief hearings, 84–87; decision to send bulk corn, 88–89; Haskell claims is "absolutely broken," 111; ARA district supervisors optimistic, 115–16; Goodrich finds Tartar Republic recovering from, 121–24; ARA directors decide to phase out famine program, 126–27
Fisher, Harold H., 83
Foellinger, Oscar, 157
France, Joseph I., 94
Frelinghuysen, Joseph, 125
Frist, Cora (Mrs. James P. Goodrich), 16–17, 51

Galpin, Perrin, 49
Garfield, James R., 159
Garner, John Nance, 161
Gibbs, Sir Philip, 72, 76
Glazunov, Aleksandr, 142
Golder, Frank A.: 110, 140, 142; influenced by Goodrich 8; accompanies Goodrich to Volga region, 58–64, 67–68; interviews A. Scheinman, 103–4; helps to arrange Kremlin meeting, 114–20; accompanies Goodrich to Leningrad and Moscow, 145–46; purchases books for Hoover War Library, 153
Goodrich, Elizabeth (mother), 14, 17
Goodrich, James P.: papers, 7–9; childhood, 14–15; education, 15–17; introduced to politics, 15–16; breaks hip, 16; legal training, 17; joins Grange and Knights of Labor, 17–18; Republican Chairman for Randolph County, 20; Republican Chairman for the Eighth District, 20; member of State Republican Committee, 20–21; Indiana Republican Chairman, 21–24; receiver of bankrupt railroad, 24–25; decides to run for governor of Indiana, 26; campaign for governor, 27–29; governorship of Indiana, 30–43; first trip to USSR, 44–81; testimony before House Foreign Affairs Committee, 84–87; vice-chairman of Purchasing Commission, 88–89; meets Alexander Gumberg, 91–92; advocates recognition of USSR, 92–94; second trip to USSR, 94–97; third trip to USSR, 110–126; views Romanov crown jewels, 113–14; meets with Soviet leaders, 116–19; tours Volga famine region, 120–25; recommends commission plan, 128–39; fourth trip to USSR, 140–55; champions 1928 candidacy of Hoover, 157–58; surprised by depression, 159–61; appalled by the New Deal, 161–68
Goodrich, John (father), 14
Goodrich, Pierre (son) 7, 17, 34, 138, 156, 165, 167
Gumberg, Alexander: 9, 137; introduced to Goodrich, 91–92; plans to accompany Goodrich to Russia,

107–8; and commission plan, 128–30; and campaign to influence Harding, 132–34

Hadley, Herbert, 25
Hammer, Armand, 126
Hammond, Dr. Lewis, 65
Hanley, J. Frank, 22–23
Hanover College, 165
Harding, Warren G.: 8, 45, 92, 107, 109, 129; supported by Goodrich in 1920, 39–41; asks Congress for Russian relief funds, 84; signs Russian famine relief bill, 87; Goodrich advises to recognize Russia, 105, 132–33; dies at San Francisco, 134
Harriman, Averell, 126
Harvey, George, 81
Haskell, Col. William N.: 57, 104, 106, 124; selected to head ARA Russian operation, 47–48; Goodrich meets at Samara, 62; accompanies Goodrich to Leningrad, 77–79; sends memo to Hoover through Goodrich, 82–83; bans individual letters by ARA personnel to US officials, 92; purges ARA personnel at Moscow, 94–96; purge approved by Hoover and Goodrich, 108; says famine is "absolutely broken," 110–11; calls conference of district supervisors, 115; accompanies Goodrich to Volga district, 120–22; asks Goodrich to restore funding for army officers assigned to ARA, 128; supports trade agreement with Russia, 130–31; urges action toward trade agreement, 133–34; accompanies Goodrich on 1925 visit to Russia, 140, 142–46
Hays, Will: 9, 37, 39, 133; selected as Indiana Republican chairman, 26–29; named head of Indiana State Council of Defense, 32; named chairman of Republican National Committee, 33; tells Hoover that Goodrich is available for Russian relief, 47
Hemenway, James A., 22
Herter, Christian A.: approves paying Goodrich's travel expenses, 49; worried ARA might be embarrassed by views of Goodrich, 106; visits Mos-

cow, 115; tours Volga district, 120, 122

Hitler, Adolf: *Mein Kampf* shocks Goodrich, 165; opposed by Goodrich, 166

Hoover, Herbert: 8, 104, 115, 134, 169; differs with Goodrich on Russian recognition, 7; briefly mentions Goodrich in *Memoirs*, 9; not supported by Goodrich for Republican nomination in 1920, 39–40; agrees to organize Russian famine relief, 46; appoints Goodrich as an ARA special investigator, 47–49; receives preliminary report from Goodrich, 75–76; summons Goodrich to Washington, 79; asserts humanitarian motives are behind Russian relief, 83; assists Goodrich in congressional testimony, 86–87; role as chairman of Purchasing Commission, 88–89; advised by Goodrich to recognize the Soviet government, 92–94; sends Goodrich to Moscow to enforce discipline, 94–97; again advised by Goodrich to recognize Soviets, 105–6; briefed by Goodrich on ARA Russian operation, 107–8; sends Goodrich on third trip to Russia, 109–110; favorably portrayed by Karl Radek, 112; advised by Goodrich to send commission to Russia, 125–26; recommends that Russian operation be reduced in scope, 126–27; endorses commission plan, 129; advised by Goodrich to open trade relations with Russia, 130–31; tries to send Goodrich to Russia under auspices of Rockefeller Foundation, 135–36; as President declines to recognize Russia, 157–58; supported by Goodrich for presidency in 1928, 157–58; appoints Goodrich to Commission on Conservation and Management of the Public Domain, 159; supported by Goodrich for reelection, 159–61; urged by Goodrich to run in 1936 against Roosevelt, 163; favored by Goodrich for 1940 Republican nomination, 166

Houghton, Alanson, 155

Hughes, Charles Evans: 8, 28, 29, 81, 92, 104, 116, 153; told by Goodrich that Soviets returning to capitalism, 74–75; blamed for sabotaging commission plan, 129–30; accused of blocking a more flexible Russian policy, 135–37; blamed by Stalin for thwarting establishment of diplomatic relations, 152

Hutchinson, Lincoln: 122, 126, 159; travels with Goodrich through Volga district, 62–64, 67–68; advises Hoover to recognize Soviets, 91; attends Goodrich interview with A. Scheinman, 103; concludes Russia has enough food to survive winter of 1922–23, 111, 115

Johnson, Sen. Hiram of California: 131; supported by Goodrich for 1920 Republican nomination, 39–40

Kalinen, Mikhail: gives lengthy speech, 142; Roosevelt suggests talks on recognition, 162

Kamenev, Lev B: 13, 134; Goodrich seeks to arrange meeting with in Kremlin, 111–14; meeting held on 19 June 1922, 116–19; attacks western imperialism (September, 1925), 145–46; criticized by Stalin, 152; executed, 164

Keller, Dr. Amelia, 34–35

Kelley, Robert F.: intense anti-Communism of, 153

Kellogg, Frank B.: influenced by anti-Communist views of Robert Kelley, 153

Kern, John, 29

Keynes, John Maynard, 146

Krassin, Leonid: 13, 81; meets Goodrich, 113–19, 151

Landon, Alf, 163–64

Lee, Edwin, 31

Lenin, Vladimir I.: 45, 80, 169; Goodrich denies having brought message from, 107; suffers stroke, 110–11; questions Hoover's motives, 112

Lewis, John, 31

Lewis, John L., 38

Lewis, Sinclair, 44

Lieber, Richard, 36, 38
Litschert, Frank: 163; shields governor's privacy, 32–33
Litvinov, Fay: demonstrates command of international affairs, 150; Goodrich's correspondence with, 153–56
Litvinov, Maxim: signs Riga pact with ARA, 46–47; attends Kremlin meeting with Goodrich, 116–19; guides Goodrich on tour of Leningrad, 141; meets Goodrich on train to Moscow, 143; discusses obstacles to recognition, 149–51; recommended by Goodrich to Roosevelt, 162; contacted by Goodrich regarding proposed 1936 Russian tour, 164
Lockwood, George, 27, 76, 157, 160
Lodge, Henry Cabot, 131–32
Lonergan, Maj. Thomas C., 95–97

Macy, John W. "Chess," 15, 17, 20
Marshall, Thomas R.: 33, 38; elected Governor of Indiana, 23; and 1916 election, 28
McCray, Warren T.: defeated by Goodrich for 1916 Republican nomination for governor of Indiana, 15, 27; opposed by Goodrich as his successor, 40; wins Indiana governorship in 1920, 41–42; convicted of mail fraud and forced to resign, 136–37; Goodrich opposes clemency, 158–59
Mellon, Andrew W., 157
Miller, John C., 80, 96
Mitchell, Mowat M., 96
Monks, Leander J., 25
Moorman, John, 136
Mote, Carl, 38; and Goodrich's campaign for governor, 27–28; named chief oil inspector by Goodrich, 31

New, Sen. Harry S.: runs for Senate in 1916, 26; elected, 29; opposes League of Nations, 44; and McCray scandal, 136

Oliver, James, 93
Ossinsky, V. V., 156

Pavlov, Dr. Ivan, 141

Quinn, Cyril J. C.: 115; Goodrich recommends as chief assistant to Haskell, 96; attends conference of district supervisors, 115

Radek, Karl: 13, 134; denounces America 111–12; defends Hoover's humanitarian motives, 112–13; denies Soviet government sponsors propaganda, 150–51; executed, 164
Ralston, Samuel M.: elected governor in 1912, 25; Goodrich criticizes in 1916 election, 28; clemency policy, 38
Recognition of Soviet Government: advocated by Lincoln Hutchinson, 91; Goodrich hints he favors, 91–92; Goodrich urges Hoover to consider, 92–94; discussed by Goodrich and Soviet leaders, 116–19; Goodrich recommends commission to explore, 125–26; Goodrich recommends to Harding, 132–33; Hughes rejects negotiations on, 137; Goodrich recommends to Coolidge, 154; ambassadors exchanged, 162. See also Borah, William E.; Gumberg, Alexander; Robins, Col. Raymond
Remmel, Arthur K., 90
Rennick, H. L., 130
Repp, George: meets Goodrich, 50; accompanies Goodrich to Moscow, 57; tours German colonies with Goodrich, 65–71; reports Volga Germans able to survive, 111, 124
Rickard, Edgar: 109, 126, 135; critical of Prof. Coolidge, 83; praises Goodrich's congressional testimony, 87; concerned Goodrich's views might embarrass ARA, 106; visits Moscow, 115; tours Volga region, 120, 122
Roberts, Henry A.: considered unqualified by Goodrich, 30; office abolished, 36–37
Robins, Col. Raymond: 9, 107–8; on Goodrich, 91, 128–29; and Russian policy, 132; influences Coolidge, 137
Robbins, John, 25
Roosevelt, Eleanor, 68
Roosevelt, Franklin D.: 7, 155, 168; and Goodrich 161, 166 Roosevelt, Theodore: 22, 25; death of, 37
Rosen, Joseph, 94–95

Rykov, Aleksii: 13, 113; and Goodrich, 116–19; executed, 164

Saunders, Shelby: Goodrich recommends dismissal, 95–96
Scheinmann, Aaron: 106, 113; interviewed by Goodrich, 103–4
Semenov, Grigori, 107
Shafroth, Will: 97; accompanies Goodrich, 98–101; Goodrich on, 110
Shively, Benjamin F., 26–27
Shumaker, Edward S., 28
Sims, Fred A.: 21, 26, 33
Skvirsky, Boris E., 129
Sokolnikov, Grigori: 13, 134; and Goodrich, 113–14, 116–19, 146
Springer, Raymond: 9; criticized by Goodrich, 166
Stalin, Joseph: 13; interviewed by Goodrich, 151–52; purges opponents, 164
Starr, Harry, 25
Strong, Dr. Anna Louise, 62

Taft, Robert A.: 14; and Goodrich, 166
Taft, William H.: 9; supported by Goodrich, 13, 25
Taggart, Tom, 29
Telford, Maj. Charles, 95–96
Toner, Edward C., 40
Trotsky, Leon: 13, 103, 110, 114; interviewed by Goodrich, 151
Tuthill, Marshall, 124

Vanscoy, Henry, 15

Van Zant, John L., 164
Vincent, Dr. George, 135

Wabash College: and Goodrich 42, 138, 165
Wahren, Ivar, 122
Walb, Clyde, 136
Wardwell, Allan, 109
Watson, Enos, 17
Watson, Sen. James: 9, 22, 36, 43, 131, 160, 168; graduates from Winchester High School, 16; reads law with Goodrich, 17; law partnership with Goodrich, 18–19; unsuccessful campaign for governor, 23; and 1916 Indiana election, 26–29; opposes League of Nations, 44; seeks 1928 Republican nomination, 157–58; attends 1940 Republican convention, 166
Wilson, Woodrow: loses Indiana in 1916 election, 28–29; fixes national coal price, 32; advised on Russia by Hoover, 83
Willkie, Wendell: opposed by Goodrich for 1940 Republican nomination, 166; Goodrich predicts will win 1940 presidential election, 166–67
Wood, Gen. Leonard: 39; promotes Wood-Goodrich Republican ticket in 1920, 37–38; Wood, Will of Indiana: 9, 157; seeks pardon for Warren T. McCray, 158–59; urged by Goodrich to cut federal salaries, 160
Wright, Homer and Edna, 99

Zinoviev, Grigori, 13, 113